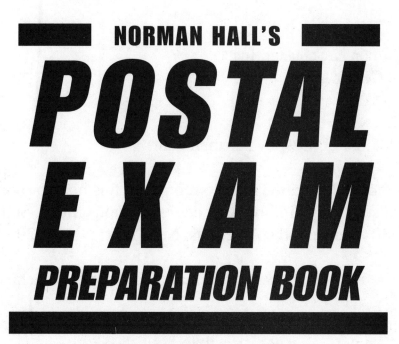

NORMAN HALL'S
POSTAL EXAM
PREPARATION BOOK

THIRD EDITION

All Major Exams Thoroughly Covered in One Book

Norman Hall

Adams Media

New York   London   Toronto   Sydney   New Delhi

Adams Media
An Imprint of Simon & Schuster, Inc.
100 Technology Center Drive
Stoughton, MA 02072

For information about special discounts for bulk purchases, please contact Simon & Schuster Special Sales at 1-866-506-1949 or business@simonandschuster.com.

The Simon & Schuster Speakers Bureau can bring authors to your live event. For more information or to book an event contact the Simon & Schuster Speakers Bureau at 1-866-248-3049 or visit our website at www.simonspeakers.com.

Manufactured in the United States of America

21

Library of Congress Cataloging-in-Publication Data has been applied for.

ISBN 978-1-59869-853-4

Table of Contents

Preface

In my twenty-plus years of preparing people to take various postal tests, it never ceases to amaze me how a large share of applicants make minimal investments toward their test preparation. Make no mistake, these are highly competitive exams. An extra one or two percentage points will make a pivotal difference in getting an interview and being subsequently hired.

Top-step postal wages are close to $25 per hour. When other benefits are included such as medical, retirement, life insurance, vacation and sick leave, to name a few, employment with the United States Postal Service is extremely desirable. Hundreds, if not thousands, of people will apply for these positions. Your use of this study guide will give you a distinct competitive edge over others. You will be able to approach the exam with complete confidence and have the ability to achieve a high test score. Well over a million people have successfully used my test preparation manuals and it will work for you. My confidence is shown through my written GUARANTEE. If, after using this material, you do not score 90 percent or higher on your postal exam, you will be entitled to a full refund from the publisher. (See back page for details.) That should demonstrate how committed I am to helping you achieve your goal of employment.

Once hired, the job satisfaction for these positions is very high and the services provided are considered to be among the most trusted and dependable in both the public and private sectors. Congratulations on your first step toward a new career!

—Norman S. Hall

Introduction

The United States Postal Service, although usually thought of as a tax-supported governmental agency, in fact, has been a private self-supporting organization since 1982. The Postal Service is the eighth largest corporation in this nation, with annual revenues of almost $65 billion. This amounts to approximately 1 percent of the total U.S. economy. With over 700,000 career employees in more than 39,000 post offices that service 146 million delivery points daily, the Postal Service is this nation's largest civilian employer. According to recent statistics (published in area updates), the types of positions within the Postal Service are as follows:

EMPLOYEES

(Statistics as of September 2007)

Total Career Employees:	**701,130**
Headquarters / Field Support Units	5,952
Inspection Service (Field)	3,049
Postmasters	26,203
Supervisors	32,013
Professional / Administrative / Technician	11,955
Clerks	214,802
Motor Vehicle Operators / Maintenance	14,730
Mail Handlers	54,980
Rural Carriers	66,212
Building and Equipment Maintenance	39,903
City Delivery Carriers	225,419
Transitionals	5,912
Total Non-career Employees	**66,708**
Substitute Rural Carriers	50,853
Postmaster Relief and Leave Replacements	9,763
Transitionals	6,092

As shown by this chart, city and rural carriers, clerks, and mail handlers comprise the largest percentage of the work force. The annual personnel turnover rate can range anywhere from 5–15 percent, and is attributable to retirements, promotions, transfers, disabilities, or employees leaving the service for unspecified personal reasons. The Postal Service, therefore, keeps active registers of qualified applicants to fill vacancies as they arise.

The frequencies of exams to the public vary. Ordinarily exams are open to the public once every one to two years. Up until recently, however, some area registers were closed for a period of three or more years due to the advent of automation and the desire to downsize the work force in compliance with leaner budgetary mandates. The Postal Service, however, did not resort to layoffs for a reduction in work force. Instead, downsizing was accomplished through early retirements and normal attrition. The post office is in fact, one of only a few corporations that have never laid off workers. Job security is tantamount to this organization.

When an area register does open, public announcements are made several weeks in advance of the exam in the local media (newspapers, TV, radio) specifying when and where individuals can apply for the test. Test applications can be picked up directly from the post office, completed, and returned to the post office prior to the announcement's closure date. Job postings are available via the Internet at *www.usps.com/employment*. By following the prompts given, you can check nationally which areas are currently accepting applications. This information is continually updated so it is to your advantage to look into this at least once a week to find new openings. Once you have found an opening that is of interest to you, you can apply online to take the exam. You will receive a test announcement number, exam type, and city/state designation along with a short list of questions that relate to basic requirements of the job. For example: are you willing to work an eight-hour shift, work varied schedules, follow established safety guidelines, etc. It is strongly suggested to answer yes to each of these questions. Conditional responses (i.e. No) may indicate a lack of sincere intent to obtain employment. After you provide your full name, Social Security number, and mailing address, you will receive a confirmation detailing your date of application. Within a few weeks, you should receive an Applicant Information Packet in the mail. This packet contains a brief overview of the written exam, a list of items you should bring with you, and sometimes a map of the exam's location will be included for your convenience. For more information on this subject, see Test-Taking Strategies.

In addition to the written exam, there are some minimum requirements that job applicants must meet for employment eligibility. You must:

- Be at least eighteen years of age at the time of appointment or be at least sixteen years of age with a high school diploma or a G.E.D.
- Be a U.S. citizen or have been granted Permanent Resident Alien status in the U.S.
- Be competent in reading and speaking English.
- Be in possession of a valid state driver's license and have a safe driving record.
- Pass a urinalysis drug screen prior to appointment.
- Meet minimum medical and health standards as set forth by the Postal Service. This normally is accomplished by sending an applicant to an appointed physician for a thorough physical. Further specifics concerning medical evaluations can be obtained by contacting the personnel department at your local post office.
- Have not received a dishonorable discharge from military service.

In addition: Men between the ages of eighteen and twenty-six must be registered with the Selective Service System in accordance to Section 3 of the Military Selective Service Act. (This requirement is subject to certain exceptions.) Selective Service Registration forms are available at any post office or, if outside the U.S., at any Consular Office.

GENERAL JOB DESCRIPTION OF PROCESSING, DISTRIBUTION AND DELIVERY POSITIONS

Mail processing and delivery is still a labor-intensive industry, despite some of the advances made in automation. Consequently, this gives a Postal Service applicant several choices. Listed below are the most common jobs available for entry-level personnel and a brief description of what is required, as well as basic salary packages. Most, if not all, of these jobs are available in metropolitan areas. Smaller cities or towns, however, which lack the necessary facilities to process mail, will have fewer positions available. The supplemental packet of information sent to you prior to the exam will stipulate what options are available for your given area.

CITY CARRIER/RURAL CARRIER: Both positions require sorting mail indoors according to the route assigned. Here, prolonged standing, walking, and being able to lift up to 70 pounds will be required. Additionally, city carriers are required to carry a mailbag on the route that can weigh as much as 35 pounds. Once mail is organized according to route schematics, it is then the responsibility of the carrier to deliver as well as collect the mail on the route (regardless of prevailing weather conditions). Driving to and from the route requires not only a valid state driver's license, but also a Government Motor Vehicle Operator's Identification Card obtained by passing a standardized driving test. Carriers are also responsible for handling accountable mails such as express mail, CODs, and registered or certified mailings. The average wage for city carrier positions is $22.79 per hour, with cost of living adjustments. Work hours are regular. **NOTE:** Rural carrier positions differ in the respect that the carrier may have to provide his or her own vehicle to deliver the mail. A valid state driver's license and a minimum of two years driving experience are required. Compensation for rural carrier associates can vary; however, the average hourly rate paid is $21.75 per hour. Additionally, equipment maintenance allowance is provided for use of a personal vehicle. Work hours can be irregular.

MAIL PROCESSOR: This is an indoor position that requires employees to stand for prolonged periods of time while loading and unloading mail from various automated processing equipment. It is desirable (not mandated) that craft employees be able to distinguish basic colors and shades. The Postal Service has adopted a color code scheme that dictates when certain mails are distributed during the course of the week. While color blindness can impair that discernment, it does not entirely preclude an employee from filling such a position. Most color-coded material provides sufficient information for correct distribution. The average wage for mail processors is $22.52 per hour with cost of living adjustments. Work hours for this craft can be irregular and include nights and weekends.

SALES SERVICES AND DISTRIBUTION ASSOCIATE: Essentially this is an indoor position that requires sorting and distribution of mail accordingly to zip code or area schematics. It may involve prolonged periods of standing, reaching, or lifting (as much as 70 pounds at one time). Associates may also be required to work with the public by conducting window services. This can involve such transactions as selling postage stamps, weighing parcels, handling express (overnight) mail, customer parcel pickup or other accountable mail such as certified or registered pieces. It can also entail fielding a wide array of customer questions about other services, or helping to solve customer problems. Associates are personally responsible for all stamp stock assigned to them and the money they receive from daily postal transactions. The average wage for this position is $22.52 with cost of living adjustments. Work hours may be irregular.

MAIL HANDLER: Employees in this craft mostly work in an industrial environment. The job requires loading and unloading sacks of packages and mail that can weigh up to 70 pounds. Some of this work will be performed inside a postal facility, while at other times it will involve working outdoors on a loading dock or platform. Applicants desiring this position must pass a short (approximately ten minutes) strength and stamina test. It simply involves being able to lift a 70-pound sack and moving it to a location a few feet away. Examiners want to be certain that you are able to accomplish such tasks without excessive exertion or, worse, hurting yourself in the attempt. Proper lifting techniques will be demonstrated prior to the test. The average wage for this position is $20.85 per hour with cost of living adjustments. Work hours for this craft may be irregular and include nights and weekends.

To further illustrate pay schedules for craft employees, the information below reflects a national agreement between the NALC (National Association of Letter Carriers union) and USPS management. The five-year agreement, brokered in October 2007, represents an 8.85 percent increase in wages combined with five separate cost of living adjustments. The basic earning schedule for a grade I City Carrier is as follows:

Step	Period Between Steps	Hourly	Yearly	Overtime	Hourly for Part-time Flexibilities
A	96 weeks	$18.52	$38,527	$27.78	$19.26
B	96 weeks	$20.20	$42,025	$30.31	$21.01
C	44 weeks	$20.85	$43,381	$31.28	$21.69
D	44 weeks	$22.10	$45,979	$33.16	$22.99
E	44 weeks	$22.27	$46,338	$33.42	$23.17
F	44 weeks	$22.45	$46,697	$33.68	$23.35
G	44 weeks	$22.62	$47,050	$33.93	$23.53

Step	Period Between Steps	Hourly	Yearly	Overtime	Hourly for Part-time Flexibilities
H	44 weeks	$22.79	$47,408	$34.19	$23.70
I	44 weeks	$22.96	$47.766	$34.45	$23.88
J	34 weeks	$23.13	$48,119	$34.70	$24.06
K	34 weeks	$23.30	$48,478	$34.96	$24.24
L	26 weeks	$23.47	$48,834	$35.22	$24.42
M	26 weeks	$23.65	$49,193	$35.48	$24.60
N	24 weeks	$23.82	$49,552	$35.73	$24.78
O	----------	$23.99	$49,907	$35.99	$24.95

The American Postal Workers Union (APWU), National Postal Mail Handlers Union (NPMHU), and the National Rural Letter Carriers Association (NRLCA) have separate labor agreements with the Postal Service. Not withstanding other contract issues, pay schedules for other craft positions are comparable to what is shown above.

Once an applicant passes the initial screening process (i.e. written exam, interview, physical, etc.) and successfully passes any necessary job simulated performance exercises, he or she is hired on a probationary basis for ninety days. During this period, supervisors closely scrutinize the candidate's performance of tasks that are required of them. The individual's motivation, ability to follow directions, and safety are taken into consideration as well. If, at any point during probation, an immediate supervisor has reason to believe an applicant does not meet expectations, the person in question is released from employment. If, on the other hand, supervisors appreciate the person's job performance and willingness to "go the extra mile," that person becomes entitled to the full complement of career employment benefits. These include:

- Job security
- Paid vacations
- Paid holidays
- Paid sick leave
- Subsidized health insurance
- Life insurance
- Promotion opportunities
- Retirement
- Flexible spending account
- Employer matched savings plan
- Compensation for suggestions

Contact the post office to which you are applying for further information about wages or benefits.

TEST TAKING STRATEGIES

When you receive the applicant information packet in the mail, a guide will be furnished that gives a detailed overview of the exam along with a letter confirming the scheduled time and place of the test. You will need this letter, a photo ID or driver's license, and two #2 pencils in order to be admitted. Under any circumstance, DO NOT arrive late for the exam. Latecomers are not permitted to take the exam and it is very unlikely you will be able to reschedule. Plan to arrive at the place of examination at least 30 minutes early. Once you are in the exam room, examiners/monitors will pass out the test answer sheets. You will be instructed to fill in your personal information (name, mailing address, Social Security Number, etc.), applicable installation office code and the test series number. You will be given the opportunity to select preferential work assignments in various offices. A note of caution should be exercised here. Typically, you will be offered four (4) separate office locations to choose to work in. Each location, depending on personnel needs, will have various positions open. One office may be a bulk mail facility that only offers mail handler positions, while others may have openings for city carriers; sales, service, and distribution associates; and mail processing clerks. Since you are only allowed to pick three (3) offices, choose those that have the widest variety of positions available. You stand a significantly better chance of having your name selected from a register. Once you make this determination, it cannot be changed. Your test score cannot be transferred to offices other than the ones you have selected. It behooves you, therefore, to sign up for other area exams as they become open. The more test scores you have on different registers, the better your chances are for a scheduled interview and subsequent employment.

Listen carefully to all instructions given by the examiners. If you are instructed to stop working because time is up, do not continue to work on the test. You will not be allowed to work on any part of the exam other than what is clearly specified. Deviation in any manner from established test procedures will result in you being disqualified from further employment consideration.

The format of exam questions is multiple choice. This makes your job a little easier because you know that one of the choices offered has to be correct. Even if the answer is not immediately apparent, you have a chance of guessing the correct answer. In addition, if you find you are running out of time in certain exercises, randomly answering the remaining items will more than likely give you a higher test score than leaving answers blank. Be aware, however, that some exercises prohibit this strategy because incorrect exam answers are counted against correct selections. Consequently, exam scores for these exercises can suffer if one guesses with reckless abandon. Exercises are noted in this book where penalty for wrong answers apply.

While multiple-choice exams are easy to complete, you may be surprised at how many people do poorly or do not pass at all because of improperly marking the answer sheet. An example of an answer blank is provided below to demonstrate how to mark an answer properly.

The following examples are answer blanks that have been improperly marked, leading to a poor test score.

Answer sheets are not hand scored. Rather, they are scanned by machine and the machine is indifferent to whatever the reason may be for sloppiness. It will score the answer wrong (even though it may, in fact, be the correct selection) if not enough effort is made to completely fill in the circle. On this same point, however, do not waste too much time filling in answers. As you work through the sample exercises in this book, you will establish an effective balance between speed and accuracy. Practice is the key.

Another costly mistake is accidentally marking answers that do not correspond to the question you are currently working on. A simple way to prevent this problem is to check every ten questions or so to verify that what was marked corresponds with the question at hand. Nothing can be more frustrating than completing all the questions given and then learn you are one answer short on the answer sheet. There will not be enough time to backtrack to discover where the error began. Also, if you decide to skip a question that you are unsure of, be certain to skip the corresponding answer blank for the same reason. One last point about marking a multiple choice answer sheet: If you change your mind about any answer, be certain to erase the original answer COMPLETELY. If two answers are apparently marked, the scanner will consider the answer incorrect. Be aware too, that statistically the first answer arrived at is generally the correct choice.

STUDY SUGGESTIONS

Postal Service examinations are not the kind of exam on which you can hope for a high test score after "cramming" the night before. Good study habits have a profound impact on how well you do on the exam. If you follow these few simple guidelines, you can approach the exam more relaxed and confident, two essential ingredients for top performance on any exam.

Regular study times should be established and tailored to your comfort. Each person's schedule is different. Some people prefer to study for one or two hours at a time and then take a break, while others prefer several hours of straight study. Regardless of how you study, it is important you do it regularly; do not rely on a marathon. You will remember the subject matter more easily and comprehend it better if you establish regular study habits.

Where you study is important also. Eliminate any distractions that can disrupt your studies. The television, telephone, and noisy children can hinder quality study time. It is suggested you set aside one room in your home as a study place and use it to isolate yourself from distractions. If you elect to use a bedroom as a study area, avoid lying in bed while you read. Otherwise, you may find yourself more inclined to sleep than to learn. It is important to have a good desk, a comfortable chair, and adequate lighting, anything less can hamper your studying. If studying in your home is not feasible, go to your local library or some other place that offers an environment conducive to study.

Again, be sure to get plenty of rest, especially the night before the examination. It is counterproductive to try to study when you are overly tired. It is also important not to skip meals. Your level of concentration during the exam can suffer if you lack proper nutrition. Coffee and other stimulants are not recommended. Although you are allowed to leave the examination room with permission, you will forfeit valuable test time. Why take the unnecessary risk of jeopardizing your test score?

PART I
Examination 460

[This page is intentionally blank.]

Address Cross Comparison

Every stage of the mail sorting process must be done accurately and efficiently. If either a Postal Clerk or Carrier misreads an address, mail is misdirected or delayed. Therefore, Postal personnel must be able to tell whether two addresses are the same or if they represent two entirely different destinations. Sometimes, differences between addresses are subtle—small differences in spelling, for example, or transposed numerals. An applicant must be able to quickly scan the address lists in this section and make an accurate determination to this effect.

At first glance, most people view this exercise as perhaps the easiest section in the exam. However, there is only a limited amount of time allowed (6 minutes) to complete the ninety-five questions given. Therefore, it is important to spend as little time as possible on each question, and yet, be thorough enough to select the correct answer without guessing. In fact, because of the time constraints, examiners will point out at the beginning of this test that you are not expected to finish.

This section of the test provides ninety-five pairs of addresses. You need to determine if each pair of addresses is different or exactly alike. The answer sheet to this test will have two choices from which you may select. Darken answer (A) if the pair of addresses are shown exactly alike. Darken answer (D) if the addresses are different. The ten pairs of sample addresses that follow will lend a general understanding of how this test is constructed. Take no more than 30 seconds to complete the samples.

1.	23351 Soundview Dr.	25331 Soundview Dr.	(A) (D)
2.	Willamette Pkwy	Willemette Pkwy	(A) (D)
3.	Boulder, CO 87523	Boulder, CO 87523	(A) (D)
4.	15-A Falcon Ridge	15-A Falcon Place	(A) (D)
5.	Cedar Rapids, IA	Cedar Rapids, IA	(A) (D)
6.	1895 SW 150th St.	1895 150th St. SE	(A) (D)
7.	Dallas, TX 73511	Dallas, TX 73511	(A) (D)
8.	1414 Laramie Ct.	1414 Laramie Ct.	(A) (D)
9.	17953 Lancaster Apt. C	17935 Lancaster Apt. C	(A) (D)
10.	1310 E 3rd Ave.	1310 E 3rd Ave.	(A) (D)

Only pair numbers 3, 5, 7, 8, and 10 are exactly alike and should have the answer Ⓐ darkened. Answer Ⓓ would be darkened for the remaining pairs (1, 2, 4, 6, and 9). If you missed any of these samples, review the pairs and determine what was overlooked. As you can see, subtle differences in either the numbers or the spelling can be unrecognizable at first glance. Most people, for one reason or another, can spot transposed numbers in either the zip code or the street address. However, applicants frequently overlook differences in addresses that sound the same. Pay particularly close attention to the addresses of this nature before marking your answer sheet. Caution exercised here will pay off in terms of a higher test score.

You may have noticed too, that while working on the sample exercises a straightedge or ruler could have helped reduce confusion. Unfortunately, such aids are not allowed in the examination room. However, you are allowed two pencils, one of which can serve as a crude straightedge, if necessary.

One other helpful trick to reduce confusion while comparing a set of addresses is to place your index finger on one column of addresses and your little finger on the other column. As you proceed with each pair, move your fingers in unison down the page. This does essentially the same thing as a straightedge. Using this method makes it substantially easier to focus your attention on just the two addresses you are comparing. You also save precious time by not having to search for where you left off in order to mark your answer sheet.

Three practice exercises are provided in this chapter. Tear the answer sheets out of the book for your convenience in marking answers. To help you get an idea of how the actual exam is conducted, you should use a kitchen timer or have someone time you for the allotted six minutes as you work each exercise. This will protect you from the unnecessary distraction of timing yourself. When time is called, do not work any further on the exercise. If you continue, you will lose the true sense of what will be required of you on the actual exam.

A scale is provided at the end of each exercise to allow you to determine your standings. Simply count the number of correct answers you have made and then subtract those that were missed. This is the one exercise in which applicants are penalized for wrong answers. Guessing answers for this part of the exam is not recommended.

ADDRESS CROSS COMPARISON/EXERCISE 1   TIME: 6 MINUTES

1. Burien Ave.   Bruin Avenue

2. 12237 Hartford Dr.   12327 Hartford Dr.

3. Marguriete Blvd.   Margurete Blvd.

4. 4731 E. 17th St.   4731 E. 17th St.

5. Truman Way   Trueman Way

6. 120-A Levenworth Ave.   120-A Levenworth Ave.

7. Cottage Blvd.   Cottage St.

8. 16-E Pinecone   16-E Pinecone

9. Ft. Worth, TX   Ft. Apache, TX

10. San Jose, CA 94371   San Jose, CA 94371

11. Deception Pass   Deseption Pass

12. 137 Hogan Ln.   137 Hogan Ln.

13. 4536 NE 103rd St.   4536 NW 103rd St.

14. Hutchison Ave.   Hutchenson Ave.

15. 30785 Elliot Bay Blvd   30785 Elliot Bay Blvd

16. Sparks, NV   Sparks, NY

17. Springfield, MS 97132   Springfield, MS 97132

18. Coos Lane   Coos Ln.

19. Evergreen, ND   Evergrein, ND

20. Butte, MT 05317   Butte, MT 03517

21. 41-RT 8 Colo, IA   41-RT 8 Colo, IA

22. Edgemont Pl.   Edgemont Place

23. 3071 Beach Dr.   3071 Beach Dr.

24.	22 Falcon E.	33 Falcon W.
25.	Anderson Heights	Andersin Heights
26.	Sparrow Hills Rd.	Eagle Hills Rd.
27.	3249 Brice Pkwy	3249 Brice Pkwy
28.	42-A Savon Circle	42-D Sabria Circle
29.	Jamestown, NJ	Jameston, NJ
30.	Victoria, BC T6J 2M8	Victoria, BC T6J 2M8
31.	359119 Galloway St.	359119 Galloway St.
32.	Rome, Georgia 36652	Rome, Georgia 36652
33.	Phinney Place	Phiney Place
34.	Constantine Cr.	Constantine Cr.
35.	44-AB Wilkes Dr.	44-AB Wilikes Dr.
36.	Ft. Collins, Colo.	Ft. Collins, CO
37.	2780 St. John Blvd	2780 St. Johns Blvd
38.	Livingston Ave.	Livingston Ave.
39.	Bloominton, Ill 61653	Bloomington, Ill 61663
40.	4802-E Blaine Pkwy	4802-W Blaine Pkwy
41.	Dallas, TX 68703	Dallas, TX 68307
42.	480-C Porter Way	480-C Porter Way
43.	Snohomish, WA	Snohamish, WA
44.	2516 Johnson Pl.	2516 Johnston Pl.
45.	3540 Jensen Way	354 Jensen Way
46.	4012 Rolling Oaks View	4012 Rolling Oaks View
47.	H-38 Harsten Blvd.	H-38 Harsten Blvd.

48.	Ankorage, AL	Anchorage, AK
49.	Petersville, KY 47159	Petersville, KY 47159
50.	3845 Reid Dr.	3844 Reid Ave.
51.	401-A Virginia Pl.	401-A Virginia Pl.
52.	10771 Dakota Point	10717 Dakota Point
53.	Faunterloy Center	Founterloy Center
54.	4013 Brussels Ct.	4013 Brussels Ct.
55.	Stovington, Conn.	Stovers, CO 43212
56.	746 Ash Place	746 Ash Pl.
57.	B-109 Country Ln.	B-109 Country Ln.
58.	Marguriette Ave.	Marguriete Ave.
59.	7140 Constitution Dr.	7140 Constitution Pl.
60.	1818-A Bloomfield Apts.	1818-A Bloomfield Apts.
61.	4099 Harbel Pkwy.	4099 Harbel Pkwy.
62.	W. Palm Beach, CA	Palm Beach, CA
63.	Phoenix, Arizona	Phoenix, AR 85021
64.	1980 S. Nipsic Pl	1980 S. Nipsic Pl.
65.	1600 Tangerine Dr.	1600 Tangerine Dr.
66.	206-C Abernathy Ct.	206-C Abernathy Ct.
67.	Newberry, W. VA	Newberry, W. VA
68.	3401 N. 19th St.	3401 W. 20th St.
69.	1280 15th Ave.	1280 13th Ave.
70.	1300 Forest Ridge	1300 Forest Ridge
71.	Montgomery Pl.	Montgomery Pl.

72.	9-D Pierce Grahm Cr.	9-D Pierce Grahm Cr.
73.	New York, NY 19104	New York, NY 19140
74.	7780 Proxmire Blvd.	8077 Proxmire Blvd.
75.	1509 Ivy Terrace	1509 Ivy Terrace
76.	275 Rampert Dr.	275 Ramport Dr.
77.	Newport, CA 99510	Newport, PA 99510
78.	1144 60th St. NW	4411 60th St. NW
79.	117 Chespeke Ct.	117 Chesepeak Ct.
80.	Willow Way E-302	Willow Way E-302
81.	672 Prairie Pl.	672 Prairie Pl.
82.	1212 Seneca Court	2121 Seneca Court
83.	9977 Mercury Blvd.	9977 Mercury Blvd.
84.	Waterloo, IA 50578	Waterloo, IA 50587
85.	14818 1st Ave.	14818 2nd Ave.
86.	1207 E. 120th Pl.	1207 E. 120th Pl.
87.	South Port, KY 98451	South Port, WY 98499
88.	Twelve Oaks, MI	Twelve Oaks, MI
89.	161 S. Duff St.	161 N. Duff St.
90.	1391 Fremont Pkwy	1931 Preemont Pkwy
91.	43 Terrington Park	43 Terrington Park
92.	Essex, MD 01426	Essex, MD 01426
93.	Covings, NM 53845	Sante Fe, NM
94.	Bessert Dr. NE	Bessert Dr. NE
95.	30921 W. Hamilton	93021 E. Hamilton

-END OF TEST-

ANSWER SHEET TO ADDRESS CROSS COMPARISON/EXERCISE 1

1. Ⓐ Ⓓ
2. Ⓐ Ⓓ
3. Ⓐ Ⓓ
4. Ⓐ Ⓓ
5. Ⓐ Ⓓ
6. Ⓐ Ⓓ
7. Ⓐ Ⓓ
8. Ⓐ Ⓓ
9. Ⓐ Ⓓ
10. Ⓐ Ⓓ
11. Ⓐ Ⓓ
12. Ⓐ Ⓓ
13. Ⓐ Ⓓ
14. Ⓐ Ⓓ
15. Ⓐ Ⓓ
16. Ⓐ Ⓓ
17. Ⓐ Ⓓ
18. Ⓐ Ⓓ
19. Ⓐ Ⓓ
20. Ⓐ Ⓓ
21. Ⓐ Ⓓ
22. Ⓐ Ⓓ
23. Ⓐ Ⓓ
24. Ⓐ Ⓓ
25. Ⓐ Ⓓ
26. Ⓐ Ⓓ
27. Ⓐ Ⓓ
28. Ⓐ Ⓓ
29. Ⓐ Ⓓ
30. Ⓐ Ⓓ
31. Ⓐ Ⓓ
32. Ⓐ Ⓓ

33. Ⓐ Ⓓ
34. Ⓐ Ⓓ
35. Ⓐ Ⓓ
36. Ⓐ Ⓓ
37. Ⓐ Ⓓ
38. Ⓐ Ⓓ
39. Ⓐ Ⓓ
40. Ⓐ Ⓓ
41. Ⓐ Ⓓ
42. Ⓐ Ⓓ
43. Ⓐ Ⓓ
44. Ⓐ Ⓓ
45. Ⓐ Ⓓ
46. Ⓐ Ⓓ
47. Ⓐ Ⓓ
48. Ⓐ Ⓓ
49. Ⓐ Ⓓ
50. Ⓐ Ⓓ
51. Ⓐ Ⓓ
52. Ⓐ Ⓓ
53. Ⓐ Ⓓ
54. Ⓐ Ⓓ
55. Ⓐ Ⓓ
56. Ⓐ Ⓓ
57. Ⓐ Ⓓ
58. Ⓐ Ⓓ
59. Ⓐ Ⓓ
60. Ⓐ Ⓓ
61. Ⓐ Ⓓ
62. Ⓐ Ⓓ
63. Ⓐ Ⓓ
64. Ⓐ Ⓓ

65. Ⓐ Ⓓ
66. Ⓐ Ⓓ
67. Ⓐ Ⓓ
68. Ⓐ Ⓓ
69. Ⓐ Ⓓ
70. Ⓐ Ⓓ
71. Ⓐ Ⓓ
72. Ⓐ Ⓓ
73. Ⓐ Ⓓ
74. Ⓐ Ⓓ
75. Ⓐ Ⓓ
76. Ⓐ Ⓓ
77. Ⓐ Ⓓ
78. Ⓐ Ⓓ
79. Ⓐ Ⓓ
80. Ⓐ Ⓓ
81. Ⓐ Ⓓ
82. Ⓐ Ⓓ
83. Ⓐ Ⓓ
84. Ⓐ Ⓓ
85. Ⓐ Ⓓ
86. Ⓐ Ⓓ
87. Ⓐ Ⓓ
88. Ⓐ Ⓓ
89. Ⓐ Ⓓ
90. Ⓐ Ⓓ
91. Ⓐ Ⓓ
92. Ⓐ Ⓓ
93. Ⓐ Ⓓ
94. Ⓐ Ⓓ
95. Ⓐ Ⓓ

(This page may be removed to mark answers.)

ADDRESS CROSS COMPARISION/EXERCISE 1 ANSWERS

1.	D	33.	D	65.	A
2.	D	34.	A	66.	A
3.	D	35.	D	67.	A
4.	A	36.	D	68.	D
5.	D	37.	D	69.	D
6.	A	38.	A	70.	A
7.	D	39.	D	71.	A
8.	A	40.	D	72.	A
9.	D	41.	D	73.	D
10.	A	42.	A	74.	D
11.	D	43.	D	75.	A
12.	A	44.	D	76.	D
13.	D	45.	D	77.	D
14.	D	46.	A	78.	D
15.	A	47.	A	79.	D
16.	D	48.	D	80.	A
17.	A	49.	A	81.	A
18.	D	50.	D	82.	D
19.	D	51.	A	83.	A
20.	D	52.	D	84.	D
21.	A	53.	D	85.	D
22.	D	54.	A	86.	A
23.	A	55.	D	87.	D
24.	D	56.	D	88.	A
25.	D	57.	A	89.	D
26.	D	58.	D	90.	D
27.	A	59.	D	91.	A
28.	D	60.	A	92.	A
29.	D	61.	A	93.	D
30.	A	62.	D	94.	A
31.	A	63.	D	95.	D
32.	A	64.	A		

If you scored:
90 or more correct, you have an excellent score.
85–89 correct, you have a good score.
84 or fewer correct, you should practice more.

ADDRESS CROSS COMPARISON/EXERCISE 2   TIME: 6 MINUTES

1.	2103 W. Highland Ave.	3102 W. Highland Ave.
2.	4609 Simpson Pkwy	4609 Simpsen Pkwy
3.	404-C Trenton Park	404-C Trentan Park
4.	Bowling Green, KY	Bowling Green, KY
5.	New Haven, CT 01975	New Haven, CT 01975
6.	Covington Cove	SW Covington Cove
7.	St. Louis, MO 48411	St. Louis, MO 41481
8.	Yuma, AZ	Yuma, AZ
9.	Santa Cruz, CA 99580	Santa Clara, CA 99580
10.	Erwin Point Dr. NW	Erwin Point Dr. NW
11.	21-C Petersberg Ave. NE	21 Petersberg Ave. NE
12.	47109 Nome Ave.	47109 Nome Ave.
13.	558 E. 160th St.	558 W. 160th St.
14.	89D Preston Blvd.	89D Preston Blvd.
15.	Harrisburg, PA 01184	Harrington, PA 08114
16.	Reno, NV 42851	Reno, NV 42851
17.	77 SE Fleming Rd.	77 SE Fleming Rd.
18.	Farmington Hills, CT	Farmingten Hills, CT
19.	1911 Jensen Way	1911 Jensen Way
20.	SW Tiffany Ct.	SW Tiffany Ct.
21.	33641 Front St.	33641 Front St.
22.	430-A McAllen Rd.	430-A McAllen Rd.
23.	791 Penny Square	719 Penny Square

24.	NE Pinchont View	NE Pinchant View
25.	6092 Wheaton Way	6092 Wheaton Way
26.	443 E. 17th St.	443 E. 107th St.
27.	Elsinore Blvd W.	Elsinore Blvd W.
28.	141 Montgomery Place	141 Montgomery Place
29.	742 Callahan Pl.	742 Calahan Pl.
30.	69 Tremont St.	96 Tremont St.
31.	1500 Pershing Blvd. Apt. 37	1500 Pershing Blvd. Apt. 37
32.	223 Finland Ave.	223 Finland Ave.
33.	Atlanta, GA 28976	Atlanta, GA 28976
34.	Gainesville, Fla 19766	Gainesville, Fla 19766
35.	2140 NW Carlson	2140 NW Carlson
36.	40301 E. Seneca	40301 NE Seneca
37.	Fremont, NE 57510	Freemont, NE 57510
38.	2020 Parkington Sq.	2020 Parkington Sq.
39.	47-D Spruce Ave.	47-D Spruce Ave.
40.	Suite N Columbia Square	Suite N Columbia Pkwy
41.	Waco, TX 55212	Waco, TX 55212
42.	278 Fontain Dr.	278 Fountain Dr.
43.	521 Essex Blvd.	521 Esser Blvd.
44.	1449 Bloomington Cr.	1449 Bloomington Cr.
45.	3032 Edgingston Way	3302 Edgingston Way
46.	14-A Hazelwood Pkwy.	14-A Hazelwood Pkwy.
47.	Island Lake Dr. NW	Island Lake Dr. NW
48.	29471 Chicago Blvd.	29417 Chicago Blvd.

49.	774 NE 72nd Ave.	774 NE 72nd Ave.
50.	Little Rock, Ark. 33741	Little Stone, Ark. 33741
51.	Norfolk, VA 11179	Norfolk, VA 11197
52.	3050 Lebaron Way	3050 Lebarron Way
53.	4640 NW 11th St.	464 NW 11th St.
54.	738 Halverson Dr.	738 Halverson Dr.
55.	12-A Nordstrom Way	12-A Nordstrom Way
56.	Presley Ct. SW	Presley Ct. SW
57.	1319 E. 22nd	1319 E. 22nd
58.	2020 Ramport St.	2020 Romport St.
59.	Forsythe Ln. E.	Forsithe Ln. E.
60.	81737 Knoll Dr.	81737 Knoll Rd.
61.	N. 40th Place	S. 40th Place
62.	207-H Evansdale W.	207-H Evansdale W.
63.	913 SW Hampshire Ln.	913 SW Hampshire Ln.
64.	25-C Flamingo Dr.	25-C Flamingo St.
65.	Boise, ID 47814	Boise, ID 47814
66.	4700 Kitsap Way	4770 Kitsap Way
67.	Chepowacket Blvd. SE	Chepowackat Blvd. SE
68.	1010 Tanner St.	10010 Tanner St.
69.	Greensboro, NC 21478	Greensberg, NC 21478
70.	Palo Alto, CA 90990	Palo Alto, CA 90990
71.	38841 Padock St.	33814 Padock St.
72.	251 E. Cascade Trail	251 E. Cascade Trail
73.	2428 Parker Place	2423 Parker Place

74.	South Shore, WA 99944	South Shore, WA 99944
75.	137 NW Symington Ct.	137 NW Symington Ct.
76.	Fairbanks, Alaska	Fairbanks, Alaska
77.	SE Karrington Blvd.	SE Carrington Blvd.
78.	11111 Tisdale Pkwy.	1111 Tisdale Pkwy.
79.	3781 E. Livingston Sq.	3781 E. Livingston Sq.
80.	Brockton, Mass. 01171	Brockton, MS 01171
81.	734 A Twin Bay	734 A Wynn Bay
82.	4000 Elsinora Beach	4000 Elsinore Beach
83.	1619 Frampton Ave.	1619 Frampton Ave.
84.	7901 Havelin Blvd.	790 Havelin Blvd.
85.	Portland, ME 00521	Portland, ME 05021
86.	Sweitzer Way SW	Sweitzer Way SW
87.	43481 Bellingham Way	43431 Bellingham Way
88.	4972 Terryington Ave.	4972 Terryington Ave.
89.	Paradise Valley, AZ	Paridise Valley, AZ
90.	13-B Westin Lake Dr.	13-B Westin Lake Dr.
91.	4100 Hildalgo Park NE	4100 Hildalgo Park NE
92.	17181 Austin Center	17181 Astin Center
93.	308 Stephenson Ave.	308 Stehensen Ave.
94.	Reno, NV 87616	Reno, NV 87616
95.	2222 S. Hoffman Dr.	2222 S. Hoffman Dr.

-END OF TEST-

ANSWER SHEET TO ADDRESS CROSS COMPARISON/EXERCISE 2

1. Ⓐ Ⓓ	33. Ⓐ Ⓓ	65. Ⓐ Ⓓ
2. Ⓐ Ⓓ	34. Ⓐ Ⓓ	66. Ⓐ Ⓓ
3. Ⓐ Ⓓ	35. Ⓐ Ⓓ	67. Ⓐ Ⓓ
4. Ⓐ Ⓓ	36. Ⓐ Ⓓ	68. Ⓐ Ⓓ
5. Ⓐ Ⓓ	37. Ⓐ Ⓓ	69. Ⓐ Ⓓ
6. Ⓐ Ⓓ	38. Ⓐ Ⓓ	70. Ⓐ Ⓓ
7. Ⓐ Ⓓ	39. Ⓐ Ⓓ	71. Ⓐ Ⓓ
8. Ⓐ Ⓓ	40. Ⓐ Ⓓ	72. Ⓐ Ⓓ
9. Ⓐ Ⓓ	41. Ⓐ Ⓓ	73. Ⓐ Ⓓ
10. Ⓐ Ⓓ	42. Ⓐ Ⓓ	74. Ⓐ Ⓓ
11. Ⓐ Ⓓ	43. Ⓐ Ⓓ	75. Ⓐ Ⓓ
12. Ⓐ Ⓓ	44. Ⓐ Ⓓ	76. Ⓐ Ⓓ
13. Ⓐ Ⓓ	45. Ⓐ Ⓓ	77. Ⓐ Ⓓ
14. Ⓐ Ⓓ	46. Ⓐ Ⓓ	78. Ⓐ Ⓓ
15. Ⓐ Ⓓ	47. Ⓐ Ⓓ	79. Ⓐ Ⓓ
16. Ⓐ Ⓓ	48. Ⓐ Ⓓ	80. Ⓐ Ⓓ
17. Ⓐ Ⓓ	49. Ⓐ Ⓓ	81. Ⓐ Ⓓ
18. Ⓐ Ⓓ	50. Ⓐ Ⓓ	82. Ⓐ Ⓓ
19. Ⓐ Ⓓ	51. Ⓐ Ⓓ	83. Ⓐ Ⓓ
20. Ⓐ Ⓓ	52. Ⓐ Ⓓ	84. Ⓐ Ⓓ
21. Ⓐ Ⓓ	53. Ⓐ Ⓓ	85. Ⓐ Ⓓ
22. Ⓐ Ⓓ	54. Ⓐ Ⓓ	86. Ⓐ Ⓓ
23. Ⓐ Ⓓ	55. Ⓐ Ⓓ	87. Ⓐ Ⓓ
24. Ⓐ Ⓓ	56. Ⓐ Ⓓ	88. Ⓐ Ⓓ
25. Ⓐ Ⓓ	57. Ⓐ Ⓓ	89. Ⓐ Ⓓ
26. Ⓐ Ⓓ	58. Ⓐ Ⓓ	90. Ⓐ Ⓓ
27. Ⓐ Ⓓ	59. Ⓐ Ⓓ	91. Ⓐ Ⓓ
28. Ⓐ Ⓓ	60. Ⓐ Ⓓ	92. Ⓐ Ⓓ
29. Ⓐ Ⓓ	61. Ⓐ Ⓓ	93. Ⓐ Ⓓ
30. Ⓐ Ⓓ	62. Ⓐ Ⓓ	94. Ⓐ Ⓓ
31. Ⓐ Ⓓ	63. Ⓐ Ⓓ	95. Ⓐ Ⓓ
32. Ⓐ Ⓓ	64. Ⓐ Ⓓ	

(This page may be removed to mark answers.)

ADDRESS CROSS COMPARISON/EXERCISE 2 ANSWERS

1.	D	33.	A	65.	A
2.	D	34.	A	66.	D
3.	D	35.	A	67.	D
4.	A	36.	D	68.	D
5.	A	37.	D	69.	D
6.	D	38.	A	70.	A
7.	D	39.	A	71.	D
8.	A	40.	D	72.	A
9.	D	41.	A	73.	D
10.	A	42.	D	74.	A
11.	D	43.	D	75.	A
12.	A	44.	A	76.	A
13.	D	45.	D	77.	D
14.	A	46.	A	78.	D
15.	D	47.	A	79.	A
16.	A	48.	D	80.	D
17.	A	49.	A	81.	D
18.	D	50.	D	82.	D
19.	A	51.	D	83.	A
20.	A	52.	D	84.	D
21.	A	53.	D	85.	D
22.	A	54.	A	86.	A
23.	D	55.	A	87.	D
24.	D	56.	A	88.	A
25.	A	57.	A	89.	D
26.	D	58.	D	90.	A
27.	A	59.	D	91.	A
28.	A	60.	D	92.	D
29.	D	61.	D	93.	D
30.	D	62.	A	94.	A
31.	A	63.	A	95.	A
32.	A	64.	D		

If you scored:

90 or more correct, you have an excellent score.
85–89 correct, you have a good score.
84 or fewer correct, you should practice more.

ADDRESS CROSS COMPARISON/EXERCISE 3   TIME: 6 MINUTES

1. 1216 W. 160th Ave.   1216 S. 160th Ave.

2. 2020 Poplar Bluff Dr.   2020 Popular Bluff Dr.

3. 131-D Wasau Terrace   131-D Wasau Terrace

4. Eau Claire, Wis. 76944   Eau Clare, Wis. 76944

5. 7088 Benton Pkwy   7088 Benton Pkwy

6. Pocatello, ID 87631   Pocatello, ID 87613

7. 19766 Rochestor Blvd.   19766 Rochestor Blvd.

8. 8755 SE Ironwood Dr.   8755 NE Ironwood Dr.

9. 6467 Ramsey Lane S.   6467 Ramsey Lane S.

10. Salida, Colo. 69481   Salada, Colo. 69418

11. 5000 Natchez CR   5000 Natchez CR

12. Chillicothe, MO 54311   Chilliclothe, MO 54311

13. 21221 Vicksburg St.   21221 Vicksburg St.

14. 50571 NE Coleman Dr.   50751 NE Coleman Dr.

15. Tucumcari, NM 60681   Tucumcary, NM 60681

16. 80-B Roswell Way SW   80-B Rosewell Way SW

17. 1612 Odessa Ave.   1612 Odessa Ave.

18. Amarillo, TX 50123   Amabrillo, TX 50123

19. 30903 Buffalo Pass   30903 Buffalo Pass

20. Hannibal, MO 45555   Hannibol, MO 45555

21. 60741 NW Ottumwa Dr.   67041 NW Ottumwa Dr.

22. 1010 Remington Ct.   1010 Remington Ct.

23. W. Palm Beach, Fla.   E. Palm Beach, Fla.

24.	80473 McComb Blvd.	80473 MacComb Blvd.
25.	6709 67th St. NW	6709 67th St. W.
26.	137-G Albert Lane	137-G Albert Lane
27.	Prescott, Ariz 84988	Prescott, Ariz 84998
28.	2070 Casper Place	2070 Casper Place
29.	603 Dexter Rd.	603 Dexter Rd.
30.	4111 Montrose Ave.	4111 Montrose Ave. NW
31.	15990 Humboldt Dr.	15909 Humboldt Dr.
32.	Pierre, SD 69009	Pierre, SD 60909
33.	4030 E. Cookie Pk.	4030 E. Cooke Pk.
34.	Missoula, MT 88083	Missoula, MD 88803
35.	33810 Mitchell Dr. SE	33810 Mitchell Dr. SE
36.	44-C Shenandoah Apts.	44-C Senandoah Apts.
37.	A-153 Roanoke Dr.	A-153 Roanoke Dr.
38.	Alpena, Mich. 47055	Alpena, Mich. 47055
39.	5151 Sherbrook	1515 Sherbrook
40.	32323 Roman Square	32323 Romon Square
41.	Charlotte, NC 13796	Charlette, NC 13796
42.	1811-B Petersberg	1811-B Peterboroughs
43.	645 Corbin St.	645 Corbin St.
44.	3044 Violet Dr. SE	3404 Violet Dr. NW
45.	450-B Deer Park	450-B Deer Place
46.	31571 Barrington Ave.	31571 Barrington Ave.
47.	3215 S. Dundee Dr.	3215 S. Dundee Dr.
48.	747 Kane St. Apt 574	747 Kane St. Apt 574

49.	189 Foxhill Ave.	189 Foxhill Ave.
50.	8752 W. Helm	8725 W. Helm
51.	1414 Millbern Rd.	1414 Millburn Rd.
52.	321-J Holdridge Dr.	321-J Holdridge Dr.
53.	351 Belvidere Pt.	351 Belvadere Pt.
54.	80913 E. Sullivan Pl.	80913 N Sullivan Pl.
55.	1314 Callahan Ln.	1314 Callahan Ln.
56.	2023 Gardner Pkwy	2023 Gardner Pkwy
57.	B-1709 Greenwood Apts.	B-1709 Greenwood Apts.
58.	1199 Hawley Ave. SW	1999 Hawley Ave. SE
59.	80019 Scribner Dr.	80019 Scribner Dr.
60.	4458 Countryside Ct.	4458 Countryside Cr.
61.	Chicago, Ill 60691	Chicago, Ill 69601
62.	513 Ivanhoe Ave.	531 Ivanhoe Ave.
63.	6050 N. Kirchoff	6500 N. Kirchoff
64.	13133 Schaumburgh Dr.	13133 Schaumburgh Dr.
65.	1705 E. Addison Center	1705 S. Addison Center
66.	104 Glen Ellyn	104 Glenn Ellyn
67.	2012-E Barber Corners	2012-E Barbara Corners
68.	99661 Westmont Ave. S.	99661 Westmont Ave. S.
69.	7001 NW Liberty View	7001 NW Liberty View
70.	125 88th St. NE	125 88th Dr. SE
71.	Wytheville, VA 15891	Wytheville, VA 15891
72.	1410 Wheaton Way	1401 Wheaton Way
73.	79090 Indian Hts. SW	79090 Indian Hts. SW

74.	345 Lambert Lane	345 Lamburt Lane
75.	17171 Camalot Dr.	17117 Camalot Dr.
76.	8873 Stickney Blvd. NE	8873 Stickney Blvd. NE
77.	C-679 Hammond Dr.	6679 Hammond Dr.
78.	140 Wilmette Ridge	140 Wilmette Ridge
79.	Bend, OR 80077	Bend, Oregon 80077
80.	Springfield, OH 39411	Springfield, OH 39441
81.	344 NE Baldwin Pt.	344 NE Baldwin Pt.
82.	14001 Prospect Dr.	14007 Prospect Dr.
83.	307 N Elm St.	307 N Elm St.
84.	409 Kittyhawk Pl	409 Kittehawk Pl
85.	16073 Algoquin Ave.	16073 Algoquin Ave. SW
86.	2000 Euclid Blvd.	2009 Euclid Blvd.
87.	7581 Lincolnshire Dr.	7581 Lincolnshire Dr.
88.	97137 Turnball Woods	97137 Turnball Woods
89.	3042 Hintz St.	3042 Hienz St.
90.	5013 Twin Orchard Ln.	5013 Twin Orchid Ln.
91.	1906 S. Central Ave.	1906 S. Central Ave.
92.	6167 Hoffman Estates	6716 Hoffman Estates
93.	4311 Devon Dr. N	4311 Devon Dr. S
94.	80118 Nickols Ave.	80118 Nickols Ave.
95.	347 N 82nd St.	347 N 82nd St.

-END OF TEST-

ANSWER SHEET TO ADDRESS CROSS COMPARISON/EXERCISE 3

1. (A) (D)	33. (A) (D)	65. (A) (D)
2. (A) (D)	34. (A) (D)	66. (A) (D)
3. (A) (D)	35. (A) (D)	67. (A) (D)
4. (A) (D)	36. (A) (D)	68. (A) (D)
5. (A) (D)	37. (A) (D)	69. (A) (D)
6. (A) (D)	38. (A) (D)	70. (A) (D)
7. (A) (D)	39. (A) (D)	71. (A) (D)
8. (A) (D)	40. (A) (D)	72. (A) (D)
9. (A) (D)	41. (A) (D)	73. (A) (D)
10. (A) (D)	42. (A) (D)	74. (A) (D)
11. (A) (D)	43. (A) (D)	75. (A) (D)
12. (A) (D)	44. (A) (D)	76. (A) (D)
13. (A) (D)	45. (A) (D)	77. (A) (D)
14. (A) (D)	46. (A) (D)	78. (A) (D)
15. (A) (D)	47. (A) (D)	79. (A) (D)
16. (A) (D)	48. (A) (D)	80. (A) (D)
17. (A) (D)	49. (A) (D)	81. (A) (D)
18. (A) (D)	50. (A) (D)	82. (A) (D)
19. (A) (D)	51. (A) (D)	83. (A) (D)
20. (A) (D)	52. (A) (D)	84. (A) (D)
21. (A) (D)	53. (A) (D)	85. (A) (D)
22. (A) (D)	54. (A) (D)	86. (A) (D)
23. (A) (D)	55. (A) (D)	87. (A) (D)
24. (A) (D)	56. (A) (D)	88. (A) (D)
25. (A) (D)	57. (A) (D)	89. (A) (D)
26. (A) (D)	58. (A) (D)	90. (A) (D)
27. (A) (D)	59. (A) (D)	91. (A) (D)
28. (A) (D)	60. (A) (D)	92. (A) (D)
29. (A) (D)	61. (A) (D)	93. (A) (D)
30. (A) (D)	62. (A) (D)	94. (A) (D)
31. (A) (D)	63. (A) (D)	95. (A) (D)
32. (A) (D)	64. (A) (D)	

(This page may be removed to mark answers.)

ADDRESS CROSS COMPARISON/EXERCISE 3 ANSWERS

1.	D	33.	D	65.	D
2.	D	34.	D	66.	D
3.	A	35.	A	67.	D
4.	D	36.	D	68.	A
5.	A	37.	A	69.	A
6.	D	38.	A	70.	D
7.	A	39.	D	71.	A
8.	D	40.	D	72.	D
9.	A	41.	D	73.	A
10.	D	42.	D	74.	D
11.	A	43.	A	75.	D
12.	D	44.	D	76.	A
13.	A	45.	D	77.	D
14.	D	46.	A	78.	A
15.	D	47.	A	79.	D
16.	D	48.	A	80.	D
17.	A	49.	A	81.	A
18.	D	50.	D	82.	D
19.	A	51.	D	83.	A
20.	D	52.	A	84.	D
21.	D	53.	D	85.	D
22.	A	54.	D	86.	D
23.	D	55.	A	87.	A
24.	D	56.	A	88.	A
25.	D	57.	A	89.	D
26.	A	58.	D	90.	D
27.	D	59.	A	91.	A
28.	A	60.	D	92.	D
29.	A	61.	D	93.	D
30.	D	62.	D	94.	A
31.	D	63.	D	95.	A
32.	D	64.	A		

If you scored:
90 or more correct, you have an excellent score.
85–89 correct, you have a good score
84 or fewer correct, you should practice more.

Memory

The second portion of this test involves memorization. Most postal employees are required to memorize city-wide route schematics in order to become proficient at sorting mail. Depending on the size of city in question, those schemes can become quite involved. If an employee cannot memorize what is required, he or she will have little chance of retaining a job beyond probation. This is no doubt a test section that many people struggle with. Doing well on this section should make the difference between excelling and settling for average. This is not meant to minimize the importance of doing well on the rest of the test. However, the other three sections of this test are fairly straight forward and most people will do fairly well on them, even if their preparation for this exam is minimal. Assuming that you do not possess a photographic memory, the memory system described in this book is designed to help you. This system of memory is actually fun to learn. Over one million people who have purchased this study guide series have applied this technique on various tests with a high degree of success. You can be guaranteed that it will work for you, too.

On the exam you will be given a key such as the one provided below that will contain twenty-five addresses in five categories (A through E). Ten addresses are plain street names while the remainder are numerical street addresses.

A	B	C	D	E
1200-1299 Brewster	6700-6799 Brewster	6900-6999 Brewster	2100-2199 Brewster	1300-1399 Brewster
Hoover Ct.	Highland St.	Beaver Ave.	Lamplight Ct.	Bellvue St.
1400-1499 Lakemont	2700-2799 Lakemont	3100-3199 Lakemont	4200-4299 Lakemont	0900-0999 Lakemont
Sycamore St.	Aspen Dr.	Johnson Ave.	Time Square	Harbor View
9200-9299 Terrace	5800-5899 Terrace	1800-1899 Terrace	8700-8799 Terrace	4300-4399 Terrace

You will be given 11 minutes to study this key at which point further reference is not permitted. You then have five minutes to answer as many of the eighty-eight questions pertaining to the key as possible.

Even if you have marginal memory skills, the techniques discussed here (imagery and association) will help you improve in this area. The technique requires you to form images in your mind related to the items to be memorized. Each of these images is then linked together in a specific order by means of association. It may sound complicated, but learning to stretch the boundaries of your imagination can be enjoyable.

A. NAMES

Street names will be among the items that need to be committed to memory for the exam. Use the following street names as examples:

Jorganson Street
Phillips Avenue
Tremont
Tricia
Edgewater Boulevard
Bloomington

Many people approach this exercise by rote memorization, or in other words, drilling the street names into their head by sheer repetition. Not only is this a boring way to memorize, but this method of recall lasts only a short time. On the other hand, imagery and association techniques can be fun and your ability to recall can be substantially extended.

Now, look at those same street names again and see what key word derivatives have been used and what images we can associate with them.

For example:

> Jorganson Street—Jogger
> Phillips Avenue—Phillips screwdriver
> Tremont—Tree
> Tricia—Tricycle
> Edgewater—Edge
> Bloomington—Blossoms

Carry the process one step further and place those key word derivatives in a bizarre context, story or situation. Using this process, we have developed the following story:

> A JOGGER with his pockets completely stuffed with PHILLIPS SCREWDRIVERS wasn't paying attention and ran into a giant TREE. After dusting himself off, he jumped on a child's TRICYCLE and pedaled to the EDGE of a pool filled with flower BLOSSOMS.

Sounds ridiculous, doesn't it? However, because of its strong images, you will not easily forget this kind of story.

Another advantage of the imagery technique is that you can remember items in their respective order by simply reviewing where they fit in relation to the other items in the story.

Look at each of the street names below and develop a story using imagery. There are no right or wrong key derivatives. What is important is that the images conjure up a clear picture in your mind and then interlink.

Work on each of these columns separately:

Country Club Dr.	Mirage Blvd.	Stoneridge Ave.	Hayward St.
Jasmine Ln.	Driftwood Pl.	University Point	Bradley Ct.
Pottery Rd.	Buckthorn	Harborview	Sunrise Dr.
Pioneer Way	Wavecrest Ct.	Old Mill Rd.	Stetson Ln.
Compass Dr.	Viking Way	Kingsley Blvd.	Springbrook
Winston Hill	Fern St.	Cardinal	Spruce Ave.

Once you have finished this exercise, cover the street names and see if you can remember all 24 items. If your four stories are bizarre enough, you can have this entire list committed to long-term memory in a short time.

B. NUMBERS

Numbers are another problem in memory recall. For most people, numbers are difficult to memorize because they are intangible. To rectify this problem, numbers can be transposed into letters so that words can be formed and associated accordingly. Below is the format for transposition. Remember this format as if it were your Social Security number because on the exam you will draw from it regularly.

0	1	2	3	4	5	6	7	8	9
/ \	/ \	/ \	/ \	|	|	|	|	|	|
G or V	B or D	C or K	F or P	M	N	R	S	T	L

(All other letters can be incorporated into words without any significance.)

For instance, let's say you are given the number 10603328157. Memorizing this number so well that you can recall it after any length of time could be very difficult. However, by using this memory system, you could use the number to spell out a variety of memorable things. Here is your chance to use your creativity!

After you have had the chance to figure out what words can code such a number, one problem becomes apparent: The more numbers you try to cram into one word, the harder it is to find a compatible word in the English vocabulary. To simplify matters, there are two alternative ways to form words. The first method is to take two numbers at a time, form a word and associate it with the next word. Dealing with the same number (10603328157) DOG could be derived from the number 10, RUG from 60, PIPE from 33, CAT from 28, BONE from 15, and S from 7. There are many ways you could imagine and link these words. One possibility would be a DOG lying on a RUG and smoking a PIPE while a CAT prances by carrying a BONE shaped like an S. This is just one way to memorize this long number. Other words and stories could work just as well.

The second alternative, which offers greater flexibility, is using words of any length but making only the first two significant letters of the word applicable to your story. For example, the word DIG/GING could represent 10 in the number 10603328157.

RAV/EN=RUG/BY=REV/OLVER=60
POP/ULATION=PUP/PY=PEP/PER=33
CAT/ERPILLAR=CAT/TLE=COT/TON=28
BIN/OCULAR=BEAN/S=DIN/NER=15

By doing this, you have larger number of words at your disposal to put into stories. With a little originality, it can be fun to see what you can imagine for any number given.

Below are exercises to help you apply this system. The first group of numbers is meant to be used as a transposition exercise. See how many different words you can use to represent each number. The second series is for practice with transposition and story fabrication. This technique may seem difficult at first, but with practice, you will enhance your memory capabilities.

I.

33	51	13	58
72	10	99	1
66	9	2	81
5	23	20	92
27	39	4	48
42	52	85	75
18	16	77	64

II.

2 3 7 9 6 0 1 1 5 6 9 2	5 0 9 3 8 2 1 0 9 7 3 2
1 4 0 7 7 9 3 2 5 6 0 9	6 7 8 0 5 3 2 1 9 2 4 4
8 5 0 9 0 5 2 3 9 1 1 7	6 7 6 8 5 2 1 6 7 8 1 0

440672139238   506077291899

933742268785   471193287616

078915032669   807051137460

Now that you have a basic grasp of how to remember street names and numbers more easily, let's take a typical test sample and break it down into the order in which the material should be memorized.

A	B	C	D	E
1200-1299 Brewster	6700-6799 Brewster	6900-6999 Brewster	2100-2199 Brewster	1300-1399 Brewster
Hoover Ct.	Highland St.	Beaver Ave.	Lamplight Ct.	Bellvue St.
1400-1499 Lakemont	2700-2799 Lakemont	3100-3199 Lakemont	4200-4299 Lakemont	0900-0999 Lakemont
Sycamore St.	Aspen Dr.	Johnson Ave.	Time Square	Harbor View
9200-9299 Terrace	5800-5899 Terrace	1800-1899 Terrace	8700-8799 Terrace	4300-4399 Terrace

What should become immediately apparent by looking at the key is the fact that all numerical addresses are redundant with respect to street name and all but the first two numbers in each address shown are redundant as well. A lot of time and effort can be saved by looking at the key in the manner shown below.

A	B	C	D	E
BREWSTER-12	67	69	21	13
Hoover Ct.	Highland St.	Beaver Ave.	Lamplight Ct.	Bellvue St.
LAKEMONT-14	27	31	42	09
Sycamore St.	Aspen Dr.	Johnson Ave.	Time Square	Harbor View
TERRACE-92	58	18	87	43

Now, each line of information needs to be set up in story format so that recall references can be easily made. As an example, let's use the sequence of numbers that represents Brewster on the exam.

A	B	C	D	E
12	67	69	21	13

There are virtually thousands of different words that can be transposed from these numbers, but for this particular illustration we'll use the words BUCKET, ROSES, ROLLING, KID and DIP. Imagine, if you will, a BUC/KET (fashioned from a huge beer can) full of ROS/ES ROL/LING down a hillside knocks over a KID trying to balance a 30-DIP ice cream cone. This is a strange story, but the underlying principle is quite effective. Not only can you reference the street name (i.e., beer represents BREW or BREWSTER) but, as long as the story's chronological order remains intact, you can easily determine the category (i.e., A through E) that each number belongs under.

For example, let's say on the test you were asked what category 1300-1399 Brewster belongs to? (Look at it as the number 13.) Referring back to the BREW-BUCKET story, the number 13 represents the word DIP. Since DIP was the last image in the story, we would know that it belongs in category E and the answer E should be marked accordingly on our answer sheet.

As another example, let's say you were asked in what category 6700-6799 Brewster belongs. Since 67 was transposed into the word ROS/ES in the BEER-BUCKET story, and it was the second image in our story, answer B would be the correct choice.

Now let's examine the next line of street names and see what kind of bizarre story can be concocted.

A	B	C	D	E
Hoover Ct.	Highland St.	Beaver Ave.	Lamplight Ct.	Bellvue St.

How about a HOOVER vacuum cleaner that has arms, both of which are waving to say HI to a BEAVER standing beneath a street LAMP with a huge BELL for a tail? Quiz yourself. At what point in the story did the beaver stand beneath the street lamp (i.e., Lamplight Ct.)? It was the fourth image in the story. Had this been an actual exam question, category D would have been marked as the answer.

As a final example to this system of memory, let's look at the third line of information in the key and work up another story format.

A	B	C	D	E
14	27	31	42	09

How about the Lakemont DAM which instead of retaining water, retains Hershey KIS/SES. At the base of the DAM was a PUD/DLE of melted chocolate that had oozed forth from a crack in the DAM. Standing in the middle of the PUDDLE was a MEC/HANIC frantically attempting to stop the leak by stuffing his GL/OVES into the crack.

At this point, you should be getting a pretty good idea of how this concept works. Transposition of numbers to letters and then back again may seem a little difficult at first. However, the more you practice at using the system, the easier it will become.

During the actual exam, you will be given a 3 minute pretest with a *sample* key and a short sample answer sheet. Examiners almost always fail to tell you that the sample key is the same key used on the rest of the exam. In other words, you will actually be provided an extra 3 minutes to study the key.

Don't bother marking the sample answer sheets in the pretest: Focus all of your attention on making up your five story lines. If you have a solid feel for your stories, you will be able to answer questions accurately and without hesitation. At the close of the first 3 minutes, the examiner will instruct you to turn the page, where the answer key is provided by itself. You are then given 3 minutes to work on your stories. After this time period is up, you will again be instructed to flip another page where the same key and a full length practice question and answer sheet will be provided. You are allotted three more minutes to either study the key or work practice exercises. Again, it is suggested that you completely ignore the practice exercises and continue working on your stories. If you feel compelled to check yourself, limit answering questions to only a few.

After the 3 minutes are up, you will be instructed to turn to the next page in your booklet, which has practice questions and an answer sheet minus the key. You have 3 minutes to work as many practice questions as you feel comfortable doing. Here again, it is strongly recommended that you simply ignore this section and continue working the stories in your mind. Close your eyes if you want to alleviate any visual distractions. If you still feel it necessary to work the practice questions, keep it to an absolute minimum. When time is up, you will be instructed to turn to the next page in the booklet which has only the key. You will be given 5 more minutes to study. At this point, you should know your five stories forward and backward. By the time the actual exam has begun, you should be able to answer all eighty-eight questions in well under 5 minutes.

A couple of words of caution are needed here. If, by chance, you somehow have a mental block to an occasional question, waste no time and skip over it. Be absolutely certain that you also skip over the corresponding answer blank. You can come back to the question later and make an educated guess, if necessary.

The second point is that the new postal exams will intentionally try to confuse you by utilizing duplicate numbers. In other words, there may be three or four 2400-2499 street addresses. Rest assured that if you keep all of your various stories in their respective orders, duplicate numbers on an exam will matter very little. The practice exams toward the back of this study guide are all comparable to what will be seen on the actual test. The practice exams in this chapter are somewhat easier due to a minimum of duplicate numbers. This will allow you to work up to a proficiency before attempting the more challenging exercises.

Before you begin any of these exercises, get yourself a timer with an alarm. Set it for the allotted time for each part of the exercise. This will spare you from losing time watching the clock. If you finish before the exam is finished, you can always check your answers once over for accuracy as well as neatness. Erase any miscellaneous marks on the answer sheet because as mentioned earlier, it can impact your test score at the time of grading. A scale is provided at the end of each exercise to allow you to determine your standings.

MEMORIZATION/EXERCISE 1

A	B	C	D	E
4200-4299 Lebo	4900-4999 Lebo	3700-3799 Lebo	4700-4799 Lebo	3900-3999 Lebo
Madrona Ave.	Aspen St.	Viking Way	Glenwood Dr.	Richards Ln.
5900-5999 Sidney	5600-5699 Sidney	5800-5899 Sidney	6700-6799 Sidney	6800-6899 Sidney
Walden Ln.	Collins Blvd.	Marric Ct.	Beachnut	National Dr.
0900-0999 Parker	0600-0699 Parker	1100-1199 Parker	1000-1099 Parker	1300-1399 Parker

(STEP 1) Study the address key above for 3 minutes.

(STEP 2) Then turn to the practice exercise on the next page and either study the key or work the practice questions provided for 3 minutes.

(STEP 3) Cover the address key (no reference permitted) and work as many of the practice exercises as possible for 3 minutes.

(STEP 4) Then turn back to this page and study the address key above for another 5 minutes.

(STEP 5) When your time is up, turn two pages over to the actual test and answer as many of the eighty-eight questions as possible within a 5 minute time frame. DO NOT exceed any of the time limits specified or look at the key while doing the actual test. If you do, you forfeit the true sense of how the real exam will be conducted.

NOTE: Remember Step 3 is purely optional. Failure to complete some or all of the practice questions given will NOT affect your test score. Time may well be better spent mentally reviewing your story fabrications.

PRACTICE MEMORIZATION/EXERCISE 1

STEP 2 TIME: 3 MINUTES
STEP 3 TIME: 3 MINUTES (cover key)

A	B	C	D	E
4200-4299 Lebo	4900-4999 Lebo	3700-3799 Lebo	4700-4799 Lebo	3900-3999 Lebo
Madrona Ave.	Aspen St.	Viking Way	Glenwood Dr.	Richards Ln.
5900-5999 Sidney	5600-5699 Sidney	5800-5899 Sidney	6700-6799 Sidney	6800-6899 Sidney
Walden Ln.	Collins Blvd.	Marric Ct.	Beachnut	National Dr.
0900-0999 Parker	0600-0699 Parker	1100-1199 Parker	1000-1099 Parker	1300-1399 Parker

1. Beachnut
2. 5600-5699 Sidney
3. Glenwood Dr.
4. 0900-0999 Parker
5. Collins Blvd.
6. 3700-3799 Lebo
7. National Dr.
8. Walden Ln.
9. 3900-3999 Lebo
10. 1100-1199 Parker
11. 6700-6799 Sidney
12. Viking Way
13. 4900-4999 Lebo
14. 1000-1099 Parker
15. 6800-6899 Sidney
16. Richards Ln.
17. Aspen St.
18. 4700-4799 Lebo
19. 1300-1399 Parker
20. Marric Ct.
21. Collins Blvd.
22. 4200-4299 Lebo
23. Madrona Ave.
24. 5800-5899 Sidney
25. 5900-5999 Sidney
26. 4900-4999 Lebo
27. 1000-1099 Parker
28. Aspen St.
29. Walden Ln.
30. 3700-3799 Lebo

31. Glenwood Dr.
32. National Dr.
33. 4700-4799 Lebo
34. 0900-0999 Parker
35. 4200-4299 Lebo
36. Beachnut
37. Collins Blvd.
38. 3900-3999 Lebo
39. 1100-1199 Parker
40. Viking Way
41. 6800-6899 Sidney
42. Madrona Ave.
43. 0600-0699 Parker
44. Marric Ct.
45. 1000-1099 Parker
46. Aspen St.
47. 3700-3799 Lebo
48. 4700-4799 Lebo
49. 5800-5899 Sidney
50. Walden Ln.
51. National Dr.
52. Glenwood Dr.
53. 1100-1199 Parker
54. 6700-6799 Sidney
55. Collins Blvd.
56. 4700-4799 Lebo
57. 1300-1399 Parker
58. 0600-0699 Parker
59. 4200-4299 Lebo
60. 6700-6799 Sidney

61. 5600-5699 Sidney
62. Richards Ln.
63. Walden Ln.
64. 4900-4999 Lebo
65. 0900-0999 Parker
66. 3700-3799 Lebo
67. Glenwood Dr.
68. 5800-5899 Sidney
69. 1300-1399 Parker
70. Marric Ct.
71. 4700-4799 Lebo
72. 0600-0699 Parker
73. Aspen St.
74. Collins Blvd.
75. 5600-5699 Sidney
76. Walden Ln.
77. Viking Way
78. 4900-4999 Lebo
79. 0900-0999 Parker
80. 1000-1099 Parker
81. 3900-3999 Lebo
82. 5600-5699 Sidney
83. Madrona Ave.
84. Beachnut
85. Richards Ln.
86. 1100-1199 Parker
87. 3900-3999 Lebo
88. 5900-5999 Sidney

PRACTICE ANSWER SHEET TO MEMORIZATION/EXERCISE 1

1. Ⓐ Ⓑ Ⓒ Ⓓ Ⓔ   31. Ⓐ Ⓑ Ⓒ Ⓓ Ⓔ   61. Ⓐ Ⓑ Ⓒ Ⓓ Ⓔ
2. Ⓐ Ⓑ Ⓒ Ⓓ Ⓔ   32. Ⓐ Ⓑ Ⓒ Ⓓ Ⓔ   62. Ⓐ Ⓑ Ⓒ Ⓓ Ⓔ
3. Ⓐ Ⓑ Ⓒ Ⓓ Ⓔ   33. Ⓐ Ⓑ Ⓒ Ⓓ Ⓔ   63. Ⓐ Ⓑ Ⓒ Ⓓ Ⓔ
4. Ⓐ Ⓑ Ⓒ Ⓓ Ⓔ   34. Ⓐ Ⓑ Ⓒ Ⓓ Ⓔ   64. Ⓐ Ⓑ Ⓒ Ⓓ Ⓔ
5. Ⓐ Ⓑ Ⓒ Ⓓ Ⓔ   35. Ⓐ Ⓑ Ⓒ Ⓓ Ⓔ   65. Ⓐ Ⓑ Ⓒ Ⓓ Ⓔ
6. Ⓐ Ⓑ Ⓒ Ⓓ Ⓔ   36. Ⓐ Ⓑ Ⓒ Ⓓ Ⓔ   66. Ⓐ Ⓑ Ⓒ Ⓓ Ⓔ
7. Ⓐ Ⓑ Ⓒ Ⓓ Ⓔ   37. Ⓐ Ⓑ Ⓒ Ⓓ Ⓔ   67. Ⓐ Ⓑ Ⓒ Ⓓ Ⓔ
8. Ⓐ Ⓑ Ⓒ Ⓓ Ⓔ   38. Ⓐ Ⓑ Ⓒ Ⓓ Ⓔ   68. Ⓐ Ⓑ Ⓒ Ⓓ Ⓔ
9. Ⓐ Ⓑ Ⓒ Ⓓ Ⓔ   39. Ⓐ Ⓑ Ⓒ Ⓓ Ⓔ   69. Ⓐ Ⓑ Ⓒ Ⓓ Ⓔ
10. Ⓐ Ⓑ Ⓒ Ⓓ Ⓔ   40. Ⓐ Ⓑ Ⓒ Ⓓ Ⓔ   70. Ⓐ Ⓑ Ⓒ Ⓓ Ⓔ
11. Ⓐ Ⓑ Ⓒ Ⓓ Ⓔ   41. Ⓐ Ⓑ Ⓒ Ⓓ Ⓔ   71. Ⓐ Ⓑ Ⓒ Ⓓ Ⓔ
12. Ⓐ Ⓑ Ⓒ Ⓓ Ⓔ   42. Ⓐ Ⓑ Ⓒ Ⓓ Ⓔ   72. Ⓐ Ⓑ Ⓒ Ⓓ Ⓔ
13. Ⓐ Ⓑ Ⓒ Ⓓ Ⓔ   43. Ⓐ Ⓑ Ⓒ Ⓓ Ⓔ   73. Ⓐ Ⓑ Ⓒ Ⓓ Ⓔ
14. Ⓐ Ⓑ Ⓒ Ⓓ Ⓔ   44. Ⓐ Ⓑ Ⓒ Ⓓ Ⓔ   74. Ⓐ Ⓑ Ⓒ Ⓓ Ⓔ
15. Ⓐ Ⓑ Ⓒ Ⓓ Ⓔ   45. Ⓐ Ⓑ Ⓒ Ⓓ Ⓔ   75. Ⓐ Ⓑ Ⓒ Ⓓ Ⓔ
16. Ⓐ Ⓑ Ⓒ Ⓓ Ⓔ   46. Ⓐ Ⓑ Ⓒ Ⓓ Ⓔ   76. Ⓐ Ⓑ Ⓒ Ⓓ Ⓔ
17. Ⓐ Ⓑ Ⓒ Ⓓ Ⓔ   47. Ⓐ Ⓑ Ⓒ Ⓓ Ⓔ   77. Ⓐ Ⓑ Ⓒ Ⓓ Ⓔ
18. Ⓐ Ⓑ Ⓒ Ⓓ Ⓔ   48. Ⓐ Ⓑ Ⓒ Ⓓ Ⓔ   78. Ⓐ Ⓑ Ⓒ Ⓓ Ⓔ
19. Ⓐ Ⓑ Ⓒ Ⓓ Ⓔ   49. Ⓐ Ⓑ Ⓒ Ⓓ Ⓔ   79. Ⓐ Ⓑ Ⓒ Ⓓ Ⓔ
20. Ⓐ Ⓑ Ⓒ Ⓓ Ⓔ   50. Ⓐ Ⓑ Ⓒ Ⓓ Ⓔ   80. Ⓐ Ⓑ Ⓒ Ⓓ Ⓔ
21. Ⓐ Ⓑ Ⓒ Ⓓ Ⓔ   51. Ⓐ Ⓑ Ⓒ Ⓓ Ⓔ   81. Ⓐ Ⓑ Ⓒ Ⓓ Ⓔ
22. Ⓐ Ⓑ Ⓒ Ⓓ Ⓔ   52. Ⓐ Ⓑ Ⓒ Ⓓ Ⓔ   82. Ⓐ Ⓑ Ⓒ Ⓓ Ⓔ
23. Ⓐ Ⓑ Ⓒ Ⓓ Ⓔ   53. Ⓐ Ⓑ Ⓒ Ⓓ Ⓔ   83. Ⓐ Ⓑ Ⓒ Ⓓ Ⓔ
24. Ⓐ Ⓑ Ⓒ Ⓓ Ⓔ   54. Ⓐ Ⓑ Ⓒ Ⓓ Ⓔ   84. Ⓐ Ⓑ Ⓒ Ⓓ Ⓔ
25. Ⓐ Ⓑ Ⓒ Ⓓ Ⓔ   55. Ⓐ Ⓑ Ⓒ Ⓓ Ⓔ   85. Ⓐ Ⓑ Ⓒ Ⓓ Ⓔ
26. Ⓐ Ⓑ Ⓒ Ⓓ Ⓔ   56. Ⓐ Ⓑ Ⓒ Ⓓ Ⓔ   86. Ⓐ Ⓑ Ⓒ Ⓓ Ⓔ
27. Ⓐ Ⓑ Ⓒ Ⓓ Ⓔ   57. Ⓐ Ⓑ Ⓒ Ⓓ Ⓔ   87. Ⓐ Ⓑ Ⓒ Ⓓ Ⓔ
28. Ⓐ Ⓑ Ⓒ Ⓓ Ⓔ   58. Ⓐ Ⓑ Ⓒ Ⓓ Ⓔ   88. Ⓐ Ⓑ Ⓒ Ⓓ Ⓔ
29. Ⓐ Ⓑ Ⓒ Ⓓ Ⓔ   59. Ⓐ Ⓑ Ⓒ Ⓓ Ⓔ
30. Ⓐ Ⓑ Ⓒ Ⓓ Ⓔ   60. Ⓐ Ⓑ Ⓒ Ⓓ Ⓔ

MEMORIZATION/EXERCISE 1   STEP 5 TIME: 5 MINUTES

1. Marric Ct.	31. 0600-0699 Parker	61. Walden Ln.
2. 4700-4799 Lebo	32. Viking Way	62. 4900-4999 Lebo
3. 6800-6899 Sidney	33. 4700-4799 Lebo	63. Glenwood Dr.
4. 4200-4299 Lebo	34. 1300-1399 Parker	64. 6700-6799 Sidney
5. 0900-0999 Parker	35. 4200-4299 Lebo	65. 1100-1199 Parker
6. Beachnut	36. Collins Blvd.	66. 4200-4299 Lebo
7. Viking Way	37. Walden Ln.	67. Marric Ct.
8. 4900-4999 Lebo	38. 5800-5899 Sidney	68. National Dr.
9. Glenwood Dr.	39. 6700-6799 Sidney	69. Collins Blvd.
10. National Dr.	40. Glenwood Dr.	70. 5900-5999 Sidney
11. Walden Ln.	41. National Dr.	71. 900-0999 Parker
12. 3700-3799 Lebo	42. 5900-5999 Sidney	72. Aspen St.
13. 1000-1099 Parker	43. Aspen St.	73. 5800-5899 Sidney
14. 6700-6799 Sidney	44. Richards Ln.	74. Beachnut
15. Richards Ln.	45. 1000-1099 Parker	75. 6800-6899 Sidney
16. 5900-5999 Sidney	46. Marric Ct.	76. 4900-4999 Lebo
17. Collins Blvd.	47. 1100-1199 Parker	77. 4200-4299 Lebo
18. Aspen St.	48. 0900-0999 Parker	78. Viking Way
19. 1100-1199 Parker	49. 6800-6899 Sidney	79. Walden Ln.
20. 1300-1399 Parker	50. 5600-5699 Sidney	80. 6700-6799 Sidney
21. Madrona Ave.	51. Beachnut	81. 1300-1399 Parker
22. 4700-4799 Lebo	52. 4200-4299 Lebo	82. 5600-5699 Sidney
23. 5600-5699 Sidney	53. Viking Way	83. Madrona Ave.
24. 4900-4999 Lebo	54. 1300-1399 Parker	84. Marric Ct.
25. Glenwood Dr.	55. Collins Blvd.	85. 3700-3799 Lebo
26. 3900-3999 Lebo	56. 0600-0699 Parker	86. Richards Ln.
27. 6800-6899 Sidney	57. 4700-4799 Lebo	87. Collins Blvd.
28. Beachnut	58. Madrona Ave.	88. 4700-4799 Lebo
29. 0900-0999 Parker	59. 3700-3799 Lebo	
30. 3700-3799 Lebo	60. Richards Ln.	

ANSWER SHEET TO MEMORIZATION/EXERCISE 1

1. Ⓐ Ⓑ Ⓒ Ⓓ Ⓔ	31. Ⓐ Ⓑ Ⓒ Ⓓ Ⓔ	61. Ⓐ Ⓑ Ⓒ Ⓓ Ⓔ
2. Ⓐ Ⓑ Ⓒ Ⓓ Ⓔ	32. Ⓐ Ⓑ Ⓒ Ⓓ Ⓔ	62. Ⓐ Ⓑ Ⓒ Ⓓ Ⓔ
3. Ⓐ Ⓑ Ⓒ Ⓓ Ⓔ	33. Ⓐ Ⓑ Ⓒ Ⓓ Ⓔ	63. Ⓐ Ⓑ Ⓒ Ⓓ Ⓔ
4. Ⓐ Ⓑ Ⓒ Ⓓ Ⓔ	34. Ⓐ Ⓑ Ⓒ Ⓓ Ⓔ	64. Ⓐ Ⓑ Ⓒ Ⓓ Ⓔ
5. Ⓐ Ⓑ Ⓒ Ⓓ Ⓔ	35. Ⓐ Ⓑ Ⓒ Ⓓ Ⓔ	65. Ⓐ Ⓑ Ⓒ Ⓓ Ⓔ
6. Ⓐ Ⓑ Ⓒ Ⓓ Ⓔ	36. Ⓐ Ⓑ Ⓒ Ⓓ Ⓔ	66. Ⓐ Ⓑ Ⓒ Ⓓ Ⓔ
7. Ⓐ Ⓑ Ⓒ Ⓓ Ⓔ	37. Ⓐ Ⓑ Ⓒ Ⓓ Ⓔ	67. Ⓐ Ⓑ Ⓒ Ⓓ Ⓔ
8. Ⓐ Ⓑ Ⓒ Ⓓ Ⓔ	38. Ⓐ Ⓑ Ⓒ Ⓓ Ⓔ	68. Ⓐ Ⓑ Ⓒ Ⓓ Ⓔ
9. Ⓐ Ⓑ Ⓒ Ⓓ Ⓔ	39. Ⓐ Ⓑ Ⓒ Ⓓ Ⓔ	69. Ⓐ Ⓑ Ⓒ Ⓓ Ⓔ
10. Ⓐ Ⓑ Ⓒ Ⓓ Ⓔ	40. Ⓐ Ⓑ Ⓒ Ⓓ Ⓔ	70. Ⓐ Ⓑ Ⓒ Ⓓ Ⓔ
11. Ⓐ Ⓑ Ⓒ Ⓓ Ⓔ	41. Ⓐ Ⓑ Ⓒ Ⓓ Ⓔ	71. Ⓐ Ⓑ Ⓒ Ⓓ Ⓔ
12. Ⓐ Ⓑ Ⓒ Ⓓ Ⓔ	42. Ⓐ Ⓑ Ⓒ Ⓓ Ⓔ	72. Ⓐ Ⓑ Ⓒ Ⓓ Ⓔ
13. Ⓐ Ⓑ Ⓒ Ⓓ Ⓔ	43. Ⓐ Ⓑ Ⓒ Ⓓ Ⓔ	73. Ⓐ Ⓑ Ⓒ Ⓓ Ⓔ
14. Ⓐ Ⓑ Ⓒ Ⓓ Ⓔ	44. Ⓐ Ⓑ Ⓒ Ⓓ Ⓔ	74. Ⓐ Ⓑ Ⓒ Ⓓ Ⓔ
15. Ⓐ Ⓑ Ⓒ Ⓓ Ⓔ	45. Ⓐ Ⓑ Ⓒ Ⓓ Ⓔ	75. Ⓐ Ⓑ Ⓒ Ⓓ Ⓔ
16. Ⓐ Ⓑ Ⓒ Ⓓ Ⓔ	46. Ⓐ Ⓑ Ⓒ Ⓓ Ⓔ	76. Ⓐ Ⓑ Ⓒ Ⓓ Ⓔ
17. Ⓐ Ⓑ Ⓒ Ⓓ Ⓔ	47. Ⓐ Ⓑ Ⓒ Ⓓ Ⓔ	77. Ⓐ Ⓑ Ⓒ Ⓓ Ⓔ
18. Ⓐ Ⓑ Ⓒ Ⓓ Ⓔ	48. Ⓐ Ⓑ Ⓒ Ⓓ Ⓔ	78. Ⓐ Ⓑ Ⓒ Ⓓ Ⓔ
19. Ⓐ Ⓑ Ⓒ Ⓓ Ⓔ	49. Ⓐ Ⓑ Ⓒ Ⓓ Ⓔ	79. Ⓐ Ⓑ Ⓒ Ⓓ Ⓔ
20. Ⓐ Ⓑ Ⓒ Ⓓ Ⓔ	50. Ⓐ Ⓑ Ⓒ Ⓓ Ⓔ	80. Ⓐ Ⓑ Ⓒ Ⓓ Ⓔ
21. Ⓐ Ⓑ Ⓒ Ⓓ Ⓔ	51. Ⓐ Ⓑ Ⓒ Ⓓ Ⓔ	81. Ⓐ Ⓑ Ⓒ Ⓓ Ⓔ
22. Ⓐ Ⓑ Ⓒ Ⓓ Ⓔ	52. Ⓐ Ⓑ Ⓒ Ⓓ Ⓔ	82. Ⓐ Ⓑ Ⓒ Ⓓ Ⓔ
23. Ⓐ Ⓑ Ⓒ Ⓓ Ⓔ	53. Ⓐ Ⓑ Ⓒ Ⓓ Ⓔ	83. Ⓐ Ⓑ Ⓒ Ⓓ Ⓔ
24. Ⓐ Ⓑ Ⓒ Ⓓ Ⓔ	54. Ⓐ Ⓑ Ⓒ Ⓓ Ⓔ	84. Ⓐ Ⓑ Ⓒ Ⓓ Ⓔ
25. Ⓐ Ⓑ Ⓒ Ⓓ Ⓔ	55. Ⓐ Ⓑ Ⓒ Ⓓ Ⓔ	85. Ⓐ Ⓑ Ⓒ Ⓓ Ⓔ
26. Ⓐ Ⓑ Ⓒ Ⓓ Ⓔ	56. Ⓐ Ⓑ Ⓒ Ⓓ Ⓔ	86. Ⓐ Ⓑ Ⓒ Ⓓ Ⓔ
27. Ⓐ Ⓑ Ⓒ Ⓓ Ⓔ	57. Ⓐ Ⓑ Ⓒ Ⓓ Ⓔ	87. Ⓐ Ⓑ Ⓒ Ⓓ Ⓔ
28. Ⓐ Ⓑ Ⓒ Ⓓ Ⓔ	58. Ⓐ Ⓑ Ⓒ Ⓓ Ⓔ	88. Ⓐ Ⓑ Ⓒ Ⓓ Ⓔ
29. Ⓐ Ⓑ Ⓒ Ⓓ Ⓔ	59. Ⓐ Ⓑ Ⓒ Ⓓ Ⓔ	
30. Ⓐ Ⓑ Ⓒ Ⓓ Ⓔ	60. Ⓐ Ⓑ Ⓒ Ⓓ Ⓔ	

ANSWERS TO MEMORIZATION/EXERCISE 1

1.	C	31.	B	61.	A
2.	D	32.	C	62.	B
3.	E	33.	D	63.	D
4.	A	34.	E	64.	D
5.	A	35.	A	65.	C
6.	D	36.	B	66.	A
7.	C	37.	A	67.	C
8.	B	38.	C	68.	E
9.	D	39.	D	69.	B
10.	E	40.	D	70.	A
11.	A	41.	E	71.	A
12.	C	42.	A	72.	B
13.	D	43.	B	73.	C
14.	D	44.	E	74.	D
15.	E	45.	D	75.	E
16.	A	46.	C	76.	B
17.	B	47.	C	77.	A
18.	B	48.	A	78.	C
19.	C	49.	E	79.	A
20.	E	50.	B	80.	D
21.	A	51.	D	81.	E
22.	D	52.	A	82.	B
23.	B	53.	C	83.	A
24.	B	54.	E	84.	C
25.	D	55.	B	85.	C
26.	E	56.	B	86.	E
27.	E	57.	D	87.	B
28.	D	58.	A	88.	D
29.	A	59.	C		
30.	C	60.	E		

If you scored:
84 or more correct, you have an excellent score.
78–83 correct, you have a good score.
77 or fewer, you should practice more.

MEMORIZATION/EXERCISE 2

A	B	C	D	E
8000-8099 Tyler	7900-7999 Tyler	8100-8199 Tyler	7800-7899 Tyler	8200-8299 Tyler
Kimble Rd.	Shorewood Dr.	Falls Place	Bradley St.	Crystal Ln.
1400-1499 Conifer	0800-0899 Conifer	2800-2899 Conifer	2500-2599 Conifer	2000-2099 Conifer
Valley View	Fletcher Bay	Gregory Ln.	Harbor Pt.	Eastlake
5700-5799 Nichols	5800-5899 Nichols	5900-5999 Nichols	6200-6299 Nichols	6100-6199 Nichols

PRACTICE MEMORIZATION/EXERCISE 2

STEP 2 TIME: 3 MINUTES
STEP 3 TIME: 3 MINUTES (cover key)

A	B	C	D	E
8000-8099 Tyler	7900-7999 Tyler	8100-8199 Tyler	7800-7899 Tyler	8200-8299 Tyler
Kimble Rd.	Shorewood Dr.	Falls Place	Bradley St.	Crystal Ln.
1400-1499 Conifer	0800-0899 Conifer	2800-2899 Conifer	2500-2599 Conifer	2000-2099 Conifer
Valley View	Fletcher Bay	Gregory Ln.	Harbor Pt.	Eastlake
5700-5799 Nichols	5800-5899 Nichols	5900-5999 Nichols	6200-6299 Nichols	6100-6199 Nichols

1. Falls Place
2. 0800-0899 Conifer
3. Kimble Rd.
4. 8100-8199 Tyler
5. 2000-2099 Conifer
6. 6100-6199 Nichols
7. Crystal Ln.
8. 6100-6199 Conifer
9. Fletcher Bay
10. Valley View
11. 5800-5899 Nichols
12. 7900-7999 Tyler
13. Bradley St.
14. 8000-8099 Tyler
15. Eastlake
16. 6100-6199 Nichols
17. 5700-5799 Nichols
18. Gregory Ln.
19. Harbor Pt.
20. 1400-1499 Conifer
21. 7800-7899 Tyler
22. Shorewood Dr.
23. 5900-5999 Nichols
24. 1400-1499 Conifer
25. 8200-8299 Tyler
26. 6100-6199 Nichols
27. Valley View
28. Crystal Ln.
29. Eastlake
30. 5700-5799 Nichols
31. 1400-1499 Conifer
32. 7800-7899 Tyler
33. 8000-8099 Tyler
34. Gregory Ln.
35. Harbor Pt.
36. 1400-1499 Conifer
37. 8100-8199 Tyler
38. 2000-2099 Conifer
39. 6100-6199 Nichols
40. Fletcher Bay
41. 2500-2599 Conifer
42. 6100-6199 Nichols
43. Kimble Rd.
44. 5900-5999 Nichols
45. Falls Place
46. 8200-8299 Tyler
47. 0800-0899 Conifer
48. 5800-5899 Nichols
49. 7900-7999 Tyler
50. Bradley St.
51. Fletcher Bay
52. 2000-2099 Conifer
53. 5800-5899 Nichols
54. 6100-6199 Nichols
55. Crystal Ln.
56. Kimble Rd.
57. 0800-0899 Conifer
58. Falls Place
59. Harbor Pt.
60. 7800-7899 Tyler
61. Shorewood Dr.
62. 5700-5799 Nichols
63. 8000-8099 Tyler
64. Valley View
65. 2500-2599 Conifer
66. 8100-8199 Tyler
67. Bradley St.
68. 1400-1499 Conifer
69. 8200-8299 Tyler
70. 6100-6199 Nichols
71. Eastlake
72. 7900-7999 Tyler
73. Gregory Ln.
74. 5900-5999 Nichols
75. Falls Place
76. Fletcher Bay
77. 0800-0899 Conifer
78. 7800-7899 Tyler
79. 5800-5899 Nichols
80. Valley View
81. Crystal Ln.
82. 8100-8199 Tyler
83. 6100-6199 Nichols
84. 1400-1499 Conifer
85. Shorewood Dr.
86. 2500-2599 Conifer
87. 7900-7999 Tyler
88. 8000-8099 Tyler

PRACTICE ANSWER SHEET TO MEMORIZATION/EXERCISE 2

1. Ⓐ Ⓑ Ⓒ Ⓓ Ⓔ   31. Ⓐ Ⓑ Ⓒ Ⓓ Ⓔ   61. Ⓐ Ⓑ Ⓒ Ⓓ Ⓔ
2. Ⓐ Ⓑ Ⓒ Ⓓ Ⓔ   32. Ⓐ Ⓑ Ⓒ Ⓓ Ⓔ   62. Ⓐ Ⓑ Ⓒ Ⓓ Ⓔ
3. Ⓐ Ⓑ Ⓒ Ⓓ Ⓔ   33. Ⓐ Ⓑ Ⓒ Ⓓ Ⓔ   63. Ⓐ Ⓑ Ⓒ Ⓓ Ⓔ
4. Ⓐ Ⓑ Ⓒ Ⓓ Ⓔ   34. Ⓐ Ⓑ Ⓒ Ⓓ Ⓔ   64. Ⓐ Ⓑ Ⓒ Ⓓ Ⓔ
5. Ⓐ Ⓑ Ⓒ Ⓓ Ⓔ   35. Ⓐ Ⓑ Ⓒ Ⓓ Ⓔ   65. Ⓐ Ⓑ Ⓒ Ⓓ Ⓔ
6. Ⓐ Ⓑ Ⓒ Ⓓ Ⓔ   36. Ⓐ Ⓑ Ⓒ Ⓓ Ⓔ   66. Ⓐ Ⓑ Ⓒ Ⓓ Ⓔ
7. Ⓐ Ⓑ Ⓒ Ⓓ Ⓔ   37. Ⓐ Ⓑ Ⓒ Ⓓ Ⓔ   67. Ⓐ Ⓑ Ⓒ Ⓓ Ⓔ
8. Ⓐ Ⓑ Ⓒ Ⓓ Ⓔ   38. Ⓐ Ⓑ Ⓒ Ⓓ Ⓔ   68. Ⓐ Ⓑ Ⓒ Ⓓ Ⓔ
9. Ⓐ Ⓑ Ⓒ Ⓓ Ⓔ   39. Ⓐ Ⓑ Ⓒ Ⓓ Ⓔ   69. Ⓐ Ⓑ Ⓒ Ⓓ Ⓔ
10. Ⓐ Ⓑ Ⓒ Ⓓ Ⓔ   40. Ⓐ Ⓑ Ⓒ Ⓓ Ⓔ   70. Ⓐ Ⓑ Ⓒ Ⓓ Ⓔ
11. Ⓐ Ⓑ Ⓒ Ⓓ Ⓔ   41. Ⓐ Ⓑ Ⓒ Ⓓ Ⓔ   71. Ⓐ Ⓑ Ⓒ Ⓓ Ⓔ
12. Ⓐ Ⓑ Ⓒ Ⓓ Ⓔ   42. Ⓐ Ⓑ Ⓒ Ⓓ Ⓔ   72. Ⓐ Ⓑ Ⓒ Ⓓ Ⓔ
13. Ⓐ Ⓑ Ⓒ Ⓓ Ⓔ   43. Ⓐ Ⓑ Ⓒ Ⓓ Ⓔ   73. Ⓐ Ⓑ Ⓒ Ⓓ Ⓔ
14. Ⓐ Ⓑ Ⓒ Ⓓ Ⓔ   44. Ⓐ Ⓑ Ⓒ Ⓓ Ⓔ   74. Ⓐ Ⓑ Ⓒ Ⓓ Ⓔ
15. Ⓐ Ⓑ Ⓒ Ⓓ Ⓔ   45. Ⓐ Ⓑ Ⓒ Ⓓ Ⓔ   75. Ⓐ Ⓑ Ⓒ Ⓓ Ⓔ
16. Ⓐ Ⓑ Ⓒ Ⓓ Ⓔ   46. Ⓐ Ⓑ Ⓒ Ⓓ Ⓔ   76. Ⓐ Ⓑ Ⓒ Ⓓ Ⓔ
17. Ⓐ Ⓑ Ⓒ Ⓓ Ⓔ   47. Ⓐ Ⓑ Ⓒ Ⓓ Ⓔ   77. Ⓐ Ⓑ Ⓒ Ⓓ Ⓔ
18. Ⓐ Ⓑ Ⓒ Ⓓ Ⓔ   48. Ⓐ Ⓑ Ⓒ Ⓓ Ⓔ   78. Ⓐ Ⓑ Ⓒ Ⓓ Ⓔ
19. Ⓐ Ⓑ Ⓒ Ⓓ Ⓔ   49. Ⓐ Ⓑ Ⓒ Ⓓ Ⓔ   79. Ⓐ Ⓑ Ⓒ Ⓓ Ⓔ
20. Ⓐ Ⓑ Ⓒ Ⓓ Ⓔ   50. Ⓐ Ⓑ Ⓒ Ⓓ Ⓔ   80. Ⓐ Ⓑ Ⓒ Ⓓ Ⓔ
21. Ⓐ Ⓑ Ⓒ Ⓓ Ⓔ   51. Ⓐ Ⓑ Ⓒ Ⓓ Ⓔ   81. Ⓐ Ⓑ Ⓒ Ⓓ Ⓔ
22. Ⓐ Ⓑ Ⓒ Ⓓ Ⓔ   52. Ⓐ Ⓑ Ⓒ Ⓓ Ⓔ   82. Ⓐ Ⓑ Ⓒ Ⓓ Ⓔ
23. Ⓐ Ⓑ Ⓒ Ⓓ Ⓔ   53. Ⓐ Ⓑ Ⓒ Ⓓ Ⓔ   83. Ⓐ Ⓑ Ⓒ Ⓓ Ⓔ
24. Ⓐ Ⓑ Ⓒ Ⓓ Ⓔ   54. Ⓐ Ⓑ Ⓒ Ⓓ Ⓔ   84. Ⓐ Ⓑ Ⓒ Ⓓ Ⓔ
25. Ⓐ Ⓑ Ⓒ Ⓓ Ⓔ   55. Ⓐ Ⓑ Ⓒ Ⓓ Ⓔ   85. Ⓐ Ⓑ Ⓒ Ⓓ Ⓔ
26. Ⓐ Ⓑ Ⓒ Ⓓ Ⓔ   56. Ⓐ Ⓑ Ⓒ Ⓓ Ⓔ   86. Ⓐ Ⓑ Ⓒ Ⓓ Ⓔ
27. Ⓐ Ⓑ Ⓒ Ⓓ Ⓔ   57. Ⓐ Ⓑ Ⓒ Ⓓ Ⓔ   87. Ⓐ Ⓑ Ⓒ Ⓓ Ⓔ
28. Ⓐ Ⓑ Ⓒ Ⓓ Ⓔ   58. Ⓐ Ⓑ Ⓒ Ⓓ Ⓔ   88. Ⓐ Ⓑ Ⓒ Ⓓ Ⓔ
29. Ⓐ Ⓑ Ⓒ Ⓓ Ⓔ   59. Ⓐ Ⓑ Ⓒ Ⓓ Ⓔ
30. Ⓐ Ⓑ Ⓒ Ⓓ Ⓔ   60. Ⓐ Ⓑ Ⓒ Ⓓ Ⓔ

MEMORIZATION/EXERCISE 2   STEP 5: 5 MINUTES

1. Gregory Ln.
2. Bradley St.
3. 2000-2099 Conifer
4. 7900-7999 Tyler
5. 0800-0899 Conifer
6. 5700-5799 Nichols
7. 2800-2899 Conifer
8. Falls Place
9. 7800-7899 Tyler
10. Crystal Ln.
11. Shorewood Dr.
12. Kimble Rd.
13. Fletcher Bay
14. 5900-5999 Nichols
15. 6200-6299 Nichols
16. Harbor Pt.
17. Valley View
18. 8200-8299 Tyler
19. 2500-2599 Conifer
20. 0800-0899 Conifer
21. 8100-8199 Tyler
22. 5700-5799 Nichols
23. 1400-1499 Conifer
24. Eastlake
25. 7800-7899 Tyler
26. 8000-8099 Tyler
27. Falls Place
28. 2500-2599 Conifer
29. Fletcher Bay
30. 0800-0899 Conifer

31. Crystal Ln.
32. 5700-5799 Nichols
33. 8100-8199 Tyler
34. 5800-5899 Nichols
35. Bradley St.
36. 2500-2599 Conifer
37. 8200-8299 Tyler
38. Valley View
39. 6100-6199 Nichols
40. Shorewood Dr.
41. 2800-2899 Conifer
42. Harbor Pt.
43. 1400-1499 Conifer
44. Kimble Rd.
45. 2000-2099 Conifer
46. 7900-7999 Tyler
47. 5900-5999 Nichols
48. Eastlake
49. 7800-7899 Tyler
50. 8000-8099 Tyler
51. Shorewood Dr.
52. Gregory Ln.
53. Harbor Pt.
54. Crystal Ln.
55. 2800-2899 Conifer
56. 5800-5899 Nichols
57. Valley View
58. 2500-2599 Conifer
59. 6100-6199 Nichols
60. 2000-2099 Conifer

61. 5700-5799 Nichols
62. Fletcher Bay
63. Falls Place
64. 8100-8199 Tyler
65. 8200-8299 Tyler
66. Bradley St.
67. 7900-7999 Tyler
68. 1400-1499 Conifer
69. Kimble Rd.
70. 0800-0899 Conifer
71. 6200-6299 Nichols
72. 5900-5999 Nichols
73. 2000-2099 Conifer
74. 2800-2899 Conifer
75. Shorewood Dr.
76. 8000-8099 Tyler
77. 5800-5899 Nichols
78. 8100-8199 Tyler
79. Harbor Pt.
80. Gregory Ln.
81. Fletcher Bay
82. Eastlake
83. 6100-6199 Nichols
84. 2500-2599 Conifer
85. 8000-8099 Tyler
86. Kimble Rd.
87. 5900-5999 Nichols
88. 2800-2899 Conifer

ANSWER SHEET TO MEMORIZATION/EXERCISE 2

1. Ⓐ Ⓑ Ⓒ Ⓓ Ⓔ	31. Ⓐ Ⓑ Ⓒ Ⓓ Ⓔ	61. Ⓐ Ⓑ Ⓒ Ⓓ Ⓔ
2. Ⓐ Ⓑ Ⓒ Ⓓ Ⓔ	32. Ⓐ Ⓑ Ⓒ Ⓓ Ⓔ	62. Ⓐ Ⓑ Ⓒ Ⓓ Ⓔ
3. Ⓐ Ⓑ Ⓒ Ⓓ Ⓔ	33. Ⓐ Ⓑ Ⓒ Ⓓ Ⓔ	63. Ⓐ Ⓑ Ⓒ Ⓓ Ⓔ
4. Ⓐ Ⓑ Ⓒ Ⓓ Ⓔ	34. Ⓐ Ⓑ Ⓒ Ⓓ Ⓔ	64. Ⓐ Ⓑ Ⓒ Ⓓ Ⓔ
5. Ⓐ Ⓑ Ⓒ Ⓓ Ⓔ	35. Ⓐ Ⓑ Ⓒ Ⓓ Ⓔ	65. Ⓐ Ⓑ Ⓒ Ⓓ Ⓔ
6. Ⓐ Ⓑ Ⓒ Ⓓ Ⓔ	36. Ⓐ Ⓑ Ⓒ Ⓓ Ⓔ	66. Ⓐ Ⓑ Ⓒ Ⓓ Ⓔ
7. Ⓐ Ⓑ Ⓒ Ⓓ Ⓔ	37. Ⓐ Ⓑ Ⓒ Ⓓ Ⓔ	67. Ⓐ Ⓑ Ⓒ Ⓓ Ⓔ
8. Ⓐ Ⓑ Ⓒ Ⓓ Ⓔ	38. Ⓐ Ⓑ Ⓒ Ⓓ Ⓔ	68. Ⓐ Ⓑ Ⓒ Ⓓ Ⓔ
9. Ⓐ Ⓑ Ⓒ Ⓓ Ⓔ	39. Ⓐ Ⓑ Ⓒ Ⓓ Ⓔ	69. Ⓐ Ⓑ Ⓒ Ⓓ Ⓔ
10. Ⓐ Ⓑ Ⓒ Ⓓ Ⓔ	40. Ⓐ Ⓑ Ⓒ Ⓓ Ⓔ	70. Ⓐ Ⓑ Ⓒ Ⓓ Ⓔ
11. Ⓐ Ⓑ Ⓒ Ⓓ Ⓔ	41. Ⓐ Ⓑ Ⓒ Ⓓ Ⓔ	71. Ⓐ Ⓑ Ⓒ Ⓓ Ⓔ
12. Ⓐ Ⓑ Ⓒ Ⓓ Ⓔ	42. Ⓐ Ⓑ Ⓒ Ⓓ Ⓔ	72. Ⓐ Ⓑ Ⓒ Ⓓ Ⓔ
13. Ⓐ Ⓑ Ⓒ Ⓓ Ⓔ	43. Ⓐ Ⓑ Ⓒ Ⓓ Ⓔ	73. Ⓐ Ⓑ Ⓒ Ⓓ Ⓔ
14. Ⓐ Ⓑ Ⓒ Ⓓ Ⓔ	44. Ⓐ Ⓑ Ⓒ Ⓓ Ⓔ	74. Ⓐ Ⓑ Ⓒ Ⓓ Ⓔ
15. Ⓐ Ⓑ Ⓒ Ⓓ Ⓔ	45. Ⓐ Ⓑ Ⓒ Ⓓ Ⓔ	75. Ⓐ Ⓑ Ⓒ Ⓓ Ⓔ
16. Ⓐ Ⓑ Ⓒ Ⓓ Ⓔ	46. Ⓐ Ⓑ Ⓒ Ⓓ Ⓔ	76. Ⓐ Ⓑ Ⓒ Ⓓ Ⓔ
17. Ⓐ Ⓑ Ⓒ Ⓓ Ⓔ	47. Ⓐ Ⓑ Ⓒ Ⓓ Ⓔ	77. Ⓐ Ⓑ Ⓒ Ⓓ Ⓔ
18. Ⓐ Ⓑ Ⓒ Ⓓ Ⓔ	48. Ⓐ Ⓑ Ⓒ Ⓓ Ⓔ	78. Ⓐ Ⓑ Ⓒ Ⓓ Ⓔ
19. Ⓐ Ⓑ Ⓒ Ⓓ Ⓔ	49. Ⓐ Ⓑ Ⓒ Ⓓ Ⓔ	79. Ⓐ Ⓑ Ⓒ Ⓓ Ⓔ
20. Ⓐ Ⓑ Ⓒ Ⓓ Ⓔ	50. Ⓐ Ⓑ Ⓒ Ⓓ Ⓔ	80. Ⓐ Ⓑ Ⓒ Ⓓ Ⓔ
21. Ⓐ Ⓑ Ⓒ Ⓓ Ⓔ	51. Ⓐ Ⓑ Ⓒ Ⓓ Ⓔ	81. Ⓐ Ⓑ Ⓒ Ⓓ Ⓔ
22. Ⓐ Ⓑ Ⓒ Ⓓ Ⓔ	52. Ⓐ Ⓑ Ⓒ Ⓓ Ⓔ	82. Ⓐ Ⓑ Ⓒ Ⓓ Ⓔ
23. Ⓐ Ⓑ Ⓒ Ⓓ Ⓔ	53. Ⓐ Ⓑ Ⓒ Ⓓ Ⓔ	83. Ⓐ Ⓑ Ⓒ Ⓓ Ⓔ
24. Ⓐ Ⓑ Ⓒ Ⓓ Ⓔ	54. Ⓐ Ⓑ Ⓒ Ⓓ Ⓔ	84. Ⓐ Ⓑ Ⓒ Ⓓ Ⓔ
25. Ⓐ Ⓑ Ⓒ Ⓓ Ⓔ	55. Ⓐ Ⓑ Ⓒ Ⓓ Ⓔ	85. Ⓐ Ⓑ Ⓒ Ⓓ Ⓔ
26. Ⓐ Ⓑ Ⓒ Ⓓ Ⓔ	56. Ⓐ Ⓑ Ⓒ Ⓓ Ⓔ	86. Ⓐ Ⓑ Ⓒ Ⓓ Ⓔ
27. Ⓐ Ⓑ Ⓒ Ⓓ Ⓔ	57. Ⓐ Ⓑ Ⓒ Ⓓ Ⓔ	87. Ⓐ Ⓑ Ⓒ Ⓓ Ⓔ
28. Ⓐ Ⓑ Ⓒ Ⓓ Ⓔ	58. Ⓐ Ⓑ Ⓒ Ⓓ Ⓔ	88. Ⓐ Ⓑ Ⓒ Ⓓ Ⓔ
29. Ⓐ Ⓑ Ⓒ Ⓓ Ⓔ	59. Ⓐ Ⓑ Ⓒ Ⓓ Ⓔ	
30. Ⓐ Ⓑ Ⓒ Ⓓ Ⓔ	60. Ⓐ Ⓑ Ⓒ Ⓓ Ⓔ	

ANSWERS TO MEMORIZATION/EXERCISE 2

1.	C	31.	E	61.	A
2.	D	32.	A	62.	B
3.	E	33.	C	63.	C
4.	B	34.	B	64.	C
5.	B	35.	D	65.	E
6.	A	36.	D	66.	D
7.	C	37.	E	67.	B
8.	C	38.	A	68.	A
9.	D	39.	E	69.	A
10.	E	40.	B	70.	B
11.	B	41.	C	71.	D
12.	A	42.	D	72.	C
13.	B	43.	A	73.	E
14.	C	44.	A	74.	C
15.	D	45.	E	75.	B
16.	D	46.	B	76.	A
17.	A	47.	C	77.	B
18.	E	48.	E	78.	C
19.	D	49.	D	79.	D
20.	B	50.	A	80.	C
21.	C	51.	B	81.	B
22.	A	52.	C	82.	E
23.	A	53.	D	83.	E
24.	E	54.	E	84.	D
25.	D	55.	C	85.	A
26.	A	56.	B	86.	A
27.	C	57.	A	87.	C
28.	D	58.	D	88.	C
29.	B	59.	E		
30.	B	60.	E		

If you scored:
84 or more correct, you have an excellent score.
78–83 correct, you have a good score.
77 or fewer correct, you should practice more.

MEMORIZATION/EXERCISE 3

A	B	C	D	E
2300-2399 Concord	2200-2299 Concord	2100-2199 Concord	2000-2099 Concord	1600-1699 Concord
Sapphire Ln.	Rockford Place	Alderwood	McGregor St.	Redwing Trail
8700-8799 Firglade	9200-9299 Firglade	9400-9499 Firglade	9700-9799 Firglade	9500-9599 Firglade
Brooklyn Rd.	Soundview	Pinehurst Dr.	Mariposa Ave.	Mission Creek
0300-0399 Madison	0400-0499 Madison	1400-1499 Madison	1500-1599 Madison	2500-2599 Madison

PRACTICE MEMORIZATION/EXERCISE 3

STEP 2 TIME: 3 MINUTES
STEP 3 TIME: 3 MINUTES (cover key)

A	B	C	D	E
2300-2399 Concord	2200-2299 Concord	2100-2199 Concord	2000-2099 Concord	1600-1699 Concord
Sapphire Ln.	Rockford Place	Alderwood	McGregor St.	Redwing Trail
8700-8799 Firglade	9200-9299 Firglade	9400-9499 Firglade	9700-9799 Firglade	9500-9599 Firglade
Brooklyn Rd.	Soundview	Pinehurst Dr.	Mariposa Ave.	Mission Creek
0300-0399 Madison	0400-0499 Madison	1400-1499 Madison	1500-1599 Madison	2500-2599 Madison

1. 2200-2299 Concord
2. Alderwood
3. 9700-9799 Firglade
4. Sapphire Ln.
5. 0400-0499 Madison
6. Mariposa Ave.
7. 9500-9599 Firglade
8. Redwing Trail
9. 2000-2099 Concord
10. Pinehurst Dr.
11. Soundview
12. 0300-0399 Madison
13. Rockford Pl.
14. McGregor St.
15. 1600-1699 Concord
16. 9400-9499 Firglade
17. Mission Creek
18. 2500-2599 Madison
19. 9200-9299 Firglade
20. Brooklyn Rd.
21. 8700-8799 Firglade
22. 1400-1499 Madison
23. 2300-2399 Concord
24. 2100-2199 Concord
25. 1500-1599 Madison
26. Redwing Trail
27. Rockford Pl.
28. Brooklyn Rd.
29. 2200-2299 Concord
30. 0300-0399 Madison

31. 2500 2599 Madison
32. 1600-1699 Concord
33. Soundview
34. 1400-1499 Madison
35. 2100-2199 Concord
36. McGregor St.
37. Mariposa Ave.
38. 9700-9799 Firglade
39. Alderwood
40. Mission Creek
41. 2300-2399 Concord
42. 9400-9499 Firglade
43. Pinehurst Dr.
44. 2000-2099 Concord
45. 9500-9599 Firglade
46. 0400-0499 Madison
47. Sapphire Ln.
48. 1500-1599 Madison
49. 9200-9299 Firglade
50. 8700-8799 Firglade
51. Rockford Pl.
52. 1600-1699 Concord
53. 9200-9299 Firglade
54. Redwing Trail
55. Soundview
56. 9700-9799 Firglade
57. Alderwood
58. 2200-2299 Concord
59. Sapphire Ln.
60. Brooklyn Rd.

61. Mission Creek
62. 2000-2099 Concord
63. Mariposa Ave.
64. 0400-0499 Madison
65. 9500-9599 Firglade
66. 2500-2599 Madison
67. 2100-2199 Concord
68. McGregor St.
69. Pinehurst Dr.
70. 0300-0399 Madison
71. 9400-9499 Firglade
72. 2300-2399 Concord
73. 8700-8799 Firglade
74. 1500-1599 Madison
75. 2000-2099 Concord
76. 9200-9299 Firglade
77. Redwing Trail
78. Brooklyn Rd.
79. Mariposa Ave.
80. 1400-1499 Madison
81. 2200-2299 Concord
82. 8700-8799 Firglade
83. 0400-0499 Madison
84. 2000-2099 Concord
85. Alderwood
86. 0300-0399 Madison
87. Pinehurst Dr.
88. 9500-9599 Firglade

PRACTICE ANSWER SHEET TO MEMORIZATION/EXERCISE 3

1. Ⓐ Ⓑ Ⓒ Ⓓ Ⓔ   31. Ⓐ Ⓑ Ⓒ Ⓓ Ⓔ   61. Ⓐ Ⓑ Ⓒ Ⓓ Ⓔ
2. Ⓐ Ⓑ Ⓒ Ⓓ Ⓔ   32. Ⓐ Ⓑ Ⓒ Ⓓ Ⓔ   62. Ⓐ Ⓑ Ⓒ Ⓓ Ⓔ
3. Ⓐ Ⓑ Ⓒ Ⓓ Ⓔ   33. Ⓐ Ⓑ Ⓒ Ⓓ Ⓔ   63. Ⓐ Ⓑ Ⓒ Ⓓ Ⓔ
4. Ⓐ Ⓑ Ⓒ Ⓓ Ⓔ   34. Ⓐ Ⓑ Ⓒ Ⓓ Ⓔ   64. Ⓐ Ⓑ Ⓒ Ⓓ Ⓔ
5. Ⓐ Ⓑ Ⓒ Ⓓ Ⓔ   35. Ⓐ Ⓑ Ⓒ Ⓓ Ⓔ   65. Ⓐ Ⓑ Ⓒ Ⓓ Ⓔ
6. Ⓐ Ⓑ Ⓒ Ⓓ Ⓔ   36. Ⓐ Ⓑ Ⓒ Ⓓ Ⓔ   66. Ⓐ Ⓑ Ⓒ Ⓓ Ⓔ
7. Ⓐ Ⓑ Ⓒ Ⓓ Ⓔ   37. Ⓐ Ⓑ Ⓒ Ⓓ Ⓔ   67. Ⓐ Ⓑ Ⓒ Ⓓ Ⓔ
8. Ⓐ Ⓑ Ⓒ Ⓓ Ⓔ   38. Ⓐ Ⓑ Ⓒ Ⓓ Ⓔ   68. Ⓐ Ⓑ Ⓒ Ⓓ Ⓔ
9. Ⓐ Ⓑ Ⓒ Ⓓ Ⓔ   39. Ⓐ Ⓑ Ⓒ Ⓓ Ⓔ   69. Ⓐ Ⓑ Ⓒ Ⓓ Ⓔ
10. Ⓐ Ⓑ Ⓒ Ⓓ Ⓔ   40. Ⓐ Ⓑ Ⓒ Ⓓ Ⓔ   70. Ⓐ Ⓑ Ⓒ Ⓓ Ⓔ
11. Ⓐ Ⓑ Ⓒ Ⓓ Ⓔ   41. Ⓐ Ⓑ Ⓒ Ⓓ Ⓔ   71. Ⓐ Ⓑ Ⓒ Ⓓ Ⓔ
12. Ⓐ Ⓑ Ⓒ Ⓓ Ⓔ   42. Ⓐ Ⓑ Ⓒ Ⓓ Ⓔ   72. Ⓐ Ⓑ Ⓒ Ⓓ Ⓔ
13. Ⓐ Ⓑ Ⓒ Ⓓ Ⓔ   43. Ⓐ Ⓑ Ⓒ Ⓓ Ⓔ   73. Ⓐ Ⓑ Ⓒ Ⓓ Ⓔ
14. Ⓐ Ⓑ Ⓒ Ⓓ Ⓔ   44. Ⓐ Ⓑ Ⓒ Ⓓ Ⓔ   74. Ⓐ Ⓑ Ⓒ Ⓓ Ⓔ
15. Ⓐ Ⓑ Ⓒ Ⓓ Ⓔ   45. Ⓐ Ⓑ Ⓒ Ⓓ Ⓔ   75. Ⓐ Ⓑ Ⓒ Ⓓ Ⓔ
16. Ⓐ Ⓑ Ⓒ Ⓓ Ⓔ   46. Ⓐ Ⓑ Ⓒ Ⓓ Ⓔ   76. Ⓐ Ⓑ Ⓒ Ⓓ Ⓔ
17. Ⓐ Ⓑ Ⓒ Ⓓ Ⓔ   47. Ⓐ Ⓑ Ⓒ Ⓓ Ⓔ   77. Ⓐ Ⓑ Ⓒ Ⓓ Ⓔ
18. Ⓐ Ⓑ Ⓒ Ⓓ Ⓔ   48. Ⓐ Ⓑ Ⓒ Ⓓ Ⓔ   78. Ⓐ Ⓑ Ⓒ Ⓓ Ⓔ
19. Ⓐ Ⓑ Ⓒ Ⓓ Ⓔ   49. Ⓐ Ⓑ Ⓒ Ⓓ Ⓔ   79. Ⓐ Ⓑ Ⓒ Ⓓ Ⓔ
20. Ⓐ Ⓑ Ⓒ Ⓓ Ⓔ   50. Ⓐ Ⓑ Ⓒ Ⓓ Ⓔ   80. Ⓐ Ⓑ Ⓒ Ⓓ Ⓔ
21. Ⓐ Ⓑ Ⓒ Ⓓ Ⓔ   51. Ⓐ Ⓑ Ⓒ Ⓓ Ⓔ   81. Ⓐ Ⓑ Ⓒ Ⓓ Ⓔ
22. Ⓐ Ⓑ Ⓒ Ⓓ Ⓔ   52. Ⓐ Ⓑ Ⓒ Ⓓ Ⓔ   82. Ⓐ Ⓑ Ⓒ Ⓓ Ⓔ
23. Ⓐ Ⓑ Ⓒ Ⓓ Ⓔ   53. Ⓐ Ⓑ Ⓒ Ⓓ Ⓔ   83. Ⓐ Ⓑ Ⓒ Ⓓ Ⓔ
24. Ⓐ Ⓑ Ⓒ Ⓓ Ⓔ   54. Ⓐ Ⓑ Ⓒ Ⓓ Ⓔ   84. Ⓐ Ⓑ Ⓒ Ⓓ Ⓔ
25. Ⓐ Ⓑ Ⓒ Ⓓ Ⓔ   55. Ⓐ Ⓑ Ⓒ Ⓓ Ⓔ   85. Ⓐ Ⓑ Ⓒ Ⓓ Ⓔ
26. Ⓐ Ⓑ Ⓒ Ⓓ Ⓔ   56. Ⓐ Ⓑ Ⓒ Ⓓ Ⓔ   86. Ⓐ Ⓑ Ⓒ Ⓓ Ⓔ
27. Ⓐ Ⓑ Ⓒ Ⓓ Ⓔ   57. Ⓐ Ⓑ Ⓒ Ⓓ Ⓔ   87. Ⓐ Ⓑ Ⓒ Ⓓ Ⓔ
28. Ⓐ Ⓑ Ⓒ Ⓓ Ⓔ   58. Ⓐ Ⓑ Ⓒ Ⓓ Ⓔ   88. Ⓐ Ⓑ Ⓒ Ⓓ Ⓔ
29. Ⓐ Ⓑ Ⓒ Ⓓ Ⓔ   59. Ⓐ Ⓑ Ⓒ Ⓓ Ⓔ
30. Ⓐ Ⓑ Ⓒ Ⓓ Ⓔ   60. Ⓐ Ⓑ Ⓒ Ⓓ Ⓔ

MEMORIZATION/EXERCISE 3

STEP 5 TIME: 5 MINUTES

1. Rockford Pl.	31. Sapphire Ln.	61. 1400-1499 Madison
2. 9400-9499 Firglade	32. Soundview	62. 0400-0499 Madison
3. Mariposa Ave.	33. Pinehurst Dr.	63. Mission Creek
4. 2300-2399 Concord	34. 9200-9299 Firglade	64. 2300-2399 Concord
5. 2500-2599 Madison	35. 2500-2599 Madison	65. Rockford Pl.
6. McGregor St.	36. McGregor St.	66. Pinehurst Dr.
7. Soundview	37. 0300-0399 Madison	67. Mariposa Ave.
8. 2200-2299 Concord	38. 1400-1499 Madison	68. 1500-1599 Madison
9. Sapphire Ln.	39. 0400-0499 Madison	69. 9200-9299 Firglade
10. 1600-1699 Concord	40. 2100-2199 Concord	70. 2500-2599 Madison
11. 9700-9799 Firglade	41. Mission Creek	71. Alderwood
12. 2100-2199 Concord	42. 2000-2099 Concord	72. 2000-2099 Concord
13. 0400-0499 Madison	43. Sapphire Ln.	73. Sapphire Ln.
14. Brooklyn Rd.	44. Rockford Pl.	74. 8700-8799 Firglade
15. 9200-9299 Firglade	45. Pinehurst Dr.	75. 2200-2299 Concord
16. 9500-9599 Firglade	46. Redwing Trail	76. 1600-1699 Concord
17. 1500-1599 Madison	47. 9700-9799 Firglade	77. 9700-9799 Firglade
18. Pinehurst Dr.	48. Mariposa Ave.	78. Rockford Pl.
19. 1400-1499 Madison	49. 2500-2599 Madison	79. 1400-1499 Madison
20. Rockford Pl.	50. 8700-8799 Firglade	80. Mission Creek
21. 8700-8799 Firglade	51. 2200-2299 Concord	81. Brooklyn Rd.
22. 2000-2099 Concord	52. Alderwood	82. 0400-0499 Madison
23. Mission Creek	53. Brooklyn Rd.	83. Pinehurst
24. Redwing Trail	54. 9200-9299 Firglade	84. 0300-0399 Madison
25. 2300-2399 Concord	55. 9400-9499 Firglade	85. 9500-9599 Firglade
26. Alderwood	56. 9700-9799 Firglade	86. Mariposa Ave.
27. 2200-2299 Concord	57. Soundview	87. McGregor St.
28. 9700-9799 Firglade	58. 0300-0399 Madison	88. Soundview
29. Mariposa Ave.	59. 1600-1699 Concord	
30. 1600-1699 Concord	60. McGregor St.	

ANSWER SHEET TO MEMORIZATION/EXERCISE 3

1. A B C D E   31. A B C D E   61. A B C D E
2. A B C D E   32. A B C D E   62. A B C D E
3. A B C D E   33. A B C D E   63. A B C D E
4. A B C D E   34. A B C D E   64. A B C D E
5. A B C D E   35. A B C D E   65. A B C D E
6. A B C D E   36. A B C D E   66. A B C D E
7. A B C D E   37. A B C D E   67. A B C D E
8. A B C D E   38. A B C D E   68. A B C D E
9. A B C D E   39. A B C D E   69. A B C D E
10. A B C D E   40. A B C D E   70. A B C D E
11. A B C D E   41. A B C D E   71. A B C D E
12. A B C D E   42. A B C D E   72. A B C D E
13. A B C D E   43. A B C D E   73. A B C D E
14. A B C D E   44. A B C D E   74. A B C D E
15. A B C D E   45. A B C D E   75. A B C D E
16. A B C D E   46. A B C D E   76. A B C D E
17. A B C D E   47. A B C D E   77. A B C D E
18. A B C D E   48. A B C D E   78. A B C D E
19. A B C D E   49. A B C D E   79. A B C D E
20. A B C D E   50. A B C D E   80. A B C D E
21. A B C D E   51. A B C D E   81. A B C D E
22. A B C D E   52. A B C D E   82. A B C D E
23. A B C D E   53. A B C D E   83. A B C D E
24. A B C D E   54. A B C D E   84. A B C D E
25. A B C D E   55. A B C D E   85. A B C D E
26. A B C D E   56. A B C D E   86. A B C D E
27. A B C D E   57. A B C D E   87. A B C D E
28. A B C D E   58. A B C D E   88. A B C D E
29. A B C D E   59. A B C D E
30. A B C D E   60. A B C D E

ANSWERS TO MEMORIZATION/EXERCISE 3

1.	B	31.	A	61.	C
2.	C	32.	B	62.	B
3.	D	33.	C	63.	E
4.	A	34.	B	64.	A
5.	E	35.	E	65.	B
6.	D	36.	D	66.	C
7.	B	37.	A	67.	D
8.	B	38.	C	68.	D
9.	A	39.	B	69.	B
10.	E	40.	C	70.	E
11.	D	41.	E	71.	C
12.	C	42.	D	72.	D
13.	B	43.	A	73.	A
14.	A	44.	B	74.	A
15.	B	45.	C	75.	B
16.	E	46.	E	76.	E
17.	D	47.	D	77.	D
18.	C	48.	D	78.	B
19.	C	49.	E	79.	C
20.	B	50.	A	80.	E
21.	A	51.	B	81.	A
22.	D	52.	C	82.	B
23.	E	53.	A	83.	C
24.	E	54.	B	84.	A
25.	A	55.	C	85.	E
26.	C	56.	D	86.	D
27.	B	57.	B	87.	D
28.	D	58.	A	88.	B
29.	D	59.	E		
30.	E	60.	D		

If you scored:
84 or more correct, you have an excellent score.
78–83 correct, you have a good score.
77 or fewer correct, you should practice more.

Number Series

Number series tests are used to determine your skill at discerning number patterns. For clerks, this has direct relevance to code recognition as information is typed into a special purpose keyboard to sort either letters or flats.

Number series tests are not difficult if you can quickly establish the pattern in the numbers listed. For example, look at the question below:

$$2 \quad 4 \quad 6 \quad 8 \quad 10 \quad 12 \quad \underline{?} \quad \underline{?}$$

As you can see, there is an addition constant of +2 between each number. Therefore, the next two numbers in the sequence should be 14 and 16.

$$2 \quad 4 \quad 6 \quad 8 \quad 10 \quad 12 \quad \underline{14} \quad \underline{16}$$
$$+2 \quad +2 \quad +2 \quad +2 \quad +2 \quad +2 \quad +2$$

Subtraction and multiplication number series are much the same as the prior example. An example of each is given below. Try to determine what the last two numbers are in each of the number sequences.

$$23 \quad 20 \quad 17 \quad 14 \quad 11 \quad 8 \quad \underline{?} \quad \underline{?}$$

$$1 \quad 3 \quad 9 \quad 27 \quad 81 \quad \underline{?} \quad \underline{?}$$

The first example shown is a subtraction number series. If you determined that there was a subtraction constant of -3 between numbers, you were correct. So the last two numbers in the first sequence should be 5 and 2.

$$23 \quad 20 \quad 17 \quad 14 \quad 11 \quad 8 \quad \underline{5} \quad \underline{2}$$
$$-3 \quad -3 \quad -3 \quad -3 \quad -3 \quad -3 \quad -3$$

The second example represents a multiplication number series. If you determined that there was a multiplication constant of 3 between the numbers in the sequence, you were right again. Therefore, the last two numbers in this series are 243 and 729.

$$1 \quad 3 \quad 9 \quad 27 \quad 81 \quad \underline{243} \quad \underline{729}$$
$$x3 \quad x3 \quad x3 \quad x3 \quad x3 \quad x3$$

The last kind of number series that will appear on the exam is an alternating number series. This kind of number sequence is a little more involved and consequently takes extra time to solve. The series involves alternating uses of addition and/or subtraction to create a pattern. A pattern may not be immediately evident but with a little diligence, it should become apparent. Two examples are given below. Try to determine what the last two numbers are in each sequence.

$$0 \quad 12 \quad 10 \quad 3 \quad 6 \quad 8 \quad 6 \quad 9 \quad \underline{?} \quad \underline{?}$$

$$0 \quad 16 \quad 17 \quad 4 \quad 18 \quad 19 \quad 8 \quad 20 \quad \underline{?} \quad \underline{?}$$

If you guessed 12 and 4, and 21 and 12, respectively you are right. You can see how these patterns can become a bit more complicated.

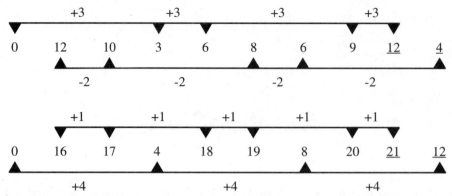

If a pattern in an alternating number series is not discernable, there is a method you can use to help. The first step involves determining the differences between each successive number in sequence. For example:

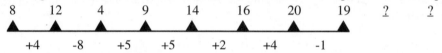

Note that there are two +4 and two +5 constants. The next step is to check these differences to see if, indeed, some kind of pattern can be established. Let's start with the +4 constant. The numbers involved are 8, 12, 16, and 20. What should become evident is that this series of four numbers represents an addition number series pattern. To better clarify the pattern, if you diagram it as shown below, it should alleviate some confusion

If there were one more answer blank, the number 24 would be the right answer. However, the addition number series pattern already established does not encompass the two answer blanks. Now, look at the remaining numbers: 4, 9, 14, and 19. Do you see a pattern emerge there? If you determined the series is another addition number series with +5 as a constant, you are correct.

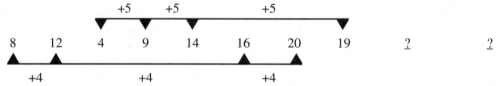

By blocking off the pattern of +5's, the answer can be determined.

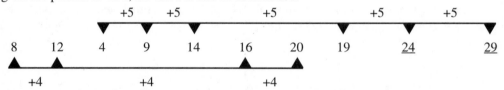

Since you are allotted only 20 minutes on the actual exam to complete twenty-four number series questions, time is of the essence. If an answer to an alternating number series question is not apparent within the scope of 30 seconds, skip the question and go on to the next one. If you have any time remaining after you have completed the test questions that you know, return to those questions you skipped, and try to solve them. If you still have trouble determining the answer, systematically plug in each of the options provided and by the process of elimination you can determine the correct answer. This is somewhat time consuming, but it is better than just guessing. Whatever the case, don't leave any answers blank. Guess only as a last resort.

For your convenience, the first number series exercise questions have been segregated into the four number series groups (i.e., addition, subtraction, multiplication, and alternating). This should clue you in as to what kind of pattern to be searching for. However, you will not be given the same convenience on number series exercises 2 and 3. On those exams, the series will be relatively well mixed for variety. The answers will provide the correct number combinations and establish the set pattern involved. Thus, you can see how the answer to the question was determined. A scale has been provided for determination of your performance on each exam.

NUMBER SERIES/EXERCISE 1   TIME: 20 MINUTES

Addition Number Series

1.   7   10   13   16   19   22   ___   ___

    A. 25, 28   C. 23, 27   E. 27, 30
    B. 23, 24   D. 25, 26

2.   24   30   36   42   48   54   ___   ___

    A. 56, 66   C. 60, 56   E. 60, 66
    B. 58, 64   D. 58, 66

3.   18   27   36   45   54   63   ___   ___

    A. 70, 81   C. 72, 81   E. 72, 83
    B. 71, 81   D. 71, 82

4.   4   20   36   52   68   84   ___   ___

    A. 96, 114   C. 100, 110   E. 110, 116
    B. 98, 110   D. 100, 116

5.   13   15   17   19   21   23   ___   ___

    A. 24, 25   C. 25, 28   E. 26, 28
    B. 27, 28   D. 25, 27

6.   1   18   35   52   69   86   ___   ___

    A. 105, 122   C. 101, 119   E. 105, 120
    B. 103, 120   D. 103, 102

Subtraction Number Series

7.   14   12   10   8   6   4   ___   ___

    A. 2, 0   C. 2, 2   E. 0, 0
    B. 4, 2   D. 0, 2

8.   174   150   126   102   78   54   ___   ___

    A. 40, 6   C. 30, 6   E. 28, 2
    B. 30, 4   D. 28, 4

9.   45   40   35   30   25   20   ___   ___

    A. 10, 5   C. 10, 15   E. 15, 10
    B. 15, 5   D. 5, 10

10.   81   72   63   54   45   36   ___   ___

    A. 18, 27   C. 17, 28   E. 27, 18
    B. 28, 17   D. 26, 18

11.   163   149   135   121   107   93   ___   ___

    A. 65, 79   C. 81, 67   E. 67, 81
    B. 79, 65   D. 79, 59

12.   1205   1088   971   854   737   620   ___   ___

    A. 386, 503   C. 503, 286   E. 500, 286
    B. 403, 386   D. 503, 386

Multiplication Number Series

13. 2   4   8   16   32   ___   ___

    A.   32, 64   C.   64, 128   E.   60, 128
    B.   64, 32   D.   60, 120

14. 4   20   100   500   2500   ___   ___

    A.   5000, 12,500   C.   62,500, 12,5000   E.   12,000, 60,000
    B.   12,500, 62,500   D.   18,500, 25,500

15. 3   9   27   81   243   ___   ___

    A.   729, 2187   C.   739, 2187   E.   723, 2187
    B.   715, 2180   D.   715, 2387

16. 1   7   49   343   ___   ___

    A.   2401, 16,807   C.   2401, 16,907   E.   4085, 17,250
    B.   2400, 16,000   D.   2400, 16,807

17. 6   12   24   48   96   ___   ___

    A.   182, 384   C.   192, 375   E.   192, 384
    B.   190, 380   D.   195, 380

18. 2   8   32   128   512   ___   ___

    A.   2408, 8192   C.   2348, 8792   E.   2040, 8029
    B.   2580, 8092   D.   2048, 8192

Alternating Number Series

19. 12   10   16   17   8   6   18   ___   ___

    A.   19, 2   C.   2, 20   E.   20, 3
    B.   4, 19   D.   19, 4

20. 7   11   3   8   13   15   19   18   ___   ___

    A.   25, 28   C.   23, 24   E.   22, 28
    B.   23, 28   D.   21, 23

21. 20   3   6   9   17   14   12   15   18   ___   ___

    A.   5,8   C.   11,8   E.   8, 11
    B.   7, 11   D.   12, 8

22. 30   20   25   28   30   35   26   40   ___   ___

    A.   45, 24   C.   47, 24   E.   41, 22
    B.   46, 25   D.   43, 25

23. 18   14   13   16   12   11   14   10   ___   ___

    A.   8, 10   C.   10, 9   E.   10, 8
    B.   9, 12   D.   12, 9

24. 36   42   35   28   45   21   14   7   ___   ___

    A.   54, 0   C.   43, 14   E.   48, 7
    B.   36, 7   D.   48, 0

ANSWER SHEET TO NUMBER SERIES/EXERCISE 1

1. Ⓐ Ⓑ Ⓒ Ⓓ Ⓔ
2. Ⓐ Ⓑ Ⓒ Ⓓ Ⓔ
3. Ⓐ Ⓑ Ⓒ Ⓓ Ⓔ
4. Ⓐ Ⓑ Ⓒ Ⓓ Ⓔ
5. Ⓐ Ⓑ Ⓒ Ⓓ Ⓔ
6. Ⓐ Ⓑ Ⓒ Ⓓ Ⓔ
7. Ⓐ Ⓑ Ⓒ Ⓓ Ⓔ
8. Ⓐ Ⓑ Ⓒ Ⓓ Ⓔ

9. Ⓐ Ⓑ Ⓒ Ⓓ Ⓔ
10. Ⓐ Ⓑ Ⓒ Ⓓ Ⓔ
11. Ⓐ Ⓑ Ⓒ Ⓓ Ⓔ
12. Ⓐ Ⓑ Ⓒ Ⓓ Ⓔ
13. Ⓐ Ⓑ Ⓒ Ⓓ Ⓔ
14. Ⓐ Ⓑ Ⓒ Ⓓ Ⓔ
15. Ⓐ Ⓑ Ⓒ Ⓓ Ⓔ
16. Ⓐ Ⓑ Ⓒ Ⓓ Ⓔ

17. Ⓐ Ⓑ Ⓒ Ⓓ Ⓔ
18. Ⓐ Ⓑ Ⓒ Ⓓ Ⓔ
19. Ⓐ Ⓑ Ⓒ Ⓓ Ⓔ
20. Ⓐ Ⓑ Ⓒ Ⓓ Ⓔ
21. Ⓐ Ⓑ Ⓒ Ⓓ Ⓔ
22. Ⓐ Ⓑ Ⓒ Ⓓ Ⓔ
23. Ⓐ Ⓑ Ⓒ Ⓓ Ⓔ
24. Ⓐ Ⓑ Ⓒ Ⓓ Ⓔ

[This page may be removed to mark answers.]

[This page is intentionally blank.]

ANSWERS TO NUMBER SERIES/EXERCISE 1

1. A. 7   10   13   16   19   22   <u>25</u>   <u>28</u>
   +3   +3   +3   +3   +3   +3   +3

2. E. 24   30   36   42   48   54   <u>60</u>   <u>66</u>
   +6   +6   +6   +6   +6   +6   +6

3. C. 18   27   36   45   54   63   <u>72</u>   <u>81</u>
   +9   +9   +9   +9   +9   +9   +9

4. D. 4   20   36   52   68   84   <u>100</u>   <u>116</u>
   +16   +16   +16   +16   +16   +16   +16

5. D. 13   15   17   19   21   23   <u>25</u>   <u>27</u>
   +2   +2   +2   +2   +2   +2   +2

6. B. 1   18   35   52   69   86   <u>103</u>   <u>120</u>
   +17   +17   +17   +17   +17   +17   +17

7. A. 14   12   10   8   6   4   <u>2</u>   <u>0</u>
   -2   -2   -2   -2   -2   -2   -2

8. C. 174   150   126   102   78   54   <u>30</u>   <u>6</u>
   -24   -24   -24   -24   -24   -24   -24

9. E. 45   40   35   30   25   20   <u>15</u>   <u>10</u>
   -5   -5   -5   -5   -5   -5   -5

10. E. 81   72   63   54   45   36   <u>27</u>   <u>18</u>
    -9   -9   -9   -9   -9   -9   -9

11. B. 163   149   135   121   107   93   <u>79</u>   <u>65</u>
    -14   -14   -14   -14   -14   -14   -14

12. D. 1205   1088   971   854   737   620   <u>503</u>   <u>386</u>
    -117   -117   -117   -117   -117   -117   -117

13. C. 2   4   8   16   32   <u>64</u>   <u>128</u>
    x2   x2   x2   x2   x2   x2

14. B. 4   20   100   500   2500   <u>12,500</u>   <u>62,500</u>
    x5   x5   x5   x5   x5   x5

15. A. 3   9   27   81   243   <u>729</u>   <u>2187</u>
    x3   x3   x3   x3   x3   x3

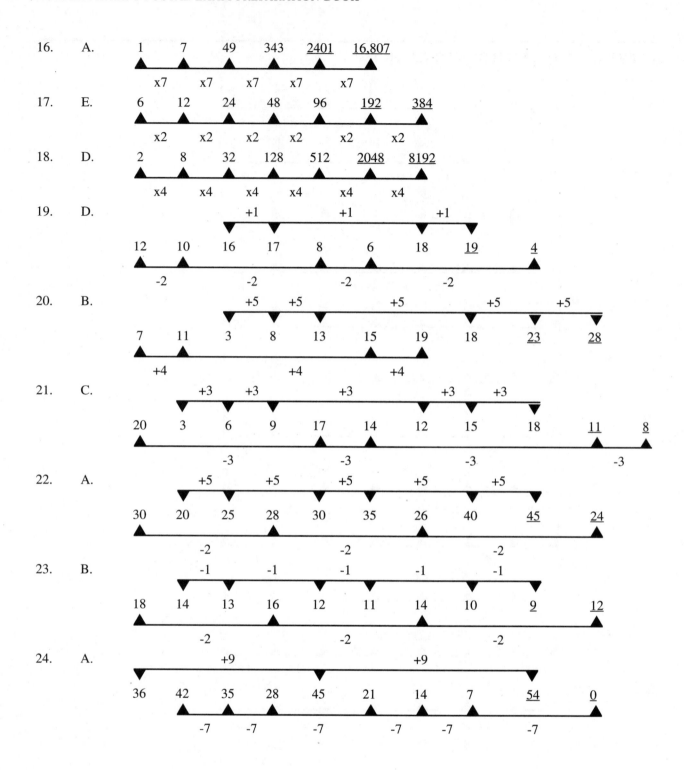

16.   A.   1   7   49   343   <u>2401</u>   <u>16,807</u>

x7   x7   x7   x7   x7

17.   E.   6   12   24   48   96   <u>192</u>   <u>384</u>

x2   x2   x2   x2   x2   x2

18.   D.   2   8   32   128   512   <u>2048</u>   <u>8192</u>

x4   x4   x4   x4   x4   x4

19.   D.   +1   +1   +1

12   10   16   17   8   6   18   <u>19</u>   <u>4</u>

-2   -2   -2   -2

20.   B.   +5   +5   +5   +5   +5

7   11   3   8   13   15   19   18   <u>23</u>   <u>28</u>

+4   +4   +4

21.   C.   +3   +3   +3   +3   +3

20   3   6   9   17   14   12   15   18   <u>11</u>   <u>8</u>

-3   -3   -3   -3

22.   A.   +5   +5   +5   +5   +5

30   20   25   28   30   35   26   40   <u>45</u>   <u>24</u>

-2   -2   -2

23.   B.   -1   -1   -1   -1   -1

18   14   13   16   12   11   14   10   <u>9</u>   <u>12</u>

-2   -2   -2

24.   A.   +9   +9

36   42   35   28   45   21   14   7   <u>54</u>   <u>0</u>

-7   -7   -7   -7   -7   -7

If you scored:
22 or more correct, you have an excellent score.
20 or 21 correct, you have a good score.
19 or fewer correct, you need more practice.

NUMBER SERIES/EXERCISE 2   TIME: 20 MINUTES

1.   12   16   20   24   28   ___   ___
   - A. 29, 32
   - B. 30, 36
   - C. 32, 24
   - D. 30, 32
   - E. 32, 36

2.   1   4   16   64   256   ___   ___
   - A. 1042, 4096
   - B. 1096, 4024
   - C. 1024, 4096
   - D. 1034, 5000
   - E. 1042, 5000

3.   21   20   18   24   15   28   ___   ___
   - A. 13, 23
   - B. 12, 32
   - C. 14, 32
   - D. 10, 30
   - E. 12, 23

4.   17   27   37   32   47   57   67   30   ___   ___
   - A. 77, 87
   - B. 77, 28
   - C. 87, 28
   - D. 87, 34
   - E. 67, 28

5.   3   6   12   24   48   ___   ___
   - A. 90, 196
   - B. 96, 129
   - C. 92, 196
   - D. 96, 192
   - E. 100, 196

6.   29   7   23   13   17   19   11   25   ___   ___
   - A. 4, 31
   - B. 4, 30
   - C. 5, 31
   - D. 31, 5
   - E. 31, 4

7.   18   12   20   28   21   36   44   ___   ___
   - A. 50, 24
   - B. 52, 34
   - C. 52, 24
   - D. 50, 34
   - E. 52, 42

8.   19   17   15   13   11   ___   ___
   - A. 10, 6
   - B. 9, 8
   - C. 9, 6
   - D. 8, 7
   - E. 9, 7

9.   14   15   23   19   32   23   ___   ___
   - A. 40, 26
   - B. 41, 27
   - C. 27, 40
   - D. 26, 14
   - E. 41, 30

10.   23   40   57   74   91   ___   ___
   - A. 98, 115
   - B. 108, 125
   - C. 103, 115
   - D. 98, 108
   - E. 118, 125

11.   4   3   5   3   7   9   ___   ___
   - A. 10, 2
   - B. 2, 11
   - C. 11, 15
   - D. 3, 10
   - E. 1, 10

12.   27   25   23   20   19   15   ___   ___
   - A. 10, 15
   - B. 12, 10
   - C. 17, 15
   - D. 15, 10
   - E. 19, 20

13.   9   18   27   36   45   ___   ___

A. 54, 63   C. 53, 64   E. 50, 63
B. 53, 63   D. 55, 64

14.   4   7   15   9   26   11   ___   ___

A. 37, 13   C. 28, 37   E. 13, 27
B. 27, 12   D. 39, 13

15.   37   40   41   39   43   46   37   ___   ___

A. 33, 48   C. 35, 49   E. 37, 50
B. 35, 48   D. 30, 49

16.   1   7   6   14   36   28   ___   ___

A. 224, 56   C. 216, 56   E. 202, 60
B. 220, 50   D. 230, 52

17.   15   20   25   30   35   40   ___   ___

A. 40, 45   C. 45, 55   E. 50, 45
B. 50, 60   D. 45, 50

18.   1   21   9   19   17   17   25   ___   ___

A. 33, 17   C. 20, 37   E. 15, 33
B. 15, 30   D. 12, 35

19.   12   40   39   24   38   37   36   36   ___   ___

A. 36, 42   C. 35, 40   E. 35, 48
B. 37, 46   D. 39, 44

20.   68   60   52   44   36   ___   ___

A. 28, 20   C. 24, 18   E. 16, 28
B. 20, 28   D. 22, 20

21.   7   12   10   14   13   16   ___   ___

A. 18, 20   C. 16, 18   E. 14, 23
B. 18, 16   D. 14, 20

22.   15   12   18   19   9   6   20   ___   ___

A. 22, 0   C. 24, 0   E. 27, 4
B. 21, 3   D. 25, 2

23.   4   12   36   108   ___   ___

A. 304, 912   C. 324, 902   E. 312, 936
B. 314, 942   D. 324, 972

24.   6   8   7   6   7   8   5   4   ___   ___

A. 2, 8   C. 2, 9   E. 0, 8
B. 1, 10   D. 3, 9

ANSWERS TO NUMBER SERIES/EXERCISE 2

1. Ⓐ Ⓑ Ⓒ Ⓓ Ⓔ
2. Ⓐ Ⓑ Ⓒ Ⓓ Ⓔ
3. Ⓐ Ⓑ Ⓒ Ⓓ Ⓔ
4. Ⓐ Ⓑ Ⓒ Ⓓ Ⓔ
5. Ⓐ Ⓑ Ⓒ Ⓓ Ⓔ
6. Ⓐ Ⓑ Ⓒ Ⓓ Ⓔ
7. Ⓐ Ⓑ Ⓒ Ⓓ Ⓔ
8. Ⓐ Ⓑ Ⓒ Ⓓ Ⓔ

9. Ⓐ Ⓑ Ⓒ Ⓓ Ⓔ
10. Ⓐ Ⓑ Ⓒ Ⓓ Ⓔ
11. Ⓐ Ⓑ Ⓒ Ⓓ Ⓔ
12. Ⓐ Ⓑ Ⓒ Ⓓ Ⓔ
13. Ⓐ Ⓑ Ⓒ Ⓓ Ⓔ
14. Ⓐ Ⓑ Ⓒ Ⓓ Ⓔ
15. Ⓐ Ⓑ Ⓒ Ⓓ Ⓔ
16. Ⓐ Ⓑ Ⓒ Ⓓ Ⓔ

17. Ⓐ Ⓑ Ⓒ Ⓓ Ⓔ
18. Ⓐ Ⓑ Ⓒ Ⓓ Ⓔ
19. Ⓐ Ⓑ Ⓒ Ⓓ Ⓔ
20. Ⓐ Ⓑ Ⓒ Ⓓ Ⓔ
21. Ⓐ Ⓑ Ⓒ Ⓓ Ⓔ
22. Ⓐ Ⓑ Ⓒ Ⓓ Ⓔ
23. Ⓐ Ⓑ Ⓒ Ⓓ Ⓔ
24. Ⓐ Ⓑ Ⓒ Ⓓ Ⓔ

[This page may be removed to mark answers.]

[This page is intentionally blank.]

1. E.   12   16   20   24   28   <u>32</u>   <u>36</u>

        +4   +4   +4   +4   +4   +4

2. C.   1   4   16   64   256   <u>1024</u>   <u>4096</u>

        x4   x4   x4   x4   x4   x4

3. B.

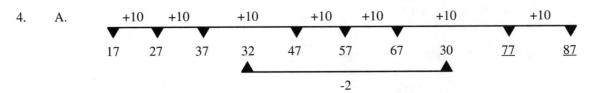

               +4   +4   +4

21   20   18   24   15   28   <u>12</u>   <u>32</u>

       -3   -3   -3

4. A.

+10   +10   +10   +10   +10   +10   +10

17   27   37   32   47   57   67   30   <u>77</u>   <u>87</u>

                     -2

5. D.   3   6   12   24   48   <u>96</u>   <u>192</u>

        x2   x2   x2   x2   x2   x2

6. C.

            +6   +6   +6   +6

29   7   23   13   17   19   11   25   <u>5</u>   <u>31</u>

       -6   -6   -6   -6

7. C.

            +8   +8   +8   +8   +8

18   12   20   28   21   36   44   <u>52</u>   <u>24</u>

            +3   +3

8. E.   19   17   15   13   11   <u>9</u>   <u>7</u>

       -2   -2   -2   -2   -2   -2

9. B.

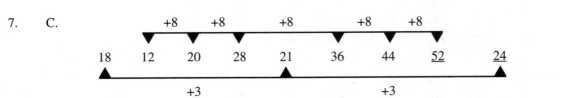

          +9   +9   +9

14   15   23   19   32   23   <u>41</u>   <u>27</u>

            +4   +4   +4

10. B.   23   40   57   74   91   <u>108</u>   <u>125</u>

        +17   +17   +17   +17   +17   +17

11. B.
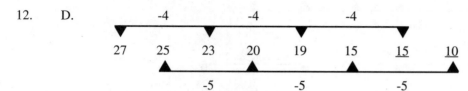

$$+2 \qquad +2 \qquad +2 \qquad +2$$
4   3   5   3   7   9   <u>2</u>   <u>11</u>
$$-1 \qquad\qquad -1$$

12. D.
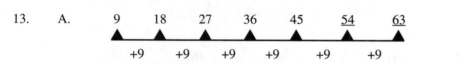

$$-4 \qquad -4 \qquad -4$$
27   25   23   20   19   15   <u>15</u>   <u>10</u>
$$-5 \qquad -5 \qquad -5$$

13. A.
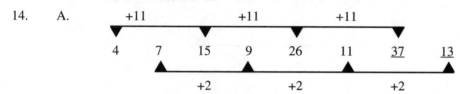

9   18   27   36   45   <u>54</u>   <u>63</u>
$$+9 \quad +9 \quad +9 \quad +9 \quad +9 \quad +9$$

14. A.
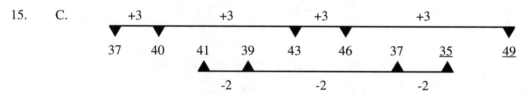

$$+11 \qquad +11 \qquad +11$$
4   7   15   9   26   11   <u>37</u>   <u>13</u>
$$+2 \qquad +2 \qquad +2$$

15. C.
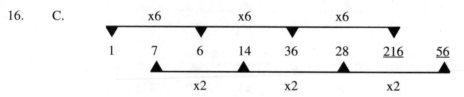

$$+3 \qquad +3 \qquad +3 \qquad +3$$
37   40   41   39   43   46   37   <u>35</u>   <u>49</u>
$$-2 \qquad -2 \qquad -2$$

16. C.
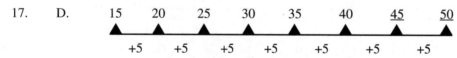

$$\times 6 \qquad \times 6 \qquad \times 6$$
1   7   6   14   36   28   <u>216</u>   <u>56</u>
$$\times 2 \qquad \times 2 \qquad \times 2$$

17. D.
15   20   25   30   35   40   <u>45</u>   <u>50</u>
$$+5 \quad +5 \quad +5 \quad +5 \quad +5 \quad +5 \quad +5$$

18. E.
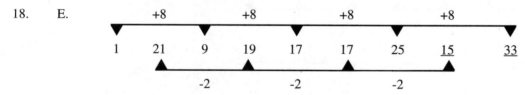

$$+8 \qquad +8 \qquad +8 \qquad +8$$
1   21   9   19   17   17   25   <u>15</u>   <u>33</u>
$$-2 \qquad -2 \qquad -2$$

19. E.
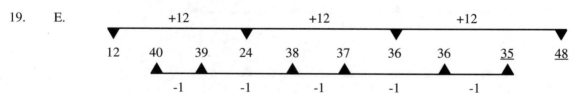

$$+12 \qquad +12 \qquad +12$$
12   40   39   24   38   37   36   36   <u>35</u>   <u>48</u>
$$-1 \quad -1 \quad -1 \quad -1 \quad -1$$

20.   A.
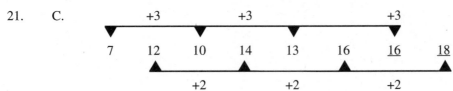

68   60   52   44   36   <u>28</u>   <u>20</u>

-8   -8   -8   -8   -8   -8

21.   C.
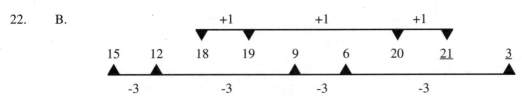

+3   +3   +3

7   12   10   14   13   16   <u>16</u>   <u>18</u>

+2   +2   +2

22.   B.

+1   +1   +1

15   12   18   19   9   6   20   <u>21</u>   <u>3</u>

-3   -3   -3   -3

23.   D.
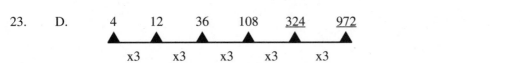

4   12   36   108   <u>324</u>   <u>972</u>

x3   x3   x3   x3   x3

24.   D.
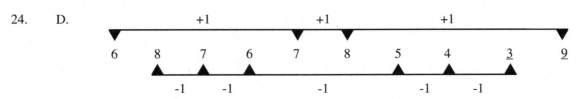

+1   +1   +1

6   8   7   6   7   8   5   4   <u>3</u>   <u>2</u>

-1   -1   -1   -1   -1

If you scored:
22 or more correct, you have an excellent score.
20 or 21 correct, you have a good score.
19 or fewer correct, you need more practice.

[This page is intentionally blank.]

NUMBER SERIES/EXERCISE 3   TIME: 20 MINUTES

1.   6   13   20   27   34   ___   ___

    A.   40, 46   C.   42, 48   E.   43, 50
    B.   41, 48   D.   40, 47

2.   19   16   13   10   7   ___   ___

    A.   4, 0   C.   5, 2   E.   4, 1
    B.   3, 0   D.   5, 3

3.   1   8   64   512   ___   ___

    A.   4069, 32,768   C.   4096, 32,768   E.   4075, 32,300
    B.   5000, 40,000   D.   4080, 32,320

4.   17   19   16   19   13   10   ___   ___

    A.   15, 6   C.   20, 8   E.   21, 6
    B.   17, 6   D.   21, 7

5.   24   27   23   25   26   27   19   ___   ___

    A.   14, 26   C.   16, 26   E.   20, 28
    B.   13, 28   D.   15, 28

6.   16   12   15   14   18   21   ___   ___

    A.   12, 24   C.   20, 19   E.   15, 19
    B.   24, 12   D.   19, 20

7.   3   21   147   ___   ___

    A.   1029, 7203   C.   1029, 7302   E.   1025, 7150
    B.   1000, 3000   D.   7203, 1028

8.   1   8   17   26   7   35   44   ___   ___

    A.   50, 13   C.   53, 12   E.   10, 56
    B.   53, 13   D.   56, 10

9.   64   80   77   75   90   70   ___   ___

    A.   105, 65   C.   103, 56   E.   103, 65
    B.   130, 70   D.   100, 65

10.   11   8   7   13   6   ___   ___

    A.   5, 14   C.   3, 10   E.   7, 20
    B.   5, 15   D.   10, 3

11.   27   34   41   48   55   62   ___   ___

    A.   69, 75   C.   69, 76   E.   75, 70
    B.   68, 76   D.   70, 75

12.   96   81   66   51   36   ___   ___

    A.   20, 6   C.   21, 6   E.   20, 3
    B.   21, 5   D.   18, 0

13. 20   17   15   19   13   11   ___   ___

    A.   18, 9   C.   6, 9   E.   17, 9
    B.   12, 9   D.   10, 2

14. 37   29   30   31   32   32   33   ___   ___

    A.   30, 27   C.   30, 28   E.   33, 27
    B.   34, 27   D.   34, 34

15. 48   58   60   63   72   68   ___   ___

    A.   80, 70   C.   84, 72   E.   90, 70
    B.   85, 73   D.   84, 73

16. 6   10   27   22   48   34   69   ___   ___

    A.   50, 70   C.   42, 88   E.   46, 90
    B.   64, 80   D.   43, 89

17. 25   22   19   16   13   ___   ___

    A.   10, 7   C.   13, 6   E.   8, 6
    B.   12, 8   D.   6, 4

18. 2   5   7   6   5   8   11   4   3   ___   ___

    A.   1, 10   C.   1, 10   E.   12, 14
    B.   2, 14   D.   10, 12

19. 20   16   12   8   ___   ___

    A.   4, 1   C.   4, 0   E.   2, 4
    B.   3, 2   D.   3, 3

20. 1   2   4   8   16   ___   ___

    A.   20, 24   C.   36, 42   E.   32, 64
    B.   32, 46   D.   30, 62

21. 14   21   3   28   35   13   ___   ___

    A.   41, 47   C.   44, 50   E.   42, 49
    B.   42, 47   D.   43, 49

22. 12   11   9   14   10   9   19   24   ___   ___

    A.   6, 5   C.   5, 6   E.   7, 5
    B.   7, 8   D.   8, 7

23. 36   42   48   54   60   66   ___   ___

    A.   70, 74   C.   73, 79   E.   75, 89
    B.   76, 86   D.   72, 78

24. 48   16   28   36   40   52   24   64   ___   ___

    A.   70, 14   C.   76, 0   E.   72, 12
    B.   76, 12   D.   64, 0

ANSWER SHEET TO NUMBER SERIES/EXERCISE 3

1. Ⓐ Ⓑ Ⓒ Ⓓ Ⓔ   9. Ⓐ Ⓑ Ⓒ Ⓓ Ⓔ   17. Ⓐ Ⓑ Ⓒ Ⓓ Ⓔ

2. Ⓐ Ⓑ Ⓒ Ⓓ Ⓔ   10. Ⓐ Ⓑ Ⓒ Ⓓ Ⓔ   18. Ⓐ Ⓑ Ⓒ Ⓓ Ⓔ

3. Ⓐ Ⓑ Ⓒ Ⓓ Ⓔ   11. Ⓐ Ⓑ Ⓒ Ⓓ Ⓔ   19. Ⓐ Ⓑ Ⓒ Ⓓ Ⓔ

4. Ⓐ Ⓑ Ⓒ Ⓓ Ⓔ   12. Ⓐ Ⓑ Ⓒ Ⓓ Ⓔ   20. Ⓐ Ⓑ Ⓒ Ⓓ Ⓔ

5. Ⓐ Ⓑ Ⓒ Ⓓ Ⓔ   13. Ⓐ Ⓑ Ⓒ Ⓓ Ⓔ   21. Ⓐ Ⓑ Ⓒ Ⓓ Ⓔ

6. Ⓐ Ⓑ Ⓒ Ⓓ Ⓔ   14. Ⓐ Ⓑ Ⓒ Ⓓ Ⓔ   22. Ⓐ Ⓑ Ⓒ Ⓓ Ⓔ

7. Ⓐ Ⓑ Ⓒ Ⓓ Ⓔ   15. Ⓐ Ⓑ Ⓒ Ⓓ Ⓔ   23. Ⓐ Ⓑ Ⓒ Ⓓ Ⓔ

8. Ⓐ Ⓑ Ⓒ Ⓓ Ⓔ   16. Ⓐ Ⓑ Ⓒ Ⓓ Ⓔ   24. Ⓐ Ⓑ Ⓒ Ⓓ Ⓔ

[This page may be removed to mark answers.]

[This page is intentionally blank.]

ANSWERS TO NUMBER SERIES/EXERCISE 3

1. B.
6	13	20	27	34	<u>41</u>	<u>48</u>

    +7   +7   +7   +7   +7   +7

2. E.
19	16	13	10	7	<u>4</u>	<u>1</u>

    -3   -3   -3   -3   -3   -3

3. C.
1	8	64	512	<u>4096</u>	<u>32,768</u>

    x8   x8   x8   x8   x8

4. D.
    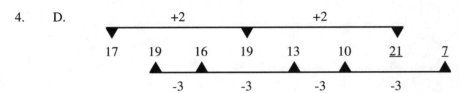

5. D.
    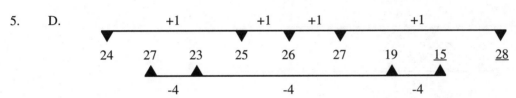

6. A.
    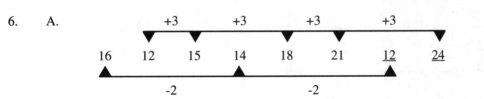

7. A.
    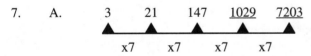

3	21	147	<u>1029</u>	<u>7203</u>

    x7   x7   x7   x7

8. B.
    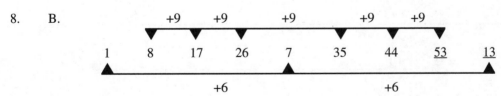

9. E.
    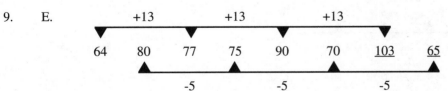

10. B.
    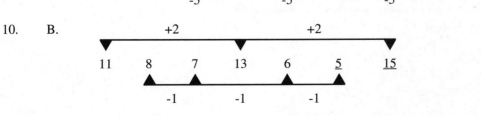

11. C. 27   34   41   48   55   62   <u>69</u>   <u>76</u>
        +7   +7   +7   +7   +7   +7   +7

12. C. 96   81   66   51   36   <u>21</u>   <u>6</u>
        -15   -15   -15   -15   -15   -15

13. A.   -1   -1
        20   17   15   19   13   11   <u>18</u>   <u>9</u>
              -2   -2   -2   -2

14. B.   -5   -5
        37   29   30   31   32   32   33   <u>34</u>   <u>27</u>
              +1   +1   +1   +1   +1

15. D.   +12   +12   +12
        48   58   60   63   72   68   <u>84</u>   <u>73</u>
              +5   +5   +5

16. E.   +21   +21   +21   +21
        6   10   27   22   48   34   69   <u>46</u>   <u>90</u>
              +12   +12   +12

17. A. 25   22   19   16   13   <u>10</u>   <u>7</u>
          -3   -3   -3   -3   -3   -3

18. B.   +3   +3   +3   +3
        2   5   7   6   5   8   11   4   3   <u>2</u>   <u>14</u>
                -1   -1   -1   -1   -1

19. C. 20   16   12   8   <u>4</u>   <u>0</u>
          -4   -4   -4   -4   -4

20. E. 1   2   4   8   16   <u>32</u>   <u>64</u>
          x2   x2   x2   x2   x2   x2

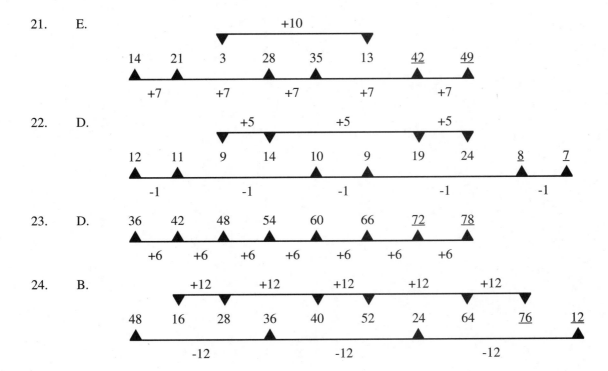

21. E.

+10

14   21   3   28   35   13   <u>42</u>   <u>49</u>

+7   +7   +7   +7   +7

22. D.

+5   +5   +5

12   11   9   14   10   9   19   24   <u>8</u>   <u>7</u>

-1   -1   -1   -1   -1

23. D.   36   42   48   54   60   66   <u>72</u>   <u>78</u>

+6   +6   +6   +6   +6   +6   +6

24. B.

+12   +12   +12   +12   +12

48   16   28   36   40   52   24   64   <u>76</u>   <u>12</u>

-12   -12   -12

If you scored:
22 or more correct, you have an excellent score.
20 or 21 correct, you have a good score.
19 or fewer correct, you need more practice.

Following Directions

This part of the exam is derived from the old Mail Handler test and is designed to determine how well you follow directions. How you perform here has bearing on the amount of time and effort required by Postal supervisory staff to train you for a specific job. Obviously, a person who needs to be told only once how to do something stands a better chance of being hired than someone who needs directions repeated. This is not a difficult test, particularly if you pay full attention to the examiner's every direction. You will be given ample time between directions to respond on your answer sheet. This is not a time-oriented section. One note of caution here: Be alert for words such as IF, OR, BUT, AND, ONLY, EXCEPT, OTHERWISE, or any other conditional terms, because they alter the instructions. Ignoring such terms will cause you to mark incorrect choices.

In the practice session that follows, a friend or relative will be needed to play the part of the test examiner. He or she will be responsible for reading the directions orally to you at a rate of 75-80 words per minute, pausing where indicated in the test. As a suggestion, have whoever you choose to help you read with a timer until they can judge what the rate of 75-80 words per minute is like. Pauses between directions should be timed also.

When you are ready to do one of the three exercises provided in this chapter, tear out those pages with the directions and give them to the person assisting you. You should be left with only the samples and answer sheets on which to mark your responses. Once a direction has been read by the examiner, it cannot be repeated. If you happen to miss part of a direction or do not understand the direction completely, you can attempt a guess at the correct answer. Place a greater emphasis on listening more closely to the next set of directions given. Most importantly, do not panic if a question has to be skipped. Overlooking one or two questions will not substantially affect your test score.

There are more answer blanks provided than there are directions on the exam, so a great deal of your answer sheet will remain blank after you have completed the test. **NOTE:** Unlike any other test section, the answer sheet in this exercise may not be filled out in numerical order. In other sections, question number 1 corresponds with answer blank number 1, question number 2 with answer blank number 2, etc. On this particular test, however, question number 1 may direct you to darken a particular letter in answer blank number 82; question number 2 may concern answer blank number 25, etc.

The correct answers to practice exams are posted at the end of each exercise. A scale has also been provided to rank your proficiency at following directions.

[This page is intentionally blank.]

FOLLOWING DIRECTIONS/EXERCISE 1

Note To Person Assisting In This Exercise:

Remove from this test guide the pages of this exercise that comprise the directions (this page and the reverse). The test applicant should be left with only the samples and the answer sheet.

Read the following directions out loud at the suggested rate of 75-80 words per minute, pausing only where indicated in parentheses. Speak as clearly as possible: Once a statement has been read, it cannot be repeated.

Examine Sample 1. (Pause 2-3 seconds.) If any of the months listed in Sample 1 can be categorized as winter months, find number 12 on your answer sheet and darken the letter E, as in "elephant." Otherwise, find number 14 on your answer sheet and darken the letter A, as in "apple." (Pause 7 seconds.)

Examine Sample 1 again. (Pause 2-3 seconds.) If more than two months begin with the letter J, as in "jack," go to number 15 on your answer sheet and darken the letter B, as in "boy." (Pause 7 seconds.) Otherwise, darken the letter C, as in "cat" on number 5 on your answer sheet. (Pause 7 seconds.)

Examine Sample 2. (Pause 2-3 seconds.) Write the number 17 in the smallest circle shown. Darken the resulting number-letter combination on your answer sheet only if there are two larger circles shown in the sample. (Pause 10 seconds.) Otherwise, write the number 16 in square D, as in "dog," and darken that number-letter combination on your answer sheet. (Pause 10 seconds.)

Examine Sample 3. (Pause 2-3 seconds.) This sample illustrates the respective number of routes originating from each of three Postal substations in a metropolitan area. Select the largest substation, designated by the highest number of routes, and write the letter C, as in "cat," beside it. (Pause 7 seconds.) Darken the resulting number-letter combination on your answer sheet. (Pause 7 seconds.)

Examine Sample 3 again. (Pause 2-3 seconds.) If the Chaney Street station has more routes than the Myers Boulevard station, write the letter B, as in "boy," beside the Clifford Avenue station. (Pause 5 seconds.) If not, write the letter A, as in "apple," beside the Myers Boulevard station. (Pause 5 seconds.) Darken the number-letter combination you have selected on your answer sheet. (Pause 7 seconds.)

Examine Sample 4. (Pause 2-3 seconds.) If the third number is greater than the second number, but less than the fifth number, write the letter A, as in "apple," beside 42. (Pause 5 seconds.) Otherwise, write the letter D, as in "dog," beside the fourth number. (Pause 5 seconds.) Darken the number-letter combination that you have selected on your answer sheet. (Pause 7 seconds.)

Examine Sample 3 again. (Pause 2-3 seconds.) Darken the letter D, as in "dog," on number 9 of your answer sheet if the Chaney Street substation has the smallest number of routes. (Pause 7 seconds.) Otherwise, go to number 82 on your answer sheet and darken the letter D, as in "dog." (Pause 7 seconds.)

Examine Sample 4 again. (Pause 2-3 seconds.) If there are any numbers greater than 53, but less than 70, write the letter B, as in "boy," beside that number and darken the resulting number-letter combination on your answer sheet. (Pause 7 seconds.) Otherwise, write the letter E, as in "elephant," beside the second number of the sample and darken that number-letter combination on your answer sheet. (Pause 10 seconds.)

Examine Sample 5. (Pause 2-3 seconds.) This sample shows four numbers, each representing a combined zip code and route direct number. The first five digits of each number identify the zip code and the last two digits represent intercity route numbers. If all of the zip codes in Sample 5 are the same and there is not a route number higher than 50, darken the letter A, as in "apple," on number 50 of your answer sheet. (Pause 10 seconds.) Otherwise, darken the letter C, as in "cat," on number 49 of your answer sheet. (Pause 7 seconds.)

Examine Sample 6. (Pause 2-3 seconds.) Write the letter A, as in "apple," beside the lowest number if the first number in the sample is less than the last number in the sample, and if there is a number greater than 91. (Pause 7 seconds.) Otherwise, write the letter E, as in "elephant," beside the number 30. (Pause 5 seconds.) Darken the number-letter combination you have selected on your answer sheet. (Pause 7 seconds.)

Examine Sample 6 again. (Pause 2-3 seconds.) Write the letter B, as in "boy," beside the number 84 if the preceding number is less than 84. (Pause 5 seconds.) Otherwise, write the letter C, as in "cat," beside 84. (Pause 5 seconds.) Darken the number-letter combination you have chosen on your answer sheet. (Pause 7 seconds.)

Examine Sample 6 one more time. (Pause 2-3 seconds.) If there is a number that is greater than 43, yet less than 53, write the letter D, as in "dog," beside it. Darken that number-letter combination on your answer sheet.

(Pause 10 seconds.) If not, go to number 14 on your answer sheet and darken the letter B, as in "boy." (Pause 7 seconds.)

Examine Sample 7. (Pause 2-3 seconds.) If Los Angeles is located in Florida, and Washington, D.C. is in California, write the number 16 on the line beside the letter E, as in "elephant." (Pause 5 seconds.) If the preceding statement is false, write the number 16 beside the letter E, as in "elephant," anyway, and darken the resulting number-letter combination on your answer sheet. (Pause 10 seconds.)

Examine Sample 8. (Pause 2-3 seconds.) Each of the five boxes show the starting and finishing times of five rural routes on a particular day. The time at the top is the rural carriers' starting time and the time listed below shows when they finished for the day. Find the carrier who spends the longest time on his or her route and write the number 10 beside the letter representing that carrier. (Pause 10 seconds.) Darken your answer sheet with this number-letter combination. (Pause 7 seconds.)

Examine Sample 8 again. (Pause 2-3 seconds.) If Carrier A, as in "apple," finished for the day before Carrier B, as in "boy," write the number 2 beside the letter A, as in "apple." (Pause 5 seconds.) Otherwise, find which of the carriers had the latest starting time and write the number 7 beside the letter representing that carrier. (Pause 7 seconds.) Darken the number-letter combination you have chosen on your answer sheet. (Pause 7 seconds.)

Examine Sample 8 one more time. (Pause 2-3 seconds.) Write the number 11 beside the letter representing the carrier with the second latest finishing time. (Pause 7 seconds.) Darken that number-letter combination on your answer sheet. (Pause 7 seconds.)

Examine Sample 9. (Pause 2-3 seconds.) Write the letter E, as in "elephant," beside the number that is in the circle and darken your answer with the resulting number-letter combination. (Pause 5 seconds.) If there is no circle in the sample, write the number 47 beside the letter within the rectangle and darken that number-letter combination on your answer sheet. (Pause 10 seconds.)

Examine Sample 10. (Pause 2-3 seconds.) If any one of the states shown in the sample is not located in the western part of the United States, go to number 36 on your answer sheet and darken the letter E, as in "elephant." (Pause 7 seconds.) Otherwise, go to number 3 on your answer sheet and darken the letter B, as in "boy." (Pause 7 seconds.)

Examine Sample 10 again. (Pause 2-3 seconds.) If any of the states listed begin with the letter C, as in "cat," go to number 49 on your answer sheet, and darken the letter C, as in "cat." (Pause 7 seconds.)

Examine Sample 11. (Pause 2-3 seconds.) If 9 is greater than 7, and 20 is less than 21, write the number 60 on the line provided and darken that number-letter combination on your answer sheet. (Pause 10 seconds.) Otherwise, go to number 23 on your answer sheet and darken the letter B, as in "boy."

Examine Sample 12. (Pause 2-3 seconds.) Find the number that is greater than 13 and less than 64, and go to that number on your answer sheet and darken the letter C, as in "cat." (Pause 10 seconds.)

Examine Sample 13. (Pause 2-3 seconds.) Choose the number that is shown in identically sized shapes and go to that number on your answer sheet and darken in the letter E, as in "elephant." (Pause 10 seconds.)

Examine Sample 14. (Pause 2-3 seconds.) If 40 is less than 69 and greater than 15, go to 40 on your answer sheet and darken the letter A, as in "apple." (Pause 7 seconds.) If not, write the letter C, as in "cat," beside the number 15 in the sample. (Pause 5 seconds.) Darken that number-letter combination on your answer sheet. (Pause 7 seconds.)

-END OF TEST-

FOLLOWING DIRECTIONS/EXERCISE 1 SAMPLES

1.   March   :   December   :   November   :   July   :   January

2.   (A)   (C)   [D]   [E]   (B)

3. | Myers Blvd.
       32___routes | | Clifford Ave.
       45___routes | | Chaney St.
       9___routes |

4.   42_____   1_____   50_____   73_____   79_____

5.   9837841   9837810   9837814   9837813

6.   43_____   27_____   84_____   91_____   30_____   52_____

7.   _____B   _____E

8. | 7:30 AM
       2:45 PM
       ___A | 7:00 AM
       2:15 PM
       ___B | 6:00 AM
       4:00 PM
       ___C | 6:45 AM
       3:30 PM
       ___D | 7:00 AM
       3:00 PM
       ___E |

9.   B_____   12_____   A_____   47_____

10.   California   :   Oregon   :   Alaska   :   Florida   :   Washington

11.   _____D

12.   13   51   64   65   80

13. ┌────┐   ⬭   ┌────┐   ⬭
     │ 20 │   (6)   │ 20 │   (6)
     └────┘   └────┘

14. _____A   15_____   69_____   40_____   _____C

ANSWER SHEET TO FOLLOWING DIRECTIONS/EXERCISE 1

1. Ⓐ Ⓑ Ⓒ Ⓓ Ⓔ   33. Ⓐ Ⓑ Ⓒ Ⓓ Ⓔ   65. Ⓐ Ⓑ Ⓒ Ⓓ Ⓔ
2. Ⓐ Ⓑ Ⓒ Ⓓ Ⓔ   34. Ⓐ Ⓑ Ⓒ Ⓓ Ⓔ   66. Ⓐ Ⓑ Ⓒ Ⓓ Ⓔ
3. Ⓐ Ⓑ Ⓒ Ⓓ Ⓔ   35. Ⓐ Ⓑ Ⓒ Ⓓ Ⓔ   67. Ⓐ Ⓑ Ⓒ Ⓓ Ⓔ
4. Ⓐ Ⓑ Ⓒ Ⓓ Ⓔ   36. Ⓐ Ⓑ Ⓒ Ⓓ Ⓔ   68. Ⓐ Ⓑ Ⓒ Ⓓ Ⓔ
5. Ⓐ Ⓑ Ⓒ Ⓓ Ⓔ   37. Ⓐ Ⓑ Ⓒ Ⓓ Ⓔ   69. Ⓐ Ⓑ Ⓒ Ⓓ Ⓔ
6. Ⓐ Ⓑ Ⓒ Ⓓ Ⓔ   38. Ⓐ Ⓑ Ⓒ Ⓓ Ⓔ   70. Ⓐ Ⓑ Ⓒ Ⓓ Ⓔ
7. Ⓐ Ⓑ Ⓒ Ⓓ Ⓔ   39. Ⓐ Ⓑ Ⓒ Ⓓ Ⓔ   71. Ⓐ Ⓑ Ⓒ Ⓓ Ⓔ
8. Ⓐ Ⓑ Ⓒ Ⓓ Ⓔ   40. Ⓐ Ⓑ Ⓒ Ⓓ Ⓔ   72. Ⓐ Ⓑ Ⓒ Ⓓ Ⓔ
9. Ⓐ Ⓑ Ⓒ Ⓓ Ⓔ   41. Ⓐ Ⓑ Ⓒ Ⓓ Ⓔ   73. Ⓐ Ⓑ Ⓒ Ⓓ Ⓔ
10. Ⓐ Ⓑ Ⓒ Ⓓ Ⓔ   42. Ⓐ Ⓑ Ⓒ Ⓓ Ⓔ   74. Ⓐ Ⓑ Ⓒ Ⓓ Ⓔ
11. Ⓐ Ⓑ Ⓒ Ⓓ Ⓔ   43. Ⓐ Ⓑ Ⓒ Ⓓ Ⓔ   75. Ⓐ Ⓑ Ⓒ Ⓓ Ⓔ
12. Ⓐ Ⓑ Ⓒ Ⓓ Ⓔ   44. Ⓐ Ⓑ Ⓒ Ⓓ Ⓔ   76. Ⓐ Ⓑ Ⓒ Ⓓ Ⓔ
13. Ⓐ Ⓑ Ⓒ Ⓓ Ⓔ   45. Ⓐ Ⓑ Ⓒ Ⓓ Ⓔ   77. Ⓐ Ⓑ Ⓒ Ⓓ Ⓔ
14. Ⓐ Ⓑ Ⓒ Ⓓ Ⓔ   46. Ⓐ Ⓑ Ⓒ Ⓓ Ⓔ   78. Ⓐ Ⓑ Ⓒ Ⓓ Ⓔ
15. Ⓐ Ⓑ Ⓒ Ⓓ Ⓔ   47. Ⓐ Ⓑ Ⓒ Ⓓ Ⓔ   79. Ⓐ Ⓑ Ⓒ Ⓓ Ⓔ
16. Ⓐ Ⓑ Ⓒ Ⓓ Ⓔ   48. Ⓐ Ⓑ Ⓒ Ⓓ Ⓔ   80. Ⓐ Ⓑ Ⓒ Ⓓ Ⓔ
17. Ⓐ Ⓑ Ⓒ Ⓓ Ⓔ   49. Ⓐ Ⓑ Ⓒ Ⓓ Ⓔ   81. Ⓐ Ⓑ Ⓒ Ⓓ Ⓔ
18. Ⓐ Ⓑ Ⓒ Ⓓ Ⓔ   50. Ⓐ Ⓑ Ⓒ Ⓓ Ⓔ   82. Ⓐ Ⓑ Ⓒ Ⓓ Ⓔ
19. Ⓐ Ⓑ Ⓒ Ⓓ Ⓔ   51. Ⓐ Ⓑ Ⓒ Ⓓ Ⓔ   83. Ⓐ Ⓑ Ⓒ Ⓓ Ⓔ
20. Ⓐ Ⓑ Ⓒ Ⓓ Ⓔ   52. Ⓐ Ⓑ Ⓒ Ⓓ Ⓔ   84. Ⓐ Ⓑ Ⓒ Ⓓ Ⓔ
21. Ⓐ Ⓑ Ⓒ Ⓓ Ⓔ   53. Ⓐ Ⓑ Ⓒ Ⓓ Ⓔ   85. Ⓐ Ⓑ Ⓒ Ⓓ Ⓔ
22. Ⓐ Ⓑ Ⓒ Ⓓ Ⓔ   54. Ⓐ Ⓑ Ⓒ Ⓓ Ⓔ   86. Ⓐ Ⓑ Ⓒ Ⓓ Ⓔ
23. Ⓐ Ⓑ Ⓒ Ⓓ Ⓔ   55. Ⓐ Ⓑ Ⓒ Ⓓ Ⓔ   87. Ⓐ Ⓑ Ⓒ Ⓓ Ⓔ
24. Ⓐ Ⓑ Ⓒ Ⓓ Ⓔ   56. Ⓐ Ⓑ Ⓒ Ⓓ Ⓔ   88. Ⓐ Ⓑ Ⓒ Ⓓ Ⓔ
25. Ⓐ Ⓑ Ⓒ Ⓓ Ⓔ   57. Ⓐ Ⓑ Ⓒ Ⓓ Ⓔ   89. Ⓐ Ⓑ Ⓒ Ⓓ Ⓔ
26. Ⓐ Ⓑ Ⓒ Ⓓ Ⓔ   58. Ⓐ Ⓑ Ⓒ Ⓓ Ⓔ   90. Ⓐ Ⓑ Ⓒ Ⓓ Ⓔ
27. Ⓐ Ⓑ Ⓒ Ⓓ Ⓔ   59. Ⓐ Ⓑ Ⓒ Ⓓ Ⓔ   91. Ⓐ Ⓑ Ⓒ Ⓓ Ⓔ
28. Ⓐ Ⓑ Ⓒ Ⓓ Ⓔ   60. Ⓐ Ⓑ Ⓒ Ⓓ Ⓔ   92. Ⓐ Ⓑ Ⓒ Ⓓ Ⓔ
29. Ⓐ Ⓑ Ⓒ Ⓓ Ⓔ   61. Ⓐ Ⓑ Ⓒ Ⓓ Ⓔ   93. Ⓐ Ⓑ Ⓒ Ⓓ Ⓔ
30. Ⓐ Ⓑ Ⓒ Ⓓ Ⓔ   62. Ⓐ Ⓑ Ⓒ Ⓓ Ⓔ   94. Ⓐ Ⓑ Ⓒ Ⓓ Ⓔ
31. Ⓐ Ⓑ Ⓒ Ⓓ Ⓔ   63. Ⓐ Ⓑ Ⓒ Ⓓ Ⓔ   95. Ⓐ Ⓑ Ⓒ Ⓓ Ⓔ
32. Ⓐ Ⓑ Ⓒ Ⓓ Ⓔ   64. Ⓐ Ⓑ Ⓒ Ⓓ Ⓔ

[This page may be removed to mark answers.]

ANSWERS TO FOLLOWING DIRECTIONS/EXERCISE 1

1.	12 E	9.	50 A	17.	47 B
2.	5 C	10.	30 E	18.	36 E
3.	17 B	11.	84 B	19.	49 C
4.	45 C	12.	52 D	20.	60 D
5.	32 A	13.	16 E	21.	51 C
6.	42 A	14.	10 C	22.	20 E
7.	9 D	15.	7 A	23.	40 A
8.	1 E	16.	11 D		

If you scored:
22 or more correct, you have an excellent score.
20 or 21 correct, you have a good score.
19 or fewer correct, you need more practice.

If you have missed any of the questions in this exercise, review the narrative and identify what you misinterpreted. Most often, applicants make errors in this section because they answer too quickly, and miss key phrases. Be sure to listen to the entire question.

FOLLOWING DIRECTIONS/EXERCISE 2

Note To Person Assisting In This Exercise:

Remove from this test guide the pages of this exercise that comprise the directions (this page and the reverse). The test applicant should be left with only the samples and the answer sheet.

Read the following directions out loud at the suggested rate of 75-80 words per minute, pausing only where indicated in parentheses. Speak as clearly as possible: Once a statement has been read, it cannot be repeated.

Examine Sample 1. (Pause 2-3 seconds.) The figures shown represent postal drop boxes, each showing respective collection times. Write the letter B, as in "boy," in the box that has the earliest collection time. (Pause 5 seconds.) Find the numbers that represent the minutes of the collection time you have selected. Go to that number on your answer sheet and darken that letter-number combination. (Pause 7 seconds.)

Examine Sample 2. (Pause 2-3 seconds.) If 30 is more than 27, and 40 is less than 41, write the letter C, as in "cat," beside number 5 in the sample. (Pause 5 seconds.) If not, write the letter E, as in "elephant," beside number 16. (Pause 5 seconds.) Darken the selected number-letter combination on your answer sheet. (Pause 7 seconds.)

Examine Sample 2 again. (Pause 2-3 seconds.) Write the letter E, as in "elephant," beside 16 if 16 is greater than 7. (Pause 5 seconds.) Otherwise, write an A, as in "apple," beside number 7. (Pause 5 seconds.) Darken your chosen number-letter combination on the answer sheet. (Pause 7 seconds.)

Examine Sample 3. (Pause 2-3 seconds.) There are three squares and two circles of different proportions. In the second to the largest square write the number 75. (Pause 7 seconds.) Darken that number-letter combination on your answer sheet. (Pause 7 seconds.)

Examine Sample 3 again. (Pause 2-3 seconds.) If 10 divided by 5 equals 3, then write the number 76 in square C, as in "cat." (Pause 5 seconds.) If not, write the number 81 in the larger circle. (Pause 5 seconds.) Darken the number-letter combination you have selected on your answer sheet. (Pause 7 seconds.)

Examine Sample 4. (Pause 2-3 seconds.) Write the letter A, as in "apple," beside the second largest number and the letter D, as in "dog," beside the largest number. (Pause 10 seconds.) Of the remaining two numbers, write the letter E, as in "elephant," beside the smallest of the two. (Pause 5 seconds.) Darken that number-letter combination on your answer sheet. (Pause 7 seconds.)

Examine Sample 5. (Pause 2-3 seconds.) The three boxes shown in this sample represent different classes of mail; each is assigned a letter to reference it. If box D, as in "dog," is a cheaper means of mailing advertisements than box A, as in "apple," find number 15 on your answer sheet and darken the letter D, as in "dog." (Pause 7 seconds.) If box D, as in "dog," is a more expensive means of mailing advertisements, then find number 3 on your answer sheet and darken the letter A, as in "apple." (Pause 7 seconds.)

Examine Sample 6. (Pause 2-3 seconds.) This sample illustrates five numbers each representing the length of a different mail route in terms of mileage. Write the letter C, as in "cat," beside the third longest route if it is over 25 miles in length. (Pause 5 seconds.) Otherwise, write the letter A, as in "apple," beside the smallest route. (Pause 5 seconds.) Darken the number-letter combination you have chosen on your answer sheet. (Pause 7 seconds.)

Examine Sample 6 again. (Pause 2-3 seconds.) Pick out the route that is more than 14 miles long, yet less than 40 miles long. (Pause 5 seconds.) Write the letter A, as in "apple," beside it. (Pause 5 seconds.) Darken the resulting number-letter combination on your answer sheet. (Pause 7 seconds.)

Examine Sample 6 one more time. (Pause 2-3 seconds.) If the longest mail route is exactly 37 miles longer than the shortest route, go to number 3 on your answer sheet and darken the letter C, as in "cat." (Pause 10 seconds.) If it is not exactly 37 miles longer, then find number 8 on your answer sheet and darken the letter E, as in "elephant." (Pause 10 seconds.)

Examine Sample 7. (Pause 2-3 seconds.) Write the letter B, as in "boy," in the triangular shape and the letter C, as in "cat," in the circular shape. (Pause 10 seconds.) If the trapezoid shape represented by the number 24 has more sides than a square, darken the number-letter combination that lies in the triangle on your answer sheet. (Pause 10 seconds.) Otherwise, darken the number-letter combination on your answer sheet that lies in the circle. (Pause 10 seconds.)

Examine Sample 8. (Pause 2-3 seconds.) This sample shows five different numbers. Each number represents the number of parcels delivered by each of five carriers on a particular day. Consider 72 the largest number and 9 the smallest number. If the second largest number is more than 50, write the letter C, as in "cat," beside number 12. (Pause 5 seconds.) Darken this number-letter combination on your answer sheet. (Pause 7 seconds.) If the second smallest number of parcels is less than 11, write the letter E, as in "elephant," beside 45 and darken that number-letter combination on your answer sheet. (Pause 10 seconds.) If none of the previous statements are true, then write the letter C, as in "cat," beside the number 9 and darken your answer sheet accordingly. (Pause 10 seconds.)

Examine Sample 9. (Pause 2-3 seconds.) Write the number 20 beside letter B, as in "boy," if Chicago is located in Alaska. (Pause 5 seconds.) If not, write the number 6 beside letter C, as in "cat," and darken that number-letter combination on your answer sheet. (Pause 10 seconds.)

Examine Sample 9 again. (Pause 2-3 seconds.) If the product of 3 times 3 is greater than the sum of 4 plus 4, then write the number 17 beside the letter E, as in "elephant." (Pause 7 seconds.) Otherwise, write the number 82 beside the letter E, as in "elephant." (Pause 5 seconds.) Darken your answer sheet with the number-letter combination that you have chosen. (Pause 7 seconds.)

Examine Sample 10. (Pause 2-3 seconds.) Sample 10 shows five Mail Volume Index figures. Index numbers located in the upper portion of each circle indicate an above-average mail volume. Index numbers located in the lower portion of each circle indicate a below-average Index figure. If circle C, as in "cat," and E, as in "elephant," each illustrate a below-average Index figure, find number 27 on your answer sheet and darken the letter D, as in "dog." (Pause 10 seconds.) However, if circle A, as in "apple," and C, as in "cat," show above average figures, find number 14 on your answer sheet and darken the letter A, as in "apple." (Pause 10 seconds.)

Examine Sample 10 again. (Pause 2-3 seconds.) If circle A, as in "apple," has a higher Index figure than circle D, as in "dog," find the number 27 on your answer sheet and darken the letter B, as in "boy." (Pause 7 seconds.) If not, find number 10 on your answer sheet and darken the letter D, as in "dog." (Pause 7 seconds.)

Examine Sample 10 one more time. (Pause 2-3 seconds.) On your answer sheet darken the number-letter combination of the highest Mail Volume Index figure. (Pause 10 seconds.)

Examine Sample 11. (Pause 2-3 seconds.) If 30 is greater than 31, write the number 30 on the line beside the letter C, as in "cat." Darken that number-letter combination on your answer sheet. (Pause 10 seconds.) If not, then write the number 30 on the line beside the letter B, as in "boy," and darken your answer sheet accordingly. (Pause 10 seconds.)

Examine Sample 9 again. (Pause 2-3 seconds.) Go to the fourth letter from the right side of the sample and write the number 32 beside it. (Pause 5 seconds.) Darken this number-letter combination on your answer sheet. (Pause 7 seconds.)

Examine Sample 11 again. (Pause 2-3 seconds.) Write the letter C, as in "cat," beside 30. Darken the number-letter combination on your answer sheet only if 30 is the largest number in the sample. (Pause 10 seconds.) Otherwise, write the letter A, as in "apple," beside 48. Darken your answer on the answer sheet. (Pause 7 seconds.)

Examine Sample 12. (Pause 2-3 seconds.) This sample has four pairs of numbers, each measuring the quantity of letters dropped in a test collection box on four consecutive Mondays. The first number in each pair represents the number of out-of-town letters and the second number represents the number of local delivery letters. If there are more out-of-town letters than there are local letters in each of the pairs, and the testing is conducted on Tuesday, go to number 93 on your answer sheet and darken the letter A, as in "apple." (Pause 7 seconds.) Otherwise, go to number 69 on your answer sheet and darken the letter B, as in "boy." (Pause 7 seconds.)

Examine Sample 12 again. (Pause 2-3 seconds.) Write the letter C, as in "cat," beside the second out-of-town mail count and darken that number-letter combination on your answer sheet. (Pause 10 seconds.)

- END OF TEST -

FOLLOWING DIRECTIONS/EXERCISE 2 SAMPLES

1.
| 1:10 PM | 1:45 PM | 10:45 PM |
| _____ | _____ | _____ |

2.   5_____   7_____   16_____

3.

_____A   _____B   _____C   _____D   _____E

4.   47_____   52_____   46_____   2_____

5.
| First Class A | Second Class C | Third Class D |

6.   4_____   13_____   41_____   40_____   24_____

7.
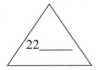
21_____   22_____   23_____   24_____

8.   12_____   18_____   9_____   72_____   45_____

9.   _____B   _____D   _____X   _____E   _____C

10.
A^{83} B_{46} C^{15} D_{10} E^{26}

11.   A_____   30_____   C_____   31_____   B_____   48_____

12.   70/10   87/14   90/3   88/69

ANSWER SHEET TO FOLLOWING DIRECTIONS/EXERCISE 2

1. Ⓐ Ⓑ Ⓒ Ⓓ Ⓔ   33. Ⓐ Ⓑ Ⓒ Ⓓ Ⓔ   65. Ⓐ Ⓑ Ⓒ Ⓓ Ⓔ
2. Ⓐ Ⓑ Ⓒ Ⓓ Ⓔ   34. Ⓐ Ⓑ Ⓒ Ⓓ Ⓔ   66. Ⓐ Ⓑ Ⓒ Ⓓ Ⓔ
3. Ⓐ Ⓑ Ⓒ Ⓓ Ⓔ   35. Ⓐ Ⓑ Ⓒ Ⓓ Ⓔ   67. Ⓐ Ⓑ Ⓒ Ⓓ Ⓔ
4. Ⓐ Ⓑ Ⓒ Ⓓ Ⓔ   36. Ⓐ Ⓑ Ⓒ Ⓓ Ⓔ   68. Ⓐ Ⓑ Ⓒ Ⓓ Ⓔ
5. Ⓐ Ⓑ Ⓒ Ⓓ Ⓔ   37. Ⓐ Ⓑ Ⓒ Ⓓ Ⓔ   69. Ⓐ Ⓑ Ⓒ Ⓓ Ⓔ
6. Ⓐ Ⓑ Ⓒ Ⓓ Ⓔ   38. Ⓐ Ⓑ Ⓒ Ⓓ Ⓔ   70. Ⓐ Ⓑ Ⓒ Ⓓ Ⓔ
7. Ⓐ Ⓑ Ⓒ Ⓓ Ⓔ   39. Ⓐ Ⓑ Ⓒ Ⓓ Ⓔ   71. Ⓐ Ⓑ Ⓒ Ⓓ Ⓔ
8. Ⓐ Ⓑ Ⓒ Ⓓ Ⓔ   40. Ⓐ Ⓑ Ⓒ Ⓓ Ⓔ   72. Ⓐ Ⓑ Ⓒ Ⓓ Ⓔ
9. Ⓐ Ⓑ Ⓒ Ⓓ Ⓔ   41. Ⓐ Ⓑ Ⓒ Ⓓ Ⓔ   73. Ⓐ Ⓑ Ⓒ Ⓓ Ⓔ
10. Ⓐ Ⓑ Ⓒ Ⓓ Ⓔ   42. Ⓐ Ⓑ Ⓒ Ⓓ Ⓔ   74. Ⓐ Ⓑ Ⓒ Ⓓ Ⓔ
11. Ⓐ Ⓑ Ⓒ Ⓓ Ⓔ   43. Ⓐ Ⓑ Ⓒ Ⓓ Ⓔ   75. Ⓐ Ⓑ Ⓒ Ⓓ Ⓔ
12. Ⓐ Ⓑ Ⓒ Ⓓ Ⓔ   44. Ⓐ Ⓑ Ⓒ Ⓓ Ⓔ   76. Ⓐ Ⓑ Ⓒ Ⓓ Ⓔ
13. Ⓐ Ⓑ Ⓒ Ⓓ Ⓔ   45. Ⓐ Ⓑ Ⓒ Ⓓ Ⓔ   77. Ⓐ Ⓑ Ⓒ Ⓓ Ⓔ
14. Ⓐ Ⓑ Ⓒ Ⓓ Ⓔ   46. Ⓐ Ⓑ Ⓒ Ⓓ Ⓔ   78. Ⓐ Ⓑ Ⓒ Ⓓ Ⓔ
15. Ⓐ Ⓑ Ⓒ Ⓓ Ⓔ   47. Ⓐ Ⓑ Ⓒ Ⓓ Ⓔ   79. Ⓐ Ⓑ Ⓒ Ⓓ Ⓔ
16. Ⓐ Ⓑ Ⓒ Ⓓ Ⓔ   48. Ⓐ Ⓑ Ⓒ Ⓓ Ⓔ   80. Ⓐ Ⓑ Ⓒ Ⓓ Ⓔ
17. Ⓐ Ⓑ Ⓒ Ⓓ Ⓔ   49. Ⓐ Ⓑ Ⓒ Ⓓ Ⓔ   81. Ⓐ Ⓑ Ⓒ Ⓓ Ⓔ
18. Ⓐ Ⓑ Ⓒ Ⓓ Ⓔ   50. Ⓐ Ⓑ Ⓒ Ⓓ Ⓔ   82. Ⓐ Ⓑ Ⓒ Ⓓ Ⓔ
19. Ⓐ Ⓑ Ⓒ Ⓓ Ⓔ   51. Ⓐ Ⓑ Ⓒ Ⓓ Ⓔ   83. Ⓐ Ⓑ Ⓒ Ⓓ Ⓔ
20. Ⓐ Ⓑ Ⓒ Ⓓ Ⓔ   52. Ⓐ Ⓑ Ⓒ Ⓓ Ⓔ   84. Ⓐ Ⓑ Ⓒ Ⓓ Ⓔ
21. Ⓐ Ⓑ Ⓒ Ⓓ Ⓔ   53. Ⓐ Ⓑ Ⓒ Ⓓ Ⓔ   85. Ⓐ Ⓑ Ⓒ Ⓓ Ⓔ
22. Ⓐ Ⓑ Ⓒ Ⓓ Ⓔ   54. Ⓐ Ⓑ Ⓒ Ⓓ Ⓔ   86. Ⓐ Ⓑ Ⓒ Ⓓ Ⓔ
23. Ⓐ Ⓑ Ⓒ Ⓓ Ⓔ   55. Ⓐ Ⓑ Ⓒ Ⓓ Ⓔ   87. Ⓐ Ⓑ Ⓒ Ⓓ Ⓔ
24. Ⓐ Ⓑ Ⓒ Ⓓ Ⓔ   56. Ⓐ Ⓑ Ⓒ Ⓓ Ⓔ   88. Ⓐ Ⓑ Ⓒ Ⓓ Ⓔ
25. Ⓐ Ⓑ Ⓒ Ⓓ Ⓔ   57. Ⓐ Ⓑ Ⓒ Ⓓ Ⓔ   89. Ⓐ Ⓑ Ⓒ Ⓓ Ⓔ
26. Ⓐ Ⓑ Ⓒ Ⓓ Ⓔ   58. Ⓐ Ⓑ Ⓒ Ⓓ Ⓔ   90. Ⓐ Ⓑ Ⓒ Ⓓ Ⓔ
27. Ⓐ Ⓑ Ⓒ Ⓓ Ⓔ   59. Ⓐ Ⓑ Ⓒ Ⓓ Ⓔ   91. Ⓐ Ⓑ Ⓒ Ⓓ Ⓔ
28. Ⓐ Ⓑ Ⓒ Ⓓ Ⓔ   60. Ⓐ Ⓑ Ⓒ Ⓓ Ⓔ   92. Ⓐ Ⓑ Ⓒ Ⓓ Ⓔ
29. Ⓐ Ⓑ Ⓒ Ⓓ Ⓔ   61. Ⓐ Ⓑ Ⓒ Ⓓ Ⓔ   93. Ⓐ Ⓑ Ⓒ Ⓓ Ⓔ
30. Ⓐ Ⓑ Ⓒ Ⓓ Ⓔ   62. Ⓐ Ⓑ Ⓒ Ⓓ Ⓔ   94. Ⓐ Ⓑ Ⓒ Ⓓ Ⓔ
31. Ⓐ Ⓑ Ⓒ Ⓓ Ⓔ   63. Ⓐ Ⓑ Ⓒ Ⓓ Ⓔ   95. Ⓐ Ⓑ Ⓒ Ⓓ Ⓔ
32. Ⓐ Ⓑ Ⓒ Ⓓ Ⓔ   64. Ⓐ Ⓑ Ⓒ Ⓓ Ⓔ

[This page may be removed to mark answers.]

ANSWERS TO FOLLOWING DIRECTIONS/EXERCISE 2

1.	10 B	9.	24 A	17.	83 A
2.	5 C	10.	3 C	18.	30 B
3.	16 E	11.	23 C	19.	32 D
4.	75 B	12.	9 C	20.	48 A
5.	81 D	13.	6 C	21.	69 B
6.	2 E	14.	17 E	22.	87 C
7.	15 D	15.	14 A		
8.	4 A	16.	27 B		

If you scored:
21 or more correct, you have an excellent score.
19 or 20 correct, you have a good score.
18 or fewer correct, you need more practice.

If you have missed any of the questions in this exercise, review the narrative and identify what you misinterpreted. Most often, applicants make errors in this section because they answer too quickly, and miss key phrases. Remember: Be sure to listen to the entire question.

FOLLOWING DIRECTIONS/EXERCISE 3

Note To Person Assisting In This Exercise:

Remove from this test guide the pages of this exercise that comprise the directions (this page and the reverse). The test applicant should be left with only the samples and the answer sheet.

Read the following directions out loud at the suggested rate of 75-80 words per minute, pausing only where indicated in parentheses. Speak as clearly as possible: Once a statement has been read, it cannot be repeated.

Examine Sample 1. (Pause 2-3 seconds.) If any of the numbers shown are greater than 122, go to number 22 on your answer sheet and darken the letter D, as in "dog." (Pause 7 seconds.) If not, go to number 23 on your answer sheet and darken the letter A, as in "apple." (Pause 7 seconds.)

Examine Sample 2. (Pause 2-3 seconds.) Write the letter E, as in "elephant," on the line provided only if the number shown is less than 51. (Pause 5 seconds.) If the number shown is greater than or equal to 51, write the letter B, as in "boy," on the line provided. (Pause 5 seconds.) Darken the number-letter combination you have selected on your answer sheet. (Pause 7 seconds.)

Examine Sample 3. (Pause 2-3 seconds.) Write the number 67 on the shortest line shown. (Pause 5 seconds.) Write the number 68 on the longest line shown. (Pause 5 seconds.) Now, darken on your answer sheet both of the number-letter combinations you have made. (Pause 12 seconds.)

Examine Sample 3 again. (Pause 2-3 seconds.) If any part of the statement that I am about to read is false, write the number 2 on line A, as in "apple." (Pause 3 seconds.) There are seven days in a week, four weeks in a month, and 12 months in a year. (Pause 5 seconds.) However, if the statement is true, write the number 1 on line A, as in "apple." (Pause 3 seconds.) Darken the number-letter combination you have selected for line A, as in "apple," on your answer sheet. (Pause 7 seconds.)

Examine Sample 4. (Pause 2-3 seconds.) Write the letter B, as in "boy," beside the highest number shown within a geometric shape. (Pause 5 seconds.) Darken the resulting number-letter combination on your answer sheet. (Pause 7 seconds.)

Examine Sample 4 again. (Pause 2-3 seconds.) Now, write the letter C, as in "cat," beside the highest number shown in the sample. (Pause 5 seconds.) Darken the number-letter combination on your answer sheet. (Pause 7 seconds.)

Examine Sample 4 one more time. (Pause 2-3 seconds.) Write the letter D, as in "dog," in the circular shape and darken the number-letter combination on your answer sheet. (Pause 10 seconds.)

Examine Sample 5. (Pause 2-3 seconds.) This sample is a record of the time each day that Mr. John Smith returned from this mail route during the week. We will assume that Mr. Smith left the office at the same time each morning to begin his route. (Pause 3 seconds.) If Mr. Smith's delivery time is improving as the week progresses, go to number 86 on your answer sheet and darken the letter E, as in "elephant." (Pause 10 seconds.) If, on the other hand, Mr. Smith seems to be taking more time to deliver his mail as the week progresses, go to number 89 on your answer sheet and darken the letter B, as in "boy." (Pause 7 seconds.)

If 40 is less than 40.5, but greater than 39, go to number 11 on your answer sheet and darken the letter D, as in "dog." (Pause 7 seconds.) Otherwise, go to number 15 on your answer sheet and darken the letter E, as in "elephant." (Pause 7 seconds.)

Examine Sample 6. (Pause 2-3 seconds.) On the line provided, write the number of letters that are needed to spell the word, "Wednesday." (Pause 10 seconds.) Darken the number-letter combination you have made on your answer sheet. (Pause 7 seconds.)

Examine Sample 7. (Pause 2-3 seconds.) Write the number 53 beside the letter A, as in "apple." (Pause 5 seconds.) If there are more than six letters shown in Sample 7, then darken the number-letter combination you have made on your answer sheet. (Pause 10 seconds.) If not, write the number 57 beside the letter C, as in "cat," and darken that number-letter combination on your answer sheet. (Pause 7 seconds.)

If New York, New York, is north of Miami, Florida, and Boston, Massachusetts, is east of San Francisco, California, go to number 38 on your answer sheet and darken the letter D, as in "dog." (Pause 10 seconds.) If any part of the previous statement is incorrect, go to number 36 on your answer sheet and darken the letter B, as in "boy." (Pause 7 seconds.)

Examine Sample 8. (Pause 2-3 seconds.) Write the number 42 beside the letter B, as in "boy." (Pause 5 seconds.) Write the number 52 beside the letter D, as in "dog." (Pause 5 seconds.) Darken the number-letter combinations you have just made on your answer sheet. (Pause 10 seconds.)

Examine Sample 9. (Pause 2-3 seconds.) Write the letter A, as in "apple," in the circle on the left side. (Pause 5 seconds.) Write the letter D, as in "dog," in the other circle. (Pause 5 seconds.) Now, write the number 17 in circle D, as in "dog," and the number 18 in circle A, as in "apple." (Pause 10 seconds.) On your answer sheet, darken both number-letter combinations shown in each of the circles. (Pause 10 seconds.)

Examine Sample 9 again. (Pause 2-3 seconds.) If circle A, as in "apple," and D, as in "dog," are the same size and interconnected, go to number 63 on your answer sheet and darken the letter E, as in "elephant." (Pause 7 seconds.) If the circles are not interconnected, go to number 23 on your answer sheet and darken the letter C, as in "cat." (Pause 7 seconds.)

Examine Sample 10. (Pause 2-3 seconds.) Write the letter A, as in "apple," on the line provided. (Pause 5 seconds.) Select the second highest number from the sequence shown and write it beside the letter you have just written. (Pause 7 seconds.) Darken the resulting number-letter combination on your answer sheet. (Pause 7 seconds.)

Examine Sample 10 again. (Pause 2-3 seconds.) Select the highest number from the sequence shown. Go to that number on your answer sheet. (Pause 5 seconds.) Darken the letter E, as in "elephant." (Pause 5 seconds.)

Examine Sample 11. (Pause 2-3 seconds.) Select the largest number shown, and completely circle it and the letter above it. (Pause 7 seconds.) Examine the last two digits of the number you have circled. Go to that number on your answer sheet. (Pause 5 seconds.) Darken the letter shown in your circle. (Pause 5 seconds.)

Examine Sample 11 again. (Pause 2-3 seconds.) If the number below D, as in "dog," is less than the number below C, as in "cat," go to number 54 on your answer sheet, and darken the letter A, as in "apple." (Pause 10 seconds.) If not, go to 54 on your answer sheet and darken the letter B, as in "boy." (Pause 7 seconds.)

If 5 is greater than 4, but less than 6, darken the letter D, as in "dog," at number 15 of your answer sheet. (Pause 7 seconds.) If not, darken the letter C, as in "cat," at number 55 on your answer sheet. (Pause 7 seconds.)

If 40 is greater than 25 plus 15, go to number 71 on your answer sheet and darken the letter E, as in "elephant." (Pause 7 seconds.) If not, go to number 71 on your answer sheet anyway and darken the letter B, as in "boy." (Pause 7 seconds.)

Examine Sample 10 again. (Pause 2-3 seconds.) If there are more than 5 numbers in the sample, go to number 33 on your answer sheet and darken the letter B, as in "boy." (Pause 7 seconds.) Otherwise, go to number 41 on your answer sheet and darken the letter A, as in "apple." (Pause 7 seconds.)

Examine Sample 1 again. (Pause 2-3 seconds.) If any of the 3 numbers shown is greater than 145, go to number 3 on your answer sheet, and darken the letter D, as in "dog." (Pause 7 seconds.) Otherwise, go to number 95 on your answer sheet and darken the letter E, as in "elephant." (Pause 5 seconds.)

-END OF TEST-

FOLLOWING DIRECTIONS/EXERCISE 3 SAMPLES

1. 147   122   130

2. 50____

3. 0_____A
    0_____C
    0_____E

4. 74____   72____   75____   77____   76____

5. 4:05 PM   4:15 PM   4:25 PM   4:35 PM   5:00 PM
    MONDAY   TUESDAY   WEDNESDAY   THURSDAY   FRIDAY

6. ____A

7. ____A   ____X   ____L   ____C   ____F   ____I

8. B____   D____

9.

10.   14   28   17   33   _____

11.   A   B   C   D
        .045   .054   .07   .45

ANSWER SHEET TO FOLLOWING DIRECTIONS/EXERCISE 3

1. (A) (B) (C) (D) (E)
2. (A) (B) (C) (D) (E)
3. (A) (B) (C) (D) (E)
4. (A) (B) (C) (D) (E)
5. (A) (B) (C) (D) (E)
6. (A) (B) (C) (D) (E)
7. (A) (B) (C) (D) (E)
8. (A) (B) (C) (D) (E)
9. (A) (B) (C) (D) (E)
10. (A) (B) (C) (D) (E)
11. (A) (B) (C) (D) (E)
12. (A) (B) (C) (D) (E)
13. (A) (B) (C) (D) (E)
14. (A) (B) (C) (D) (E)
15. (A) (B) (C) (D) (E)
16. (A) (B) (C) (D) (E)
17. (A) (B) (C) (D) (E)
18. (A) (B) (C) (D) (E)
19. (A) (B) (C) (D) (E)
20. (A) (B) (C) (D) (E)
21. (A) (B) (C) (D) (E)
22. (A) (B) (C) (D) (E)
23. (A) (B) (C) (D) (E)
24. (A) (B) (C) (D) (E)
25. (A) (B) (C) (D) (E)
26. (A) (B) (C) (D) (E)
27. (A) (B) (C) (D) (E)
28. (A) (B) (C) (D) (E)
29. (A) (B) (C) (D) (E)
30. (A) (B) (C) (D) (E)
31. (A) (B) (C) (D) (E)
32. (A) (B) (C) (D) (E)

33. (A) (B) (C) (D) (E)
34. (A) (B) (C) (D) (E)
35. (A) (B) (C) (D) (E)
36. (A) (B) (C) (D) (E)
37. (A) (B) (C) (D) (E)
38. (A) (B) (C) (D) (E)
39. (A) (B) (C) (D) (E)
40. (A) (B) (C) (D) (E)
41. (A) (B) (C) (D) (E)
42. (A) (B) (C) (D) (E)
43. (A) (B) (C) (D) (E)
44. (A) (B) (C) (D) (E)
45. (A) (B) (C) (D) (E)
46. (A) (B) (C) (D) (E)
47. (A) (B) (C) (D) (E)
48. (A) (B) (C) (D) (E)
49. (A) (B) (C) (D) (E)
50. (A) (B) (C) (D) (E)
51. (A) (B) (C) (D) (E)
52. (A) (B) (C) (D) (E)
53. (A) (B) (C) (D) (E)
54. (A) (B) (C) (D) (E)
55. (A) (B) (C) (D) (E)
56. (A) (B) (C) (D) (E)
57. (A) (B) (C) (D) (E)
58. (A) (B) (C) (D) (E)
59. (A) (B) (C) (D) (E)
60. (A) (B) (C) (D) (E)
61. (A) (B) (C) (D) (E)
62. (A) (B) (C) (D) (E)
63. (A) (B) (C) (D) (E)
64. (A) (B) (C) (D) (E)

65. (A) (B) (C) (D) (E)
66. (A) (B) (C) (D) (E)
67. (A) (B) (C) (D) (E)
68. (A) (B) (C) (D) (E)
69. (A) (B) (C) (D) (E)
70. (A) (B) (C) (D) (E)
71. (A) (B) (C) (D) (E)
72. (A) (B) (C) (D) (E)
73. (A) (B) (C) (D) (E)
74. (A) (B) (C) (D) (E)
75. (A) (B) (C) (D) (E)
76. (A) (B) (C) (D) (E)
77. (A) (B) (C) (D) (E)
78. (A) (B) (C) (D) (E)
79. (A) (B) (C) (D) (E)
80. (A) (B) (C) (D) (E)
81. (A) (B) (C) (D) (E)
82. (A) (B) (C) (D) (E)
83. (A) (B) (C) (D) (E)
84. (A) (B) (C) (D) (E)
85. (A) (B) (C) (D) (E)
86. (A) (B) (C) (D) (E)
87. (A) (B) (C) (D) (E)
88. (A) (B) (C) (D) (E)
89. (A) (B) (C) (D) (E)
90. (A) (B) (C) (D) (E)
91. (A) (B) (C) (D) (E)
92. (A) (B) (C) (D) (E)
93. (A) (B) (C) (D) (E)
94. (A) (B) (C) (D) (E)
95. (A) (B) (C) (D) (E)

[This page may be removed to mark answers.]

ANSWERS TO FOLLOWING DIRECTIONS/EXERCISE 3

1.	22 D	10.	11 D	19.	28 A
2.	50 E	11.	9 A	20.	33 E
3.	67 E	12.	57 C	21.	45 D
4.	68 C	13.	38 D	22.	54 B
5.	1 A	14.	42 B	23.	15 D
6.	75 B	15.	52 D	24.	71 B
7.	77 C	16.	18 A	25.	41 A
8.	72 D	17.	17 D	26.	3 D
9.	89 B	18.	23 C		

If you scored:
24 or more correct, you have an excellent score.
22 or 23 correct, you have a good score.
21 or fewer correct, you should practice more.

If you have missed any of the questions in this exercise, review the narrative and identify what you misinterpreted. Most often, applicants make errors in this section because they answer too quickly, and miss key phrases. Remember: Be sure to listen to the entire question.

NOTE: The rest of this study guide has been dedicated to full-length practice exams which incorporate each of the four sections studied earlier. You will need the assistance of someone to time you for each part of the exam as well as narrate the FOLLOWING DIRECTIONS portion of the test. To gain a comprehensive feel for the actual exam, work the entire practice exam (i.e., complete each of the four sections provided) in one session, allowing only a 3-5 minute break between exercises. Be certain not to continue working on an exercise when the allotted time is up. Going beyond the time allotted will only skew your test results. Make it a point to alleviate any potential distractions prior to beginning the exam. Disruptive kids, an inquisitive spouse, telephone calls, etc., can all have a detrimental impact on test preparation.

Try to simulate exam room conditions as best you can. That way, you can approach the real exam with a true sense of confidence and preparation—two factors critical to the achievement of a high test score.

Exam 1

**DO NOT OPEN THIS TEST BOOKLET UNTIL
YOU ARE TOLD TO START BY THE INDIVIDUAL
ASSISTING YOU IN THIS EXERCISE.**

[This page is intentionally blank.]

ADDRESS CROSS COMPARISON/EXAM 1   TIME: 6 MINUTES

1.	E Miami Blvd.	E Miami Blvd.
2.	121 Burroughs Way	12 Burroughs Way
3.	1489 Van Meter St.	1489 Van Metor St.
4.	2379 Holiday Ave.	2379 Holliday Ave.
5.	Atlanta, Georgia 26711	Atlanta, Georgia 26711
6.	17666 Bolivar Ln	17666 Bolevar Ln
7.	12-A Kingsley Blvd. SE	12-A Kinsley Blvd. SE
8.	4456 Lamplight Sq	4654 Lamplight Sq
9.	17171 Bonteview St.	17177 Bonteview St.
10.	1396 Moonlight Bay	1396 Moonlight Bay
11.	Las Vegas, Nevada 67088	Las Vegas, Nev. 67088
12.	Tucson, Ariz 82050	Tuscon, Ariz. 82050
13.	Hampton Blvd. SW	Hampton Blvd. SW
14.	11 Bonn St. S	11 Bonn St. N.
15.	418 9th Ave. NE	481 9th Ave. SW
16.	1000 Terrace St.	10000 Terrace St.
17.	7478 E. Wellington	7478 E. Wellington
18.	Plainsville, NE 69719	Planesville, NE 69719
19.	Faunterloy Pkwy NW	Faunterloy Pkwy NW
20.	212-B Seaview Place	212-B Seaview Point
21.	Little Rock, Ark. 58009	Little Rock, Ark. 58009
22.	158 Johnathon Ln.	158 Jonathon Ln.
23.	Route 4, Box 4342	Route 4, Box 4342

24.	9315 Labador Park SE	9351 Labador Park
25.	Crysanthanum Place SW	Crysanthinum Place SW
26.	Fullerton, CA 97097	Fullerton, CA 97097
27.	3407 Knotingham Dr.	3407 Knottingham Dr.
28.	323 N Warner Ave.	332 N Warner Ave.
29.	1816 Vermont Pl.	1618 Vermont Pl.
30.	Minneapolis, MN 49401	Minneapolis, Minn. 49401
31.	13-J Briginham Rd.	13-J Brigingham Rd.
32.	NW Constance Bay	NW Constance Bay
33.	3388 Joplin Center	8833 Joplin Central
34.	684 11th St. NE	684 13th St. NE
35.	210 Harmont Place	210 Hormont Place
36.	Tooele, Utah 82102	Tooele, Utah 81202
37.	1717 W Carver Dr.	1717 W Carver Dr.
38.	546 W Galveston Ln.	546 W Galveston Blvd.
39.	New York, NY 00723	Newark, NY 00723
40.	3941 Belmont Way SE	3941 Belmont Way SE
41.	87-D University Village	87-D Univarsity Village
42.	713 Monroe Dr.	713 Monroe Dr.
43.	2211 Northwestern Rd.	1122 Northwestern Rd.
44.	140-C Hawthrone Ct.	140-C Hawthorn Ct.
45.	720 NW Kellogg	720 NW Kellogg
46.	2419 S. Douglas	2419 S. Douglas
47.	Holyoke, Mass. 04211	Holyoke, Miss. 02411
48.	B-707 Pierce Circle	B-707 Pierce Circle

49.	13251 Harding Ave.	13251 Harding Ave.
50.	2531 Eisenhower Blvd.	2531 Eisenhower Blvd.
51.	110 Main St. NE	110 Main St. NE
52.	22619 Hayes Point	22619 Heyes Point
53.	435 Wilmoth Dr.	453 Wilmoth Dr.
54.	Bakersville, NC 23718	Bakersville, NC 23718
55.	338-E Lighthouse Pt.	338-E Lighthouse Pt.
56.	214 O'Neil Dr. NW	214 O'Neil Dr. SW
57.	4516 Mulberry Pkwy	4516 Mulberry Pkwy
58.	Greenbriar Circle	S. Greenbriar Circle
59.	7000 Marston Ct.	70000 Marston Ct.
60.	3501 Jensen Way	3501 Jantzen Way
61.	Murfreesboro, TN	Murfreesboro, TN 38914
62.	Paducah, Kentucky 35114	Paducah, Kentucky 35114
63.	10074 Jackson Square	10704 Jackson Square
64.	330 E 42nd Ave.	330 E 42nd Ave.
65.	1111 Bouldergrant	1117 Bouldergrant
66.	119 SW Symington Way	119 SW Symington Way
67.	3939 Concord Ave.	9393 Concord Ave.
68.	Dubuque, IA 56013	Dubuque, IA 56013
69.	41-F Blanchard Dr.	41-C Blanchard Dr.
70.	901 K Stables Ln	901 K. Stabbles Ln
71.	N. Shoshonee Pl.	N. Shoshownee Pl.
72.	222 Welch Ave. SW	222 Welch Ave. SW
73.	1515 N 1st Ave.	1515 1st Ave. S

74.	103-C King Terrace	103-C King Terrace
75.	4466 Baltic Ave.	4646 Baltic Ave.
76.	Augusta, Maine 00111	Augusta, Maine 01011
77.	New Albany St. SW	Old Albany St. SW
78.	A-115 25th Ave. S.	A-115 22nd Ave. S.
79.	17677 Belfair Square	17677 Belfair Square
80.	3731 Washington Blvd.	3731 Washinton Blvd.
81.	2029 Isaquah Ln.	2029 Isaquah Ln.
82.	Kansas City, Kansas 47320	Kansas City, MO 47320
83.	NW Macnally Dr. 1-B	NW Mcnally Dr. 1-B
84.	3078 S. George St.	30078 Saint George St.
85.	40473 Paulson Dr. S	40473 Paulson Dr. S
86.	Jacksonville, FL 27119	Jacksonville, Fla. 27119
87.	2000 Ebeneezor Place	2000 Ebaneezor Place
88.	1212 Ballen Lake Way	1212 Ballon Lake Way
89.	16-B Lester Blvd.	61-B Lester Blvd.
90.	4392 Crestwood Park	4392 Crestwood Park
91.	78990 Norweigan Trail	78990 Norweigen Trail
92.	327 S. Hazel Ct.	327 N. Hazel Ct.
93.	Cincinnati, Ohio 48921	Cinncinati, Ohio 48921
94.	RR 4, Box 414-S	RR 4, Box 41-4S
95.	Provo, UT	Provo, UT

ANSWER SHEET TO ADDRESS CROSS COMPARISON/EXAM 1

1. Ⓐ Ⓓ
2. Ⓐ Ⓓ
3. Ⓐ Ⓓ
4. Ⓐ Ⓓ
5. Ⓐ Ⓓ
6. Ⓐ Ⓓ
7. Ⓐ Ⓓ
8. Ⓐ Ⓓ
9. Ⓐ Ⓓ
10. Ⓐ Ⓓ
11. Ⓐ Ⓓ
12. Ⓐ Ⓓ
13. Ⓐ Ⓓ
14. Ⓐ Ⓓ
15. Ⓐ Ⓓ
16. Ⓐ Ⓓ
17. Ⓐ Ⓓ
18. Ⓐ Ⓓ
19. Ⓐ Ⓓ
20. Ⓐ Ⓓ
21. Ⓐ Ⓓ
22. Ⓐ Ⓓ
23. Ⓐ Ⓓ
24. Ⓐ Ⓓ
25. Ⓐ Ⓓ
26. Ⓐ Ⓓ
27. Ⓐ Ⓓ
28. Ⓐ Ⓓ
29. Ⓐ Ⓓ
30. Ⓐ Ⓓ
31. Ⓐ Ⓓ
32. Ⓐ Ⓓ

33. Ⓐ Ⓓ
34. Ⓐ Ⓓ
35. Ⓐ Ⓓ
36. Ⓐ Ⓓ
37. Ⓐ Ⓓ
38. Ⓐ Ⓓ
39. Ⓐ Ⓓ
40. Ⓐ Ⓓ
41. Ⓐ Ⓓ
42. Ⓐ Ⓓ
43. Ⓐ Ⓓ
44. Ⓐ Ⓓ
45. Ⓐ Ⓓ
46. Ⓐ Ⓓ
47. Ⓐ Ⓓ
48. Ⓐ Ⓓ
49. Ⓐ Ⓓ
50. Ⓐ Ⓓ
51. Ⓐ Ⓓ
52. Ⓐ Ⓓ
53. Ⓐ Ⓓ
54. Ⓐ Ⓓ
55. Ⓐ Ⓓ
56. Ⓐ Ⓓ
57. Ⓐ Ⓓ
58. Ⓐ Ⓓ
59. Ⓐ Ⓓ
60. Ⓐ Ⓓ
61. Ⓐ Ⓓ
62. Ⓐ Ⓓ
63. Ⓐ Ⓓ
64. Ⓐ Ⓓ

65. Ⓐ Ⓓ
66. Ⓐ Ⓓ
67. Ⓐ Ⓓ
68. Ⓐ Ⓓ
69. Ⓐ Ⓓ
70. Ⓐ Ⓓ
71. Ⓐ Ⓓ
72. Ⓐ Ⓓ
73. Ⓐ Ⓓ
74. Ⓐ Ⓓ
75. Ⓐ Ⓓ
76. Ⓐ Ⓓ
77. Ⓐ Ⓓ
78. Ⓐ Ⓓ
79. Ⓐ Ⓓ
80. Ⓐ Ⓓ
81. Ⓐ Ⓓ
82. Ⓐ Ⓓ
83. Ⓐ Ⓓ
84. Ⓐ Ⓓ
85. Ⓐ Ⓓ
86. Ⓐ Ⓓ
87. Ⓐ Ⓓ
88. Ⓐ Ⓓ
89. Ⓐ Ⓓ
90. Ⓐ Ⓓ
91. Ⓐ Ⓓ
92. Ⓐ Ⓓ
93. Ⓐ Ⓓ
94. Ⓐ Ⓓ
95. Ⓐ Ⓓ

(This page may be removed to mark answers.)

[This page is intentionally blank.]

MEMORIZATION/EXAM 1

A	B	C	D	E
6000-6099 Sullivan Regency Dr. 7000-7099 Payton Roosevelt Pl. 0500-0599 Clare	7000-7099 Sullivan Cameron Pt. 7300-7399 Payton Cantershire 0800-0899 Clare	7300-7399 Sullivan Elizabeth 7500-7599 Payton Sunrise Dr. 1300-1399 Clare	7700-7799 Sullivan Stenman Ave. 7700-7799 Payton Converse Pl. 1500-1599 Clare	8000-8099 Sullivan Varsity Ln. 7900-7999 Payton Daphne St. 2400-2499 Clare

NOTE: Follow the same step-by-step format established for the memorization exercise studied earlier. (See page 41.)

PRACTICE MEMORIZATION/EXAM 1

A	B	C	D	E
6000-6099 Sullivan	7000-7099 Sullivan	7300-7399 Sullivan	7700-7799 Sullivan	8000-8099 Sullivan
Regency Dr.	Cameron Pt.	Elizabeth	Stenman Ave.	Varsity Ln.
7000-7099 Payton	7300-7399 Payton	7500-7599 Payton	7700-7799 Payton	7900-7999 Payton
Roosevelt Pl.	Cantershire	Sunrise Dr.	Converse Pl.	Daphne St.
0500-0599 Clare	0800-0899 Clare	1300-1399 Clare	1500-1599 Clare	2400-2499 Clare

1. 7300-7399 Payton
2. Cameron Pt.
3. Sunrise Dr.
4. 1500-1599 Clare
5. 8000-8099 Sullivan
6. 7000-7099 Payton
7. Regency Dr.
8. 1300-1399 Clare
9. Stenman Ave.
10. Daphne St.
11. 7900-7999 Payton
12. 7300-7399 Sullivan
13. 2400-2499 Clare
14. Cantershire
15. Roosevelt Pl.
16. 0500-0599 Clare
17. Elizabeth
18. Converse Pl.
19. Varsity Ln.
20. 7700-7799 Sullivan
21. 7500-7599 Payton
22. 7000-7099 Sullivan
23. 0800-0899 Clare
24. 6000-6099 Sullivan
25. 7700-7799 Payton
26. Daphne St.
27. 1300-1399 Clare
28. 7700-7799 Sullivan
29. Elizabeth
30. Cantershire

31. 7900-7999 Payton
32. 1500-1599 Clare
33. Roosevelt Pl.
34. 2400-2499 Clare
35. 7000-7099 Sullivan
36. 6000-6099 Sullivan
37. 7000-7099 Payton
38. Stenman Ave.
39. 8000-8099 Sullivan
40. 7300-7399 Payton
41. Cameron Pt.
42. Regency Dr.
43. Sunrise Dr.
44. 0500-0599 Clare
45. 7500-7599 Payton
46. Converse Pl.
47. 7000-7099 Payton
48. 7300-7399 Sullivan
49. 7700-7799 Payton
50. Varsity Ln.
51. 0800-0899 Clare
52. Stenman Ave.
53. 7000-7099 Payton
54. 2400-2499 Clare
55. Elizabeth
56. 7500-7599 Payton
57. Varsity Ln.
58. Cantershire
59. Daphne St.
60. 8000-8099 Sullivan

61. 7300-7399 Payton
62. Roosevelt Pl.
63. 7700-7799 Sullivan
64. 7700-7799 Payton
65. Regency Dr.
66. Sunrise Dr.
67. Cameron Pt.
68. 1300-1399 Clare
69. 7300-7399 Sullivan
70. 0800-0899 Clare
71. 0500-0599 Clare
72. 7900-7999 Payton
73. Converse Pl.
74. 7700-7799 Payton
75. 7000-7099 Sullivan
76. 7300-7399 Payton
77. 1300-1399 Clare
78. 7700-7799 Payton
79. 2400-2499 Clare
80. Stenman Ave.
81. Cantershire
82. 0500-0599 Clare
83. 7300-7399 Sullivan
84. Elizabeth
85. Cameron Pt.
86. 0800-0899 Clare
87. Converse Pl.
88. 1300-1399 Clare

PRACTICE ANSWER SHEET TO MEMORIZATION/EXAM 1

1. Ⓐ Ⓑ Ⓒ Ⓓ Ⓔ   31. Ⓐ Ⓑ Ⓒ Ⓓ Ⓔ   61. Ⓐ Ⓑ Ⓒ Ⓓ Ⓔ
2. Ⓐ Ⓑ Ⓒ Ⓓ Ⓔ   32. Ⓐ Ⓑ Ⓒ Ⓓ Ⓔ   62. Ⓐ Ⓑ Ⓒ Ⓓ Ⓔ
3. Ⓐ Ⓑ Ⓒ Ⓓ Ⓔ   33. Ⓐ Ⓑ Ⓒ Ⓓ Ⓔ   63. Ⓐ Ⓑ Ⓒ Ⓓ Ⓔ
4. Ⓐ Ⓑ Ⓒ Ⓓ Ⓔ   34. Ⓐ Ⓑ Ⓒ Ⓓ Ⓔ   64. Ⓐ Ⓑ Ⓒ Ⓓ Ⓔ
5. Ⓐ Ⓑ Ⓒ Ⓓ Ⓔ   35. Ⓐ Ⓑ Ⓒ Ⓓ Ⓔ   65. Ⓐ Ⓑ Ⓒ Ⓓ Ⓔ
6. Ⓐ Ⓑ Ⓒ Ⓓ Ⓔ   36. Ⓐ Ⓑ Ⓒ Ⓓ Ⓔ   66. Ⓐ Ⓑ Ⓒ Ⓓ Ⓔ
7. Ⓐ Ⓑ Ⓒ Ⓓ Ⓔ   37. Ⓐ Ⓑ Ⓒ Ⓓ Ⓔ   67. Ⓐ Ⓑ Ⓒ Ⓓ Ⓔ
8. Ⓐ Ⓑ Ⓒ Ⓓ Ⓔ   38. Ⓐ Ⓑ Ⓒ Ⓓ Ⓔ   68. Ⓐ Ⓑ Ⓒ Ⓓ Ⓔ
9. Ⓐ Ⓑ Ⓒ Ⓓ Ⓔ   39. Ⓐ Ⓑ Ⓒ Ⓓ Ⓔ   69. Ⓐ Ⓑ Ⓒ Ⓓ Ⓔ
10. Ⓐ Ⓑ Ⓒ Ⓓ Ⓔ   40. Ⓐ Ⓑ Ⓒ Ⓓ Ⓔ   70. Ⓐ Ⓑ Ⓒ Ⓓ Ⓔ
11. Ⓐ Ⓑ Ⓒ Ⓓ Ⓔ   41. Ⓐ Ⓑ Ⓒ Ⓓ Ⓔ   71. Ⓐ Ⓑ Ⓒ Ⓓ Ⓔ
12. Ⓐ Ⓑ Ⓒ Ⓓ Ⓔ   42. Ⓐ Ⓑ Ⓒ Ⓓ Ⓔ   72. Ⓐ Ⓑ Ⓒ Ⓓ Ⓔ
13. Ⓐ Ⓑ Ⓒ Ⓓ Ⓔ   43. Ⓐ Ⓑ Ⓒ Ⓓ Ⓔ   73. Ⓐ Ⓑ Ⓒ Ⓓ Ⓔ
14. Ⓐ Ⓑ Ⓒ Ⓓ Ⓔ   44. Ⓐ Ⓑ Ⓒ Ⓓ Ⓔ   74. Ⓐ Ⓑ Ⓒ Ⓓ Ⓔ
15. Ⓐ Ⓑ Ⓒ Ⓓ Ⓔ   45. Ⓐ Ⓑ Ⓒ Ⓓ Ⓔ   75. Ⓐ Ⓑ Ⓒ Ⓓ Ⓔ
16. Ⓐ Ⓑ Ⓒ Ⓓ Ⓔ   46. Ⓐ Ⓑ Ⓒ Ⓓ Ⓔ   76. Ⓐ Ⓑ Ⓒ Ⓓ Ⓔ
17. Ⓐ Ⓑ Ⓒ Ⓓ Ⓔ   47. Ⓐ Ⓑ Ⓒ Ⓓ Ⓔ   77. Ⓐ Ⓑ Ⓒ Ⓓ Ⓔ
18. Ⓐ Ⓑ Ⓒ Ⓓ Ⓔ   48. Ⓐ Ⓑ Ⓒ Ⓓ Ⓔ   78. Ⓐ Ⓑ Ⓒ Ⓓ Ⓔ
19. Ⓐ Ⓑ Ⓒ Ⓓ Ⓔ   49. Ⓐ Ⓑ Ⓒ Ⓓ Ⓔ   79. Ⓐ Ⓑ Ⓒ Ⓓ Ⓔ
20. Ⓐ Ⓑ Ⓒ Ⓓ Ⓔ   50. Ⓐ Ⓑ Ⓒ Ⓓ Ⓔ   80. Ⓐ Ⓑ Ⓒ Ⓓ Ⓔ
21. Ⓐ Ⓑ Ⓒ Ⓓ Ⓔ   51. Ⓐ Ⓑ Ⓒ Ⓓ Ⓔ   81. Ⓐ Ⓑ Ⓒ Ⓓ Ⓔ
22. Ⓐ Ⓑ Ⓒ Ⓓ Ⓔ   52. Ⓐ Ⓑ Ⓒ Ⓓ Ⓔ   82. Ⓐ Ⓑ Ⓒ Ⓓ Ⓔ
23. Ⓐ Ⓑ Ⓒ Ⓓ Ⓔ   53. Ⓐ Ⓑ Ⓒ Ⓓ Ⓔ   83. Ⓐ Ⓑ Ⓒ Ⓓ Ⓔ
24. Ⓐ Ⓑ Ⓒ Ⓓ Ⓔ   54. Ⓐ Ⓑ Ⓒ Ⓓ Ⓔ   84. Ⓐ Ⓑ Ⓒ Ⓓ Ⓔ
25. Ⓐ Ⓑ Ⓒ Ⓓ Ⓔ   55. Ⓐ Ⓑ Ⓒ Ⓓ Ⓔ   85. Ⓐ Ⓑ Ⓒ Ⓓ Ⓔ
26. Ⓐ Ⓑ Ⓒ Ⓓ Ⓔ   56. Ⓐ Ⓑ Ⓒ Ⓓ Ⓔ   86. Ⓐ Ⓑ Ⓒ Ⓓ Ⓔ
27. Ⓐ Ⓑ Ⓒ Ⓓ Ⓔ   57. Ⓐ Ⓑ Ⓒ Ⓓ Ⓔ   87. Ⓐ Ⓑ Ⓒ Ⓓ Ⓔ
28. Ⓐ Ⓑ Ⓒ Ⓓ Ⓔ   58. Ⓐ Ⓑ Ⓒ Ⓓ Ⓔ   88. Ⓐ Ⓑ Ⓒ Ⓓ Ⓔ
29. Ⓐ Ⓑ Ⓒ Ⓓ Ⓔ   59. Ⓐ Ⓑ Ⓒ Ⓓ Ⓔ
30. Ⓐ Ⓑ Ⓒ Ⓓ Ⓔ   60. Ⓐ Ⓑ Ⓒ Ⓓ Ⓔ

MEMORIZATION/EXAM 1

STEP 5 TIME: 5 MINUTES

1. Regency Dr.
2. Sunrise Dr.
3. 7300-7399 Payton
4. 7700-7799 Sullivan
5. Varsity Ln.
6. 1300-1399 Clare
7. 7000-7099 Sullivan
8. 0500-0599 Clare
9. Converse Pl.
10. Daphne St.
11. Elizabeth
12. 2400-2499 Clare
13. Cantershire
14. 6000-6099 Sullivan
15. Stenman Ave.
16. 7700-7799 Payton
17. 8000-8099 Sullivan
18. 7500-7599 Payton
19. 0800-0899 Clare
20. Cameron Pt.
21. Roosevelt Pl.
22. 1500-1599 Clare
23. 7900-7999 Payton
24. 7300-7399 Sullivan
25. 7000-7099 Payton
26. Converse Pl.
27. Stenman Ave.
28. 0500-0599 Clare
29. Regency Dr.
30. Elizabeth

31. Roosevelt Pl.
32. 6000-6099 Sullivan
33. 7300-7399 Payton
34. 7700-7799 Sullivan
35. Sunrise Dr.
36. Cantershire
37. 7900-7999 Payton
38. 1500-1599 Clare
39. 7300-7399 Sullivan
40. Cameron Pt.
41. Daphne St.
42. 1300-1399 Clare
43. 7000-7099 Payton
44. Varsity Ln.
45. 7000-7099 Sullivan
46. 2400-2499 Clare
47. 8000-8099 Sullivan
48. 7700-7799 Payton
49. 0800-0899 Clare
50. 7500-7599 Payton
51. Cantershire
52. 2400-2499 Clare
53. 0800-0899 Clare
54. 7700-7799 Payton
55. Sunrise Dr.
56. 7700-7799 Sullivan
57. Stenman Ave.
58. 8000-8099 Sullivan
59. Varsity Ln.
60. 7500-7599 Payton

61. 7000-7099 Sullivan
62. 7000-7099 Payton
63. Daphne St.
64. Roosevelt Pl.
65. Regency Dr.
66. Elizabeth
67. 7900-7999 Payton
68. 1300-1399 Clare
69. 7300-7399 Sullivan
70. 7300-7399 Payton
71. 6000-6099 Sullivan
72. 1500-1599 Clare
73. 0500-0599 Clare
74. Converse Pl.
75. Cameron Pt.
76. 7000-7099 Sullivan
77. 7700-7799 Payton
78. Varsity Ln.
79. 7000-7099 Payton
80. Cantershire
81. 7500-7599 Payton
82. 1300-1399 Clare
83. 0800-0899 Clare
84. 2400-2499 Clare
85. Converse Pl.
86. Regency Dr.
87. 7300-7399 Sullivan
88. 8000-8099 Sullivan

ANSWER SHEET TO MEMORIZATION/EXAM 1

1. Ⓐ Ⓑ Ⓒ Ⓓ Ⓔ   31. Ⓐ Ⓑ Ⓒ Ⓓ Ⓔ   61. Ⓐ Ⓑ Ⓒ Ⓓ Ⓔ
2. Ⓐ Ⓑ Ⓒ Ⓓ Ⓔ   32. Ⓐ Ⓑ Ⓒ Ⓓ Ⓔ   62. Ⓐ Ⓑ Ⓒ Ⓓ Ⓔ
3. Ⓐ Ⓑ Ⓒ Ⓓ Ⓔ   33. Ⓐ Ⓑ Ⓒ Ⓓ Ⓔ   63. Ⓐ Ⓑ Ⓒ Ⓓ Ⓔ
4. Ⓐ Ⓑ Ⓒ Ⓓ Ⓔ   34. Ⓐ Ⓑ Ⓒ Ⓓ Ⓔ   64. Ⓐ Ⓑ Ⓒ Ⓓ Ⓔ
5. Ⓐ Ⓑ Ⓒ Ⓓ Ⓔ   35. Ⓐ Ⓑ Ⓒ Ⓓ Ⓔ   65. Ⓐ Ⓑ Ⓒ Ⓓ Ⓔ
6. Ⓐ Ⓑ Ⓒ Ⓓ Ⓔ   36. Ⓐ Ⓑ Ⓒ Ⓓ Ⓔ   66. Ⓐ Ⓑ Ⓒ Ⓓ Ⓔ
7. Ⓐ Ⓑ Ⓒ Ⓓ Ⓔ   37. Ⓐ Ⓑ Ⓒ Ⓓ Ⓔ   67. Ⓐ Ⓑ Ⓒ Ⓓ Ⓔ
8. Ⓐ Ⓑ Ⓒ Ⓓ Ⓔ   38. Ⓐ Ⓑ Ⓒ Ⓓ Ⓔ   68. Ⓐ Ⓑ Ⓒ Ⓓ Ⓔ
9. Ⓐ Ⓑ Ⓒ Ⓓ Ⓔ   39. Ⓐ Ⓑ Ⓒ Ⓓ Ⓔ   69. Ⓐ Ⓑ Ⓒ Ⓓ Ⓔ
10. Ⓐ Ⓑ Ⓒ Ⓓ Ⓔ   40. Ⓐ Ⓑ Ⓒ Ⓓ Ⓔ   70. Ⓐ Ⓑ Ⓒ Ⓓ Ⓔ
11. Ⓐ Ⓑ Ⓒ Ⓓ Ⓔ   41. Ⓐ Ⓑ Ⓒ Ⓓ Ⓔ   71. Ⓐ Ⓑ Ⓒ Ⓓ Ⓔ
12. Ⓐ Ⓑ Ⓒ Ⓓ Ⓔ   42. Ⓐ Ⓑ Ⓒ Ⓓ Ⓔ   72. Ⓐ Ⓑ Ⓒ Ⓓ Ⓔ
13. Ⓐ Ⓑ Ⓒ Ⓓ Ⓔ   43. Ⓐ Ⓑ Ⓒ Ⓓ Ⓔ   73. Ⓐ Ⓑ Ⓒ Ⓓ Ⓔ
14. Ⓐ Ⓑ Ⓒ Ⓓ Ⓔ   44. Ⓐ Ⓑ Ⓒ Ⓓ Ⓔ   74. Ⓐ Ⓑ Ⓒ Ⓓ Ⓔ
15. Ⓐ Ⓑ Ⓒ Ⓓ Ⓔ   45. Ⓐ Ⓑ Ⓒ Ⓓ Ⓔ   75. Ⓐ Ⓑ Ⓒ Ⓓ Ⓔ
16. Ⓐ Ⓑ Ⓒ Ⓓ Ⓔ   46. Ⓐ Ⓑ Ⓒ Ⓓ Ⓔ   76. Ⓐ Ⓑ Ⓒ Ⓓ Ⓔ
17. Ⓐ Ⓑ Ⓒ Ⓓ Ⓔ   47. Ⓐ Ⓑ Ⓒ Ⓓ Ⓔ   77. Ⓐ Ⓑ Ⓒ Ⓓ Ⓔ
18. Ⓐ Ⓑ Ⓒ Ⓓ Ⓔ   48. Ⓐ Ⓑ Ⓒ Ⓓ Ⓔ   78. Ⓐ Ⓑ Ⓒ Ⓓ Ⓔ
19. Ⓐ Ⓑ Ⓒ Ⓓ Ⓔ   49. Ⓐ Ⓑ Ⓒ Ⓓ Ⓔ   79. Ⓐ Ⓑ Ⓒ Ⓓ Ⓔ
20. Ⓐ Ⓑ Ⓒ Ⓓ Ⓔ   50. Ⓐ Ⓑ Ⓒ Ⓓ Ⓔ   80. Ⓐ Ⓑ Ⓒ Ⓓ Ⓔ
21. Ⓐ Ⓑ Ⓒ Ⓓ Ⓔ   51. Ⓐ Ⓑ Ⓒ Ⓓ Ⓔ   81. Ⓐ Ⓑ Ⓒ Ⓓ Ⓔ
22. Ⓐ Ⓑ Ⓒ Ⓓ Ⓔ   52. Ⓐ Ⓑ Ⓒ Ⓓ Ⓔ   82. Ⓐ Ⓑ Ⓒ Ⓓ Ⓔ
23. Ⓐ Ⓑ Ⓒ Ⓓ Ⓔ   53. Ⓐ Ⓑ Ⓒ Ⓓ Ⓔ   83. Ⓐ Ⓑ Ⓒ Ⓓ Ⓔ
24. Ⓐ Ⓑ Ⓒ Ⓓ Ⓔ   54. Ⓐ Ⓑ Ⓒ Ⓓ Ⓔ   84. Ⓐ Ⓑ Ⓒ Ⓓ Ⓔ
25. Ⓐ Ⓑ Ⓒ Ⓓ Ⓔ   55. Ⓐ Ⓑ Ⓒ Ⓓ Ⓔ   85. Ⓐ Ⓑ Ⓒ Ⓓ Ⓔ
26. Ⓐ Ⓑ Ⓒ Ⓓ Ⓔ   56. Ⓐ Ⓑ Ⓒ Ⓓ Ⓔ   86. Ⓐ Ⓑ Ⓒ Ⓓ Ⓔ
27. Ⓐ Ⓑ Ⓒ Ⓓ Ⓔ   57. Ⓐ Ⓑ Ⓒ Ⓓ Ⓔ   87. Ⓐ Ⓑ Ⓒ Ⓓ Ⓔ
28. Ⓐ Ⓑ Ⓒ Ⓓ Ⓔ   58. Ⓐ Ⓑ Ⓒ Ⓓ Ⓔ   88. Ⓐ Ⓑ Ⓒ Ⓓ Ⓔ
29. Ⓐ Ⓑ Ⓒ Ⓓ Ⓔ   59. Ⓐ Ⓑ Ⓒ Ⓓ Ⓔ
30. Ⓐ Ⓑ Ⓒ Ⓓ Ⓔ   60. Ⓐ Ⓑ Ⓒ Ⓓ Ⓔ

[This page is intentionally blank.]

NUMBER SERIES/EXAM 1   TIME: 20 MINUTES

1.   14   5   17   4   20   3   23   ___   ___
   A.   26, 12
   B.   1, 24
   C.   1, 25
   D.   2, 25
   E.   2, 26

2.   9   9   10   15   11   21   ___   ___
   A.   11, 27
   B.   12, 27
   C.   27, 11
   D.   27, 12
   E.   12, 12

3.   3   4   7   9   11   14   15   ___   ___
   A.   19, 19
   B.   13, 19
   C.   11, 19
   D.   12, 18
   E.   18, 18

4.   28   14   21   18   14   22   ___   ___
   A.   20, 15
   B.   16, 20
   C.   7, 26
   D.   21, 23
   E.   26, 7

5.   6   1   12   6   18   36   ___   ___
   A.   24, 261
   B.   24, 216
   C.   42, 216
   D.   42, 48
   E.   48, 58

6.   21   16   17   18   20   19   18   19   20   ___   ___
   A.   21, 18
   B.   20, 17
   C.   19, 18
   D.   21, 17
   E.   18, 20

7.   49   40   36   39   31   22   42   ___   ___
   A.   45, 13
   B.   45, 12
   C.   46, 12
   D.   12, 46
   E.   49, 39

8. 32   39   5   13   46   53   21   ___   ___

    A. 29, 60
    B. 60, 29
    C. 39, 60
    D. 60, 39
    E. 39, 39

9. 3   9   8   3   8   7   3   7   ___   ___

    A. 3, 6
    B. 6, 6
    C. 7, 2
    D. 5, 6
    E. 6, 3

10. 0   0   12   10   24   36   20   48   ___   ___

    A. 56, 26
    B. 60, 30
    C. 56, 30
    D. 30, 60
    E. 62, 26

11. 16   17   19   20   23   24   ___   ___

    A. 29, 30
    B. 29, 28
    C. 28, 29
    D. 27, 28
    E. 28, 27

12. 16   27   27   18   29   29   20   ___   ___

    A. 30, 30
    B. 31, 22
    C. 31, 31
    D. 22, 31
    E. 32, 30

13. 4   6   9   11   14   16   19   ___   ___

    A. 21, 25
    B. 25, 24
    C. 24, 24
    D. 23, 24
    E. 21, 24

14. 81   8   18   28   72   38   48   58   63   68   78   ___   ___

    A. 54, 88
    B. 88, 54
    C. 88, 69
    D. 54, 69
    E. 72, 88

15.   9   3   3   9   4   4   4   9   5   5   ___   ___

- A. 5, 9
- B. 5, 5
- C. 9, 5
- D. 9, 6
- E. 6, 9

16.   2   2   0   9   9   10   16   16   ___   ___

- A. 18, 20
- B. 20, 18
- C. 23, 23
- D. 20, 23
- E. 21, 27

17.   1   0   5   3   0   5   9   0   5   ___   ___

- A. 27, 0
- B. 23, 0
- C. 18, 0
- D. 36, 0
- E. 22, 0

18.   18   16   9   8   14   12   7   ___   ___

- A. 6, 11
- B. 10, 9
- C. 6, 10
- D. 10, 11
- E. 11, 11

19.   0   5   7   9   1   7   9   11   2   9   11   ___   ___

- A. 3, 12
- B. 3, 13
- C. 3, 10
- D. 13, 4
- E. 13, 3

20.   9   13   12   11   7   12   11   10   5   11   10   ___   ___

- A. 9, 4
- B. 9, 3
- C. 9, 9
- D. 8, 3
- E. 8, 4

21.   0   2   4   3   2   4   6   6   2   4   6   8   ___   ___

- A. 9, 2
- B. 8, 2
- C. 8, 3
- D. 2, 9
- E. 6, 9

22. 2 0 4 4 6 8 8 12 ___ ___

    A. 10, 16
    B. 10, 14
    C. 16, 14
    D. 14, 16
    E. 10, 12

23. 0 1 2 4 1 8 16 32 2 64 128 ___ ___

    A. 252, 3
    B. 256, 3
    C. 250, 4
    D. 4, 256
    E. 3, 252

24. 71 47 63 55 55 63 47 ___ ___

    A. 39, 31
    B. 31, 39
    C. 71, 39
    D. 42, 39
    E. 39, 71

ANSWER SHEET TO NUMBER SERIES/EXAM 1

1. (A) (B) (C) (D) (E)   9. (A) (B) (C) (D) (E)   17. (A) (B) (C) (D) (E)

2. (A) (B) (C) (D) (E)   10. (A) (B) (C) (D) (E)   18. (A) (B) (C) (D) (E)

3. (A) (B) (C) (D) (E)   11. (A) (B) (C) (D) (E)   19. (A) (B) (C) (D) (E)

4. (A) (B) (C) (D) (E)   12. (A) (B) (C) (D) (E)   20. (A) (B) (C) (D) (E)

5. (A) (B) (C) (D) (E)   13. (A) (B) (C) (D) (E)   21. (A) (B) (C) (D) (E)

6. (A) (B) (C) (D) (E)   14. (A) (B) (C) (D) (E)   22. (A) (B) (C) (D) (E)

7. (A) (B) (C) (D) (E)   15. (A) (B) (C) (D) (E)   23. (A) (B) (C) (D) (E)

8. (A) (B) (C) (D) (E)   16. (A) (B) (C) (D) (E)   24. (A) (B) (C) (D) (E)

[This page may be removed to mark answers.]

[This page is intentionally blank.]

FOLLOWING DIRECTIONS/EXAM 1

Note To Person Assisting In this Exam:

Remove from this test guide the pages of this exam that comprise the directions to be read out loud. The test applicant should be left with only the sample sheet and answer sheet. Read the following directions out loud at the suggested rate of 75-80 words per minute, pausing only where indicated in parentheses. Speak as clearly as possible: Once a statement has been read, it cannot be repeated.

Examine Sample 1. (Pause 2-3 seconds.) Write the letter E, as in "elephant," beside the fourth highest number of the number series shown. Darken that number-letter combination on your answer sheet. (Pause 5 seconds.)

Examine Sample 1 again. (Pause 2-3 seconds.) If the third number is 10 less than the fourth number and 20 more than the first number, write the letter B, as in "boy," beside the first number shown in the sample. (Pause 2 seconds.) Now darken the number-letter combination you have selected on your answer sheet. (Pause 5 seconds.)

Examine Sample 2. (Pause 2-3 seconds.) Draw a line under the smallest odd number shown if it is less than the sum of the first two numbers in the series. (Pause 5 seconds.) Otherwise, draw a line under the largest even number shown in the sample. (Pause 2 seconds.) Now, go to the number underlined on your answer sheet and darken the letter A, as in "apple." (Pause 5 seconds.)

Examine Sample 2 again. (Pause 2-3 seconds.) If the numbers 9 and 10 are the largest two even numbers shown in the sample, write the letter D, as in "dog," beside the first number shown in the sample. (Pause 2 seconds.) Otherwise, write the letter D, as in "dog," beside the second number shown in the sample. (Pause 2 seconds.) Now, darken the number-letter combination you have selected on your answer sheet. (Pause 5 seconds.)

Examine Sample 2 one more time. (Pause 2-3 seconds.) If the third number in the sample is less than the sum of the first two numbers, write the letter E, as in "elephant," beside the fifth number. (Pause 2 seconds.) However, if the fourth number is equal to the sum of the first two numbers in the sample, write the letter E, as in "elephant," beside the last number in the sample. (Pause 2 seconds.) Otherwise, write the letter B, as in "boy," beside the first number in the sample. (Pause 2 seconds.) Darken the number-letter combination you chose on your answer sheet. (Pause 5 seconds.)

Examine Sample 3. (Pause 2-3 seconds.) Write the letters D, as in "dog," and C, as in "cat," in the two smallest circles, respectively. If the number that you wrote the letter C, as in "cat," is less than the number you wrote the letter D, as in "dog," then write the letter B, as in "boy," beside the number in the last circle in the sample. (Pause 2 seconds.) Otherwise, go to the first circle shown in the sample and write the letter C, as in "cat." (Pause 2 seconds.) Now darken the number-letter combination you have selected on your answer sheet. (Pause 5 seconds.)

Examine Sample 3 again. (Pause 2-3 seconds.) Write the letter E, as in "elephant," in the first and third circle from the left. (Pause 5 seconds.) Between the two circles just mentioned, select the circle with the highest number and mark that number-letter combination on your answer sheet. (Pause 5 seconds.)

Examine Sample 4. (Pause 2-3 seconds.) Write the letter C, as in "cat," in the smaller circle shown if the number in the rectangle is higher than the number in the larger circle. (Pause 2 seconds.) Otherwise, write the letter A, as in "apple," beside the number in the triangle. (Pause 2 seconds.) Darken the number-letter combination you selected on your answer sheet. (Pause 5 seconds.)

Examine Sample 4 again. (Pause 2-3 seconds.) If any of the numbers within the geometric shapes are greater than 43 or less than 23, go to number 13 on your answer sheet and darken the letter B, as in "boy." (Pause 5 seconds.) Otherwise, go to number 12 on your answer sheet and darken the letter D, as in "dog." (Pause 5 seconds.)

Examine Sample 4 one more time. (Pause 2-3 seconds.) Write the letters E, as in "elephant," D, as in "dog," and B, as in "boy," in the larger circle, triangle, and square respectively. (Pause 7 seconds.) Now, darken each of those number-letter combinations on your answer sheet. (Pause 10 seconds.)

Examine Sample 5. (Pause 2-3 seconds.) Write the number 61 beside the third letter in the alphabet and darken that number-letter combination on your answer sheet. (Pause 5 seconds.)

Examine Sample 5 again. (Pause 2-3 seconds.) Write the number 71 beside the last letter in the sample if that is the first letter in the alphabet. (Pause 2 seconds.) Otherwise, write the number 86 beside the second letter from the right. (Pause 2 seconds.) Darken the number-letter combination you have selected on your answer sheet. (Pause 5 seconds.)

Examine Sample 6. (Pause 2-3 seconds.) Each pair of numbers shown in the sample represents a route number and its corresponding length in miles. Assume, for now, that the shorter routes comprise business districts, while the longer routes are rural. (Pause 2-3 seconds.) Select the route number that is most likely to be business oriented and go to that same number on your answer sheet. Darken the letter C, as in "cat." (Pause 5 seconds.)

Examine Sample 6 again. (Pause 2-3 seconds.) Using the same guidelines as described in the previous question, select the route number that is the most rural and go to that same number on your answer sheet and darken the letter E, as in "elephant." (Pause 5 seconds.)

Examine Sample 4 again. (Pause 2-3 seconds.) If the second number is less than the third number, but greater than the fourth number, go to number 92 on your answer sheet and darken the letter A, as in "apple." (Pause 2 seconds.) Otherwise, go to the same number that is shown in the rectangle on your answer sheet and darken the letter D, as in "dog." (Pause 5 seconds.)

Examine Sample 7. (Pause 2-3 seconds.) Each of the letters shown designate postal substations and their respective closing times on Saturdays. (Pause 2-3 seconds.) Go to number 30 on your answer sheet and darken the letter that represents the substation that remains open after 5:00 P.M. (Pause 5 seconds.)

Examine Sample 7 again. (Pause 2-3 seconds.) If substation A, as in "apple," closes before substation D, as in "dog," and substation C, as in "cat," go to number 70 on your answer sheet and darken the letter E, as in "elephant." (Pause 2 seconds.) Otherwise, go to number 1 on your answer sheet and darken the letter E, as in "elephant." (Pause 5 seconds.)

Examine Sample 8. (Pause 2-3 seconds.) Go to the smallest number shown in the sample on your answer sheet and darken the letter B, as in "boy," if the first number in the sample is less than the last number in the sample. (Pause 2 seconds.) Otherwise, go to number 78 on your answer sheet and darken the letter C, as in "cat." (Pause 5 seconds.)

Examine Sample 8 again. (Pause 2-3 seconds.) If the third number from the right is greater than the third number from the left, go to number 82 on your answer sheet and darken the letter E, as in "elephant." Otherwise, go to the same number on your answer sheet that I just mentioned and darken the letter B, as in "boy," instead. (Pause 5 seconds.)

Examine Sample 9. (Pause 2-3 seconds.) Write the letter A, as in "apple," beside both numbers shown in the sample if the first number is less than the second. (Pause 5 seconds.) However, if the opposite is true, write the number 33 beside the letter D, as in "dog," and the number 36 beside the letter A, as in "apple." (Pause 2 seconds.) Now, darken the number-letter combinations you have selected on your answer sheet. (Pause 7 seconds.)

Examine Sample 10. (Pause 2-3 seconds.) Each of the numbers shown represents five different zip codes. Assume the higher numbered zip codes represent destinations that are further west. (Pause 2 seconds.) Go to number 2 on your answer sheet and darken the letter that represents the zip code that would be considered the easternmost destination given. (Pause 5 seconds.)

Examine Sample 10 again. (Pause 2-3 seconds.) Now, underline the first two digits of the zip code that represents the second most western destination given. Go to that number on your answer sheet and darken the letter that corresponds to the zip code selected. (Pause 5 seconds.)

Examine Sample 11. (Pause 2-3 seconds.) If 7 is greater than the sum of 3 plus 3, but less than the product of 3 times 3, write the number 27 beside the letter shown. (Pause 2 seconds.) Otherwise, write the letter E, as in "elephant," beside the number shown. (Pause 2 seconds.) Now darken the number-letter combination you have selected on your answer sheet. (Pause 5 seconds.)

-END OF TEST-

FOLLOWING DIRECTIONS/EXAM 1 SAMPLES

1.   25_____   35_____   45_____   55_____   65_____   75_____

2.   2   4   6   7   8   9   10

3.   51_____   52_____   53_____   54_____   55_____

4.   23_____   24_____   29_____   42_____   43_____

5.   _____A   _____C   _____B   _____E   _____D

6.   14/30   9/15   15/8   16/2   95/14

7.   A   B   C   D
      | 12 NOON | | 5:30 PM | | 5:00 PM | | 3:00 PM |

8.   738   645   125   50   892

9.   33_____   _____D   36_____   A_____

10.
A	B	C	D	E
65322	65311	65221	65111	70500

11.   ____C   17____

ANSWER SHEET TO FOLLOWING DIRECTIONS/EXAM 1

1. A B C D E   33. A B C D E   65. A B C D E
2. A B C D E   34. A B C D E   66. A B C D E
3. A B C D E   35. A B C D E   67. A B C D E
4. A B C D E   36. A B C D E   68. A B C D E
5. A B C D E   37. A B C D E   69. A B C D E
6. A B C D E   38. A B C D E   70. A B C D E
7. A B C D E   39. A B C D E   71. A B C D E
8. A B C D E   40. A B C D E   72. A B C D E
9. A B C D E   41. A B C D E   73. A B C D E
10. A B C D E   42. A B C D E   74. A B C D E
11. A B C D E   43. A B C D E   75. A B C D E
12. A B C D E   44. A B C D E   76. A B C D E
13. A B C D E   45. A B C D E   77. A B C D E
14. A B C D E   46. A B C D E   78. A B C D E
15. A B C D E   47. A B C D E   79. A B C D E
16. A B C D E   48. A B C D E   80. A B C D E
17. A B C D E   49. A B C D E   81. A B C D E
18. A B C D E   50. A B C D E   82. A B C D E
19. A B C D E   51. A B C D E   83. A B C D E
20. A B C D E   52. A B C D E   84. A B C D E
21. A B C D E   53. A B C D E   85. A B C D E
22. A B C D E   54. A B C D E   86. A B C D E
23. A B C D E   55. A B C D E   87. A B C D E
24. A B C D E   56. A B C D E   88. A B C D E
25. A B C D E   57. A B C D E   89. A B C D E
26. A B C D E   58. A B C D E   90. A B C D E
27. A B C D E   59. A B C D E   91. A B C D E
28. A B C D E   60. A B C D E   92. A B C D E
29. A B C D E   61. A B C D E   93. A B C D E
30. A B C D E   62. A B C D E   94. A B C D E
31. A B C D E   63. A B C D E   95. A B C D E
32. A B C D E   64. A B C D E

[This page may be removed to mark answers.]

[This page is intentionally blank.]

ANSWERS TO ADDRESS CROSS COMPARISON/EXAM 1

1.	A	33.	D	65.	D
2.	D	34.	D	66.	A
3.	D	35.	D	67.	D
4.	D	36.	D	68.	A
5.	A	37.	A	69.	D
6.	D	38.	D	70.	D
7.	D	39.	D	71.	D
8.	D	40.	A	72.	A
9.	D	41.	D	73.	D
10.	A	42.	A	74.	A
11.	D	43.	D	75.	D
12.	D	44.	D	76.	D
13.	A	45.	A	77.	D
14.	D	46.	A	78.	D
15.	D	47.	D	79.	A
16.	D	48.	A	80.	D
17.	A	49.	A	81.	A
18.	D	50.	A	82.	D
19.	A	51.	A	83.	D
20.	D	52.	D	84.	D
21.	A	53.	D	85.	A
22.	D	54.	A	86.	D
23.	A	55.	A	87.	D
24.	D	56.	D	88.	D
25.	D	57.	A	89.	D
26.	A	58.	D	90.	A
27.	D	59.	D	91.	D
28.	D	60.	D	92.	D
29.	D	61.	D	93.	D
30.	D	62.	A	94.	D
31.	D	63.	D	95.	A
32.	A	64.	A		

ANSWERS TO MEMORIZATION/EXAM 1

1.	A	31.	A	61.	B
2.	C	32.	A	62.	A
3.	B	33.	B	63.	E
4.	D	34.	D	64.	A
5.	E	35.	C	65.	A
6.	C	36.	B	66.	C
7.	B	37.	E	67.	E
8.	A	38.	D	68.	C
9.	D	39.	C	69.	C
10.	E	40.	B	70.	B
11.	C	41.	E	71.	A
12.	E	42.	C	72.	D
13.	B	43.	A	73.	A
14.	A	44.	E	74.	D
15.	D	45.	B	75.	B
16.	D	46.	E	76.	B
17.	E	47.	E	77.	D
18.	C	48.	D	78.	E
19.	B	49.	B	79.	A
20.	B	50.	C	80.	B
21.	A	51.	B	81.	C
22.	D	52.	E	82.	C
23.	E	53.	B	83.	B
24.	C	54.	D	84.	E
25.	A	55.	C	85.	D
26.	D	56.	D	86.	A
27.	D	57.	D	87.	C
28.	A	58.	E	88.	E
29.	A	59.	E		
30.	C	60.	C		

ANSWERS TO NUMBER SERIES/EXAM 1

1. E.

	-1		-1		-1			
14	5	17	4	20	3	23	2	26
	+3		+3		+3		+3	

2. B.

	+1		+1		+1		
9	9	10	15	11	21	12	27
		+6		+6		+6	

3. A.

	+4		+4		+4		+4	
3	4	7	9	11	14	15	19	19
		+5		+5		+5		

4. C.

	+4		+4		+4		
28	14	21	18	14	22	7	26
	-7		-7		-7		

5. B.

	x6		x6		x6		
6	1	12	6	18	36	24	216
	+6		+6		+6		

6. D.

		-1			-1	-1			-1		
21	16	17	18	20	19	18	19	20	21	17	
	+1	+1			+1			+1	+1		

7. A.

	-9		-9		-9		-9	
49	40	36	39	31	22	42	45	13
		+3		+3		+3		

8. A.

		+8		+8		+8		
32	39	5	13	46	53	21	29	60
	+7		+7		+7		+7	

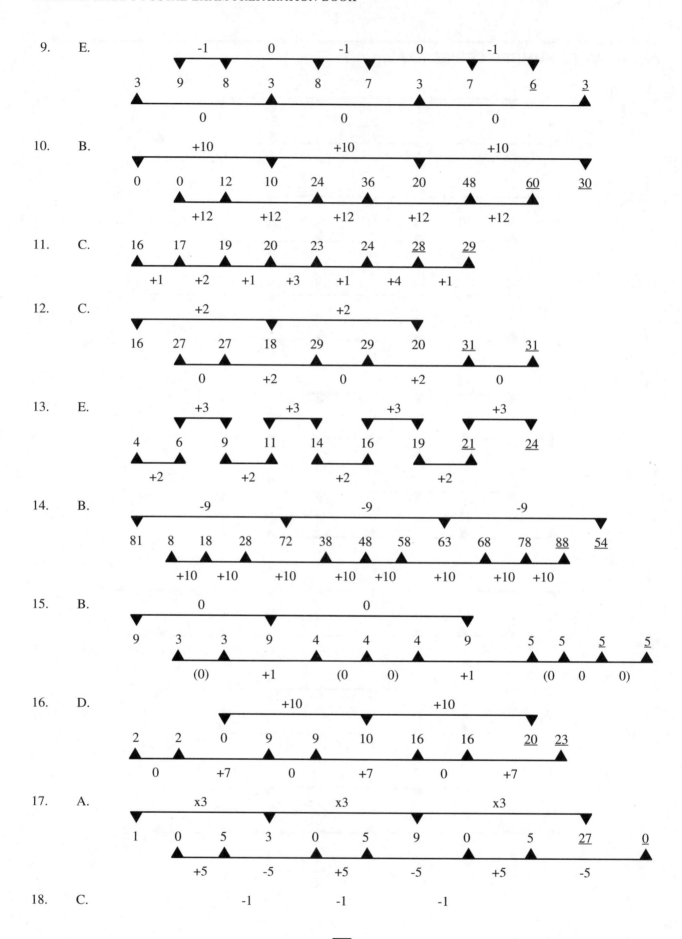

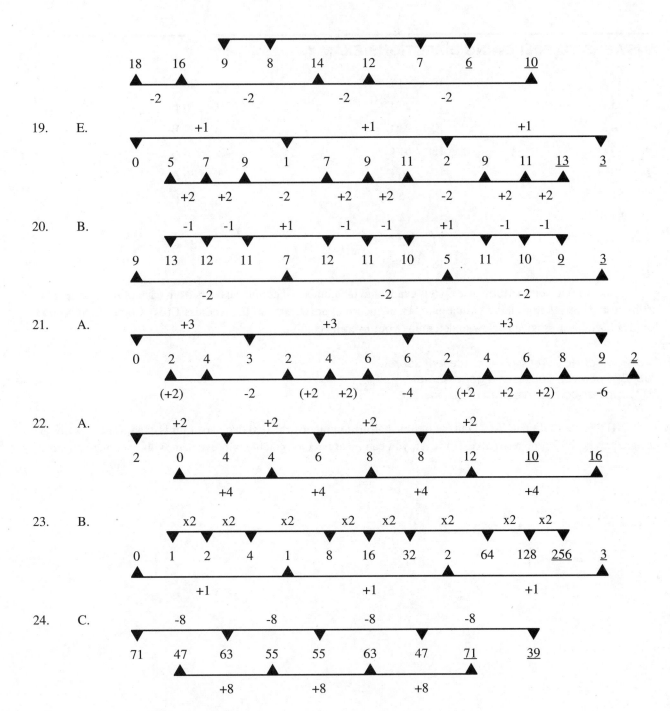

ANSWERS TO FOLLOWING DIRECTIONS/EXAM 1

1.	45 E	10.	24 E	19.	70 E
2.	25 B	11.	29 D	20.	50 B
3.	10 A	12.	23 B	21.	82 B
4.	4 D	13.	61 C	22.	33 A
5.	2 B	14.	86 E	23.	36 A
6.	51 C	15.	16 C	24.	2 D
7.	53 E	16.	14 E	25.	65 A
8.	43 C	17.	42 D	26.	27 C
9.	12 D	18.	30 B		

To determine your performance on this exam, add the number of correct answers from each of the four sections of the test. Subtract from this total the number of incorrect answers from the Address Cross Comparison section. Ratings have been provided below to determine your overall standing.

225–233 correct, you have an excellent score.
208–224 correct, you have a good score.
207 or fewer correct requires more practice.

NOTE: Don't despair if you ran out of time before completing the first two parts of this exam. These exams are designed to be very time restrictive. However, you can be assured of notable improvement with continued practice.

Exam 2

**DO NOT OPEN THIS TEST BOOKLET UNTIL
YOU ARE TOLD TO START BY THE INDIVIDUAL
ASSISTING YOU IN THIS EXERCISE.**

[This page is intentionally blank.]

ADDRESS CROSS COMPARISON/EXAM 2   TIME: 6 MINUTES

1.	1502 Tallagson Blvd.	1502 Talagson Blvd.
2.	19720 Harrison Dr.	19720 Harrison Ave.
3.	102 9th Ave. SW	102 9th Ave. SW
4.	18771 Fairmont Pl. NW	18771 Fairmont Pl. NE
5.	16-E Pebble Beach	16-W Pebble Beach
6.	Poulsbo, Wash. 98370	Poulsbo, Wash. 98370
7.	4213 NE Lincoln Pkwy	4123 NE Lincoln Pkwy
8.	67967 Tukwilla Rd.	67697 Tukwilla Rd.
9.	Ames, IA 50010	Ames, IA 50010
10.	2020 Whiteford Rd. SW	2020 Whiteford Rd. SE
11.	Alturas, Calif. 90081	Alturas, Calif. 90801
12.	Beacon Fall, Conn. 01091	Bacon Falls, Conn. 01091
13.	841 W. Liberty Ct.	814 W. Liberty Ct.
14.	1646 SW Lassie Ln.	1646 NE Lassie Lane
15.	29580 Mt. View Ridge	29850 Mt. View Ridge
16.	47751 Orseth Circle	47751 Orseth Circle
17.	Kaumakani, Hawaii	Kaumokani, Hawaii
18.	14189 Frontier Ave.	14198 Frontier Ave.
19.	Keyport, Wash. 98686	Keyport, Wash. 98686
20.	13455 S Spirit Ct.	13455 S Sirit Ct.
21.	Cass, Illinois	Cass, Ilinois
22.	E. Nesika Bay Rd.	E. Nesika Bay Rd.
23.	20895 Melson Dr.	20995 Melson Dr.

24.	Shelby, New York	Shelby, New York
25.	11-B Cedar Heights, Ark.	11-B Cedar Heights, Ark.
26.	Hernando, Florida 11212	Hernando, Florida 11221
27.	453 Canyon Dr.	4581 Canyon Dr.
28.	Yuma, Arizona 80010	Yuma, Arizona 80010
29.	11B Shadow Ct. Apts.	113 Shadow Ct. Apts.
30.	77127 Brair Cliff Rd.	77127 Briter Cliff Rd.
31.	10101 N. Blackberry Ln.	10101 N. Blackberry Ln.
32.	105-C Trevor Pl. SW	105-C Trevor Pt. SW
33.	Billings, Montana	Billings, Montana
34.	C-707 Clover Park	C-707 Clover Park
35.	Trail Ridge, MO 51181	Trail Ridge, MA 51181
36.	Tombstone, NM 72912	Tombstone, NM 72912
37.	19 Edgewater Ct. SW	19 Edgewater Circle SW
38.	11541 Suquamish Dr.	11541 Suqamish Dr.
39.	809 E Lemolo Square	908 E. Lemolo Square
40.	137-A Mulholland SE	137-A Mullholland SE
41.	Quakersville, PA 10044	Quakersville, PA 10404
42.	244 Johnston Place	2441 Johnston Place
43.	185 N Division Dr.	185 Division Ave. NW
44.	10071 Pacific Blvd.	10071 Atlantic Blvd.
45.	Crestview Ct. Apt 433	Crestview Ct. Apt 433
46.	7711 Rindal St.	7711 Rindall St.
47.	22252 Woodward Way	22225 Woodward Way

48.	15733 Virginia Point	15737 Virginia Point
49.	903 Knollward Pkwy	903 Nollward Pkwy
50.	San Juan Island	San Juan Islands
51.	14073 Sawdust Trail	14073 Sawdust Trail
52.	Bloomingdale, CA 30081	Bloomingdale, GA 30018
53.	Bridgeview, Del. 05811	Bridgeview, Del. SW
54.	202 21st Street NE	202 21st Ave. NE
55.	169340 Peterson Blvd.	169340 Petersun Blvd.
56.	995 Indianola Square	985 Indianola Square
57.	H.M. Asgard Apts.	H.M. Atgard Apts.
58.	Brownsville, TX 77811	Brownsville, TX 77811
59.	Apache Jct., AZ	Apache Jct., AZ
60.	Denver, CO 89036	Denver, Colorado
61.	B-1936 Lisir Circle	B-1936 Lisir Circle
62.	33810 Melody Lane	33810 Meludy Lane
63.	13102 Dogwood Dr.	13012 Dogwood Dr.
64.	Butte, MT 89721	Butte, MT 89721
65.	W. Des Moines, IA 50010	W. Des Moines, IA 50011
66.	Bristol Rapids, Mich.	Bristal Rapids, Mich.
67.	101-D Hoover St. NE	101-D Hover St. NE
68.	48444 Lakeside Shore	48454 Lakeside Shore
69.	12121 8th Ave. N	12121 8th Ave. N
70.	Clay, North Carolina	Clay, South Carolina
71.	Sunnydale, CA 99011	Sunnydale, CA 99011

72.	Albany, NY 09337	Albany, NM 88179
73.	Bloomington, Illinois	Blomington, Illinois
74.	East Ely, Nevada 72017	West Ely, Nevada 72017
75.	Bonscillica, WY 77811	Bonscillica, WY 77811
76.	A-1340 Wingsong Apts.	A-1340 Windsong Apts.
77.	Brighton, NH 08814	Brighton, NM 08814
78.	Snoqualamine Pass, WA	Snoqualamine Pass, VA
79.	223411 Wavecrest Ave.	22341 Wavecrest Ave.
80.	NW Forest Creek Pk.	NW Forest Creek Pt.
81.	59983 Stottlemeyer Rd.	59983 Stottlemeyer Rd.
82.	333 Chesnut Blvd. SW	888 Chestnut Blvd. SW
83.	Silverton Bay, CA	Silverten Bay, CA
84.	Admirality Pt, WA	Admirality Point, OR
85.	1656 N Sherman Hill Rd.	1656 N Sherman Hill Rd.
86.	Vista Center, OK 58090	Vista Canter, OK 58090
87.	S. Brockton Square	S. Brockson Square
88.	23-B Lincolnside Apts.	23-B Linconside Apts.
89.	71333 Bayberry Pkwy	71333 Bayberry Pkwy
90.	35556 Sunde Rd.	35556 Sundae Rd.
91.	9001 Arizona Ave.	9001 Arizona Ave.
92.	276598 Loveland Dr.	27659 Loveland Dr. S
93.	160 Bridle Pt. NE	160 Briddle Pt. NE
94.	126 8th Ave. SW	126 8th Ave. SW
95.	78441 Oyster Bay Lane	78414 Oyster Bay Lane

ANSWER SHEET TO ADDRESS CROSS COMPARISON/EXAM 2

1. (A) (D)
2. (A) (D)
3. (A) (D)
4. (A) (D)
5. (A) (D)
6. (A) (D)
7. (A) (D)
8. (A) (D)
9. (A) (D)
10. (A) (D)
11. (A) (D)
12. (A) (D)
13. (A) (D)
14. (A) (D)
15. (A) (D)
16. (A) (D)
17. (A) (D)
18. (A) (D)
19. (A) (D)
20. (A) (D)
21. (A) (D)
22. (A) (D)
23. (A) (D)
24. (A) (D)
25. (A) (D)
26. (A) (D)
27. (A) (D)
28. (A) (D)
29. (A) (D)
30. (A) (D)
31. (A) (D)
32. (A) (D)

33. (A) (D)
34. (A) (D)
35. (A) (D)
36. (A) (D)
37. (A) (D)
38. (A) (D)
39. (A) (D)
40. (A) (D)
41. (A) (D)
42. (A) (D)
43. (A) (D)
44. (A) (D)
45. (A) (D)
46. (A) (D)
47. (A) (D)
48. (A) (D)
49. (A) (D)
50. (A) (D)
51. (A) (D)
52. (A) (D)
53. (A) (D)
54. (A) (D)
55. (A) (D)
56. (A) (D)
57. (A) (D)
58. (A) (D)
59. (A) (D)
60. (A) (D)
61. (A) (D)
62. (A) (D)
63. (A) (D)
64. (A) (D)

65. (A) (D)
66. (A) (D)
67. (A) (D)
68. (A) (D)
69. (A) (D)
70. (A) (D)
71. (A) (D)
72. (A) (D)
73. (A) (D)
74. (A) (D)
75. (A) (D)
76. (A) (D)
77. (A) (D)
78. (A) (D)
79. (A) (D)
80. (A) (D)
81. (A) (D)
82. (A) (D)
83. (A) (D)
84. (A) (D)
85. (A) (D)
86. (A) (D)
87. (A) (D)
88. (A) (D)
89. (A) (D)
90. (A) (D)
91. (A) (D)
92. (A) (D)
93. (A) (D)
94. (A) (D)
95. (A) (D)

(This page may be removed to mark answers.)

[This page is intentionally blank.]

MEMORIZATION/EXAM 2 STEP 1 TIME: 3 MINUTES
STEP 4 TIME: 5 MINUTES

A	B	C	D	E
0900-0999 Jacobsen	1400-1499 Jacobsen	2700-2799 Jacobsen	3700-3799 Jacobsen	4000-4099 Jacobsen
Glenwood Way	Echo Valley Rd.	Sea Vista Dr.	Huntington Ln.	Jasper Ct.
1800-1899 Douglas	2300-2399 Douglas	2400-2499 Douglas	2500-2599 Douglas	2600-2699 Douglas
Shamrock Pl.	Cedar Trail	Hendrickson	Coho Run.	Theodore St.
1400-1499 Hostmark	2400-2499 Hostmark	3700-3799 Hostmark	4100-4199 Hostmark	5100-5199 Hostmark

NOTE: Follow the same step-by-step format established for the memorization exercises studied earlier. (See page 41.)

PRACTICE MEMORIZATION/EXAM 2

STEP 2 TIME: 3 MINUTES
STEP 3 TIME: 3 MINUTES (cover key)

A	B	C	D	E
0900-0999 Jacobsen	1400-1499 Jacobsen	2700-2799 Jacobsen	3700-3799 Jacobsen	4000-4099 Jacobsen
Glenwood Way	Echo Valley Rd.	Sea Vista Dr.	Huntington Ln.	Jasper Ct.
1800-1899 Douglas	2300-2399 Douglas	2400-2499 Douglas	2500-2599 Douglas	2600-2699 Douglas
Shamrock Pl.	Cedar Trail	Hendrickson	Coho Run.	Theodore St.
1400-1499 Hostmark	2400-2499 Hostmark	3700-3799 Hostmark	4100-4199 Hostmark	5100-5199 Hostmark

1. 2400-2499 Douglas
2. Coho Run
3. Jasper Ct.
4. 2400-2499 Hostmark
5. Echo Valley Rd.
6. 1800-1899 Douglas
7. 3700-3799 Jacobsen
8. Theodore St.
9. Hendrickson
10. 0900-0999 Jacobsen
11. Cedar Trail
12. Sea Vista Dr.
13. 2600-2699 Douglas
14. Huntington Ln.
15. 1400-1499 Hostmark
16. 1400-1499 Jacobsen
17. 3700-3799 Hostmark
18. 2500-2599 Douglas
19. 5100-5199 Hostmark
20. 2700-2799 Jacobsen
21. 2300-2399 Douglas
22. Shamrock Pl.
23. Glenwood Way
24. 4100-4199 Hostmark
25. 4000-4099 Jacobsen
26. 2300-2399 Douglas
27. 5100-5199 Hostmark
28. 1400-1499 Jacobsen
29. 2600-2699 Douglas
30. Sea Vista Dr.

31. 2500-2599 Douglas
32. 1400-1499 Hostmark
33. Glenwood Way
34. 4000-4099 Jacobsen
35. 2700-2799 Jacobsen
36. Shamrock Pl.
37. Theodore St.
38. 4100-4199 Hostmark
39. Echo Valley Rd.
40. Cedar Trail
41. Jasper Ct.
42. 3700-3799 Jacobsen
43. 2400-2499 Douglas
44. Coho Run
45. 1800-1899 Douglas
46. Hendrickson
47. Huntington Ln.
48. 0900-0999 Jacobsen
49. 3700-3799 Hostmark
50. 2400-2499 Hostmark
51. 2700-2799 Jacobsen
52. 4100-4199 Hostmark
53. Shamrock Pl.
54. Cedar Trail
55. 3700-3799 Jacobsen
56. Coho Run
57. 1400-1499 Jacobsen
58. 2300-2399 Douglas
59. Hendrickson
60. 0900-0999 Jacobsen

61. 1800-1899 Douglas
62. Jasper Ct.
63. 4000-4099 Jacobsen
64. Huntington Ln.
65. 3700-3799 Hostmark
66. 2400-2499 Hostmark
67. Echo Valley Rd.
68. Theodore St.
69. 2400-2499 Douglas
70. Glenwood Way
71. Sea Vista Dr.
72. 5100-5199 Hostmark
73. 2600-2699 Douglas
74. 2500-2599 Douglas
75. 1400-1499 Hostmark
76. Jasper Ct.
77. 1400-1499 Jacobsen
78. 1800-1899 Douglas
79. Coho Run
80. 2700-2799 Jacobsen
81. 4000-4099 Jacobsen
82. 2400-2499 Hostmark
83. Shamrock Pl.
84. Glenwood Way
85. 3700-3799 Jacobsen
86. 2300-2399 Douglas
87. 0900-0999 Jacobsen
88. 5100-5199 Hostmark

PRACTICE ANSWER SHEET TO MEMORIZATION/EXAM 2

1. Ⓐ Ⓑ Ⓒ Ⓓ Ⓔ   31. Ⓐ Ⓑ Ⓒ Ⓓ Ⓔ   61. Ⓐ Ⓑ Ⓒ Ⓓ Ⓔ
2. Ⓐ Ⓑ Ⓒ Ⓓ Ⓔ   32. Ⓐ Ⓑ Ⓒ Ⓓ Ⓔ   62. Ⓐ Ⓑ Ⓒ Ⓓ Ⓔ
3. Ⓐ Ⓑ Ⓒ Ⓓ Ⓔ   33. Ⓐ Ⓑ Ⓒ Ⓓ Ⓔ   63. Ⓐ Ⓑ Ⓒ Ⓓ Ⓔ
4. Ⓐ Ⓑ Ⓒ Ⓓ Ⓔ   34. Ⓐ Ⓑ Ⓒ Ⓓ Ⓔ   64. Ⓐ Ⓑ Ⓒ Ⓓ Ⓔ
5. Ⓐ Ⓑ Ⓒ Ⓓ Ⓔ   35. Ⓐ Ⓑ Ⓒ Ⓓ Ⓔ   65. Ⓐ Ⓑ Ⓒ Ⓓ Ⓔ
6. Ⓐ Ⓑ Ⓒ Ⓓ Ⓔ   36. Ⓐ Ⓑ Ⓒ Ⓓ Ⓔ   66. Ⓐ Ⓑ Ⓒ Ⓓ Ⓔ
7. Ⓐ Ⓑ Ⓒ Ⓓ Ⓔ   37. Ⓐ Ⓑ Ⓒ Ⓓ Ⓔ   67. Ⓐ Ⓑ Ⓒ Ⓓ Ⓔ
8. Ⓐ Ⓑ Ⓒ Ⓓ Ⓔ   38. Ⓐ Ⓑ Ⓒ Ⓓ Ⓔ   68. Ⓐ Ⓑ Ⓒ Ⓓ Ⓔ
9. Ⓐ Ⓑ Ⓒ Ⓓ Ⓔ   39. Ⓐ Ⓑ Ⓒ Ⓓ Ⓔ   69. Ⓐ Ⓑ Ⓒ Ⓓ Ⓔ
10. Ⓐ Ⓑ Ⓒ Ⓓ Ⓔ   40. Ⓐ Ⓑ Ⓒ Ⓓ Ⓔ   70. Ⓐ Ⓑ Ⓒ Ⓓ Ⓔ
11. Ⓐ Ⓑ Ⓒ Ⓓ Ⓔ   41. Ⓐ Ⓑ Ⓒ Ⓓ Ⓔ   71. Ⓐ Ⓑ Ⓒ Ⓓ Ⓔ
12. Ⓐ Ⓑ Ⓒ Ⓓ Ⓔ   42. Ⓐ Ⓑ Ⓒ Ⓓ Ⓔ   72. Ⓐ Ⓑ Ⓒ Ⓓ Ⓔ
13. Ⓐ Ⓑ Ⓒ Ⓓ Ⓔ   43. Ⓐ Ⓑ Ⓒ Ⓓ Ⓔ   73. Ⓐ Ⓑ Ⓒ Ⓓ Ⓔ
14. Ⓐ Ⓑ Ⓒ Ⓓ Ⓔ   44. Ⓐ Ⓑ Ⓒ Ⓓ Ⓔ   74. Ⓐ Ⓑ Ⓒ Ⓓ Ⓔ
15. Ⓐ Ⓑ Ⓒ Ⓓ Ⓔ   45. Ⓐ Ⓑ Ⓒ Ⓓ Ⓔ   75. Ⓐ Ⓑ Ⓒ Ⓓ Ⓔ
16. Ⓐ Ⓑ Ⓒ Ⓓ Ⓔ   46. Ⓐ Ⓑ Ⓒ Ⓓ Ⓔ   76. Ⓐ Ⓑ Ⓒ Ⓓ Ⓔ
17. Ⓐ Ⓑ Ⓒ Ⓓ Ⓔ   47. Ⓐ Ⓑ Ⓒ Ⓓ Ⓔ   77. Ⓐ Ⓑ Ⓒ Ⓓ Ⓔ
18. Ⓐ Ⓑ Ⓒ Ⓓ Ⓔ   48. Ⓐ Ⓑ Ⓒ Ⓓ Ⓔ   78. Ⓐ Ⓑ Ⓒ Ⓓ Ⓔ
19. Ⓐ Ⓑ Ⓒ Ⓓ Ⓔ   49. Ⓐ Ⓑ Ⓒ Ⓓ Ⓔ   79. Ⓐ Ⓑ Ⓒ Ⓓ Ⓔ
20. Ⓐ Ⓑ Ⓒ Ⓓ Ⓔ   50. Ⓐ Ⓑ Ⓒ Ⓓ Ⓔ   80. Ⓐ Ⓑ Ⓒ Ⓓ Ⓔ
21. Ⓐ Ⓑ Ⓒ Ⓓ Ⓔ   51. Ⓐ Ⓑ Ⓒ Ⓓ Ⓔ   81. Ⓐ Ⓑ Ⓒ Ⓓ Ⓔ
22. Ⓐ Ⓑ Ⓒ Ⓓ Ⓔ   52. Ⓐ Ⓑ Ⓒ Ⓓ Ⓔ   82. Ⓐ Ⓑ Ⓒ Ⓓ Ⓔ
23. Ⓐ Ⓑ Ⓒ Ⓓ Ⓔ   53. Ⓐ Ⓑ Ⓒ Ⓓ Ⓔ   83. Ⓐ Ⓑ Ⓒ Ⓓ Ⓔ
24. Ⓐ Ⓑ Ⓒ Ⓓ Ⓔ   54. Ⓐ Ⓑ Ⓒ Ⓓ Ⓔ   84. Ⓐ Ⓑ Ⓒ Ⓓ Ⓔ
25. Ⓐ Ⓑ Ⓒ Ⓓ Ⓔ   55. Ⓐ Ⓑ Ⓒ Ⓓ Ⓔ   85. Ⓐ Ⓑ Ⓒ Ⓓ Ⓔ
26. Ⓐ Ⓑ Ⓒ Ⓓ Ⓔ   56. Ⓐ Ⓑ Ⓒ Ⓓ Ⓔ   86. Ⓐ Ⓑ Ⓒ Ⓓ Ⓔ
27. Ⓐ Ⓑ Ⓒ Ⓓ Ⓔ   57. Ⓐ Ⓑ Ⓒ Ⓓ Ⓔ   87. Ⓐ Ⓑ Ⓒ Ⓓ Ⓔ
28. Ⓐ Ⓑ Ⓒ Ⓓ Ⓔ   58. Ⓐ Ⓑ Ⓒ Ⓓ Ⓔ   88. Ⓐ Ⓑ Ⓒ Ⓓ Ⓔ
29. Ⓐ Ⓑ Ⓒ Ⓓ Ⓔ   59. Ⓐ Ⓑ Ⓒ Ⓓ Ⓔ
30. Ⓐ Ⓑ Ⓒ Ⓓ Ⓔ   60. Ⓐ Ⓑ Ⓒ Ⓓ Ⓔ

MEMORIZATION/EXAM 2 STEP 5: 5 MINUTES

1. 2600-2699 Douglas
2. Huntington Ln.
3. 3700-3799 Hostmark
4. Cedar Trail
5. 2500-2599 Douglas
6. Glenwood Way
7. 5100-5199 Hostmark
8. Sea Vista Dr.
9. 1400-1499 Jacobsen
10. 4100-4199 Hostmark
11. Theodore St.
12. 0900-0999 Jacobsen
13. Shamrock Pl.
14. Jasper Ct.
15. 3700-3799 Jacobsen
16. Echo Valley Rd.
17. 2400-2499 Douglas
18. 2700-2799 Jacobsen
19. 1800-1899 Douglas
20. Coho Run
21. 4000-4099 Jacobsen
22. Hendrickson
23. 2400-2499 Hostmark
24. 2300-2399 Douglas
25. 1400-1499 Hostmark
26. 2700-2799 Jacobsen
27. 3700-3799 Jacobsen
28. Coho Run
29. Echo Valley Rd.
30. 2400-2499 Douglas

31. 4000-4099 Jacobsen
32. 2400-2499 Hostmark
33. Shamrock Pl.
34. 1800-1899 Douglas
35. Hendrickson
36. 1400-1499 Hostmark
37. Jasper Ct.
38. Cedar Trail
39. 2600-2699 Douglas
40. 3700-3799 Hostmark
41. Huntington Ln.
42. Glenwood Way
43. 2500-2599 Douglas
44. Sea Vista Dr.
45. Theodore St.
46. 4100-4199 Hostmark
47. 5100-5199 Hostmark
48. 1400-1499 Jacobsen
49. 0900-0999 Jacobsen
50. 2300-2399 Douglas
51. Huntington Ln.
52. 2600-2699 Douglas
53. Jasper Ct.
54. 3700-3799 Hostmark
55. Cedar Trail
56. 2400-2499 Hostmark
57. 2500-2599 Douglas
58. 4100-4199 Hostmark
59. Glenwood Way
60. 0900-0999 Jacobsen

61. Sea Vista Dr.
62. 5100-5199 Hostmark
63. Shamrock Pl.
64. 1400-1499 Hostmark
65. Echo Valley Rd.
66. 1800-1899 Douglas
67. Hendrickson
68. Theodore St.
69. 1400-1499 Jacobsen
70. 2300-2399 Douglas
71. 4000-4099 Jacobsen
72. Coho Run
73. 2400-2499 Douglas
74. 3700-3799 Jacobsen
75. 2700-2799 Jacobsen
76. Cedar Trail
77. Shamrock Pl.
78. 2400-2499 Hostmark
79. 2600-2699 Douglas
80. 4100-4199 Hostmark
81. Sea Vista Dr.
82. 0900-0999 Jacobsen
83. 1400-1499 Jacobsen
84. Glenwood Way
85. Jasper Ct.
86. Huntington Ln.
87. 3700-3799 Jacobsen
88. Hendrickson

ANSWER SHEET TO MEMORIZATION/EXAM 2

1. Ⓐ Ⓑ Ⓒ Ⓓ Ⓔ
2. Ⓐ Ⓑ Ⓒ Ⓓ Ⓔ
3. Ⓐ Ⓑ Ⓒ Ⓓ Ⓔ
4. Ⓐ Ⓑ Ⓒ Ⓓ Ⓔ
5. Ⓐ Ⓑ Ⓒ Ⓓ Ⓔ
6. Ⓐ Ⓑ Ⓒ Ⓓ Ⓔ
7. Ⓐ Ⓑ Ⓒ Ⓓ Ⓔ
8. Ⓐ Ⓑ Ⓒ Ⓓ Ⓔ
9. Ⓐ Ⓑ Ⓒ Ⓓ Ⓔ
10. Ⓐ Ⓑ Ⓒ Ⓓ Ⓔ
11. Ⓐ Ⓑ Ⓒ Ⓓ Ⓔ
12. Ⓐ Ⓑ Ⓒ Ⓓ Ⓔ
13. Ⓐ Ⓑ Ⓒ Ⓓ Ⓔ
14. Ⓐ Ⓑ Ⓒ Ⓓ Ⓔ
15. Ⓐ Ⓑ Ⓒ Ⓓ Ⓔ
16. Ⓐ Ⓑ Ⓒ Ⓓ Ⓔ
17. Ⓐ Ⓑ Ⓒ Ⓓ Ⓔ
18. Ⓐ Ⓑ Ⓒ Ⓓ Ⓔ
19. Ⓐ Ⓑ Ⓒ Ⓓ Ⓔ
20. Ⓐ Ⓑ Ⓒ Ⓓ Ⓔ
21. Ⓐ Ⓑ Ⓒ Ⓓ Ⓔ
22. Ⓐ Ⓑ Ⓒ Ⓓ Ⓔ
23. Ⓐ Ⓑ Ⓒ Ⓓ Ⓔ
24. Ⓐ Ⓑ Ⓒ Ⓓ Ⓔ
25. Ⓐ Ⓑ Ⓒ Ⓓ Ⓔ
26. Ⓐ Ⓑ Ⓒ Ⓓ Ⓔ
27. Ⓐ Ⓑ Ⓒ Ⓓ Ⓔ
28. Ⓐ Ⓑ Ⓒ Ⓓ Ⓔ
29. Ⓐ Ⓑ Ⓒ Ⓓ Ⓔ
30. Ⓐ Ⓑ Ⓒ Ⓓ Ⓔ

31. Ⓐ Ⓑ Ⓒ Ⓓ Ⓔ
32. Ⓐ Ⓑ Ⓒ Ⓓ Ⓔ
33. Ⓐ Ⓑ Ⓒ Ⓓ Ⓔ
34. Ⓐ Ⓑ Ⓒ Ⓓ Ⓔ
35. Ⓐ Ⓑ Ⓒ Ⓓ Ⓔ
36. Ⓐ Ⓑ Ⓒ Ⓓ Ⓔ
37. Ⓐ Ⓑ Ⓒ Ⓓ Ⓔ
38. Ⓐ Ⓑ Ⓒ Ⓓ Ⓔ
39. Ⓐ Ⓑ Ⓒ Ⓓ Ⓔ
40. Ⓐ Ⓑ Ⓒ Ⓓ Ⓔ
41. Ⓐ Ⓑ Ⓒ Ⓓ Ⓔ
42. Ⓐ Ⓑ Ⓒ Ⓓ Ⓔ
43. Ⓐ Ⓑ Ⓒ Ⓓ Ⓔ
44. Ⓐ Ⓑ Ⓒ Ⓓ Ⓔ
45. Ⓐ Ⓑ Ⓒ Ⓓ Ⓔ
46. Ⓐ Ⓑ Ⓒ Ⓓ Ⓔ
47. Ⓐ Ⓑ Ⓒ Ⓓ Ⓔ
48. Ⓐ Ⓑ Ⓒ Ⓓ Ⓔ
49. Ⓐ Ⓑ Ⓒ Ⓓ Ⓔ
50. Ⓐ Ⓑ Ⓒ Ⓓ Ⓔ
51. Ⓐ Ⓑ Ⓒ Ⓓ Ⓔ
52. Ⓐ Ⓑ Ⓒ Ⓓ Ⓔ
53. Ⓐ Ⓑ Ⓒ Ⓓ Ⓔ
54. Ⓐ Ⓑ Ⓒ Ⓓ Ⓔ
55. Ⓐ Ⓑ Ⓒ Ⓓ Ⓔ
56. Ⓐ Ⓑ Ⓒ Ⓓ Ⓔ
57. Ⓐ Ⓑ Ⓒ Ⓓ Ⓔ
58. Ⓐ Ⓑ Ⓒ Ⓓ Ⓔ
59. Ⓐ Ⓑ Ⓒ Ⓓ Ⓔ
60. Ⓐ Ⓑ Ⓒ Ⓓ Ⓔ

61. Ⓐ Ⓑ Ⓒ Ⓓ Ⓔ
62. Ⓐ Ⓑ Ⓒ Ⓓ Ⓔ
63. Ⓐ Ⓑ Ⓒ Ⓓ Ⓔ
64. Ⓐ Ⓑ Ⓒ Ⓓ Ⓔ
65. Ⓐ Ⓑ Ⓒ Ⓓ Ⓔ
66. Ⓐ Ⓑ Ⓒ Ⓓ Ⓔ
67. Ⓐ Ⓑ Ⓒ Ⓓ Ⓔ
68. Ⓐ Ⓑ Ⓒ Ⓓ Ⓔ
69. Ⓐ Ⓑ Ⓒ Ⓓ Ⓔ
70. Ⓐ Ⓑ Ⓒ Ⓓ Ⓔ
71. Ⓐ Ⓑ Ⓒ Ⓓ Ⓔ
72. Ⓐ Ⓑ Ⓒ Ⓓ Ⓔ
73. Ⓐ Ⓑ Ⓒ Ⓓ Ⓔ
74. Ⓐ Ⓑ Ⓒ Ⓓ Ⓔ
75. Ⓐ Ⓑ Ⓒ Ⓓ Ⓔ
76. Ⓐ Ⓑ Ⓒ Ⓓ Ⓔ
77. Ⓐ Ⓑ Ⓒ Ⓓ Ⓔ
78. Ⓐ Ⓑ Ⓒ Ⓓ Ⓔ
79. Ⓐ Ⓑ Ⓒ Ⓓ Ⓔ
80. Ⓐ Ⓑ Ⓒ Ⓓ Ⓔ
81. Ⓐ Ⓑ Ⓒ Ⓓ Ⓔ
82. Ⓐ Ⓑ Ⓒ Ⓓ Ⓔ
83. Ⓐ Ⓑ Ⓒ Ⓓ Ⓔ
84. Ⓐ Ⓑ Ⓒ Ⓓ Ⓔ
85. Ⓐ Ⓑ Ⓒ Ⓓ Ⓔ
86. Ⓐ Ⓑ Ⓒ Ⓓ Ⓔ
87. Ⓐ Ⓑ Ⓒ Ⓓ Ⓔ
88. Ⓐ Ⓑ Ⓒ Ⓓ Ⓔ

[This page is intentionally blank.]

NUMBER SERIES/EXAM 2   TIME: 20 MINUTES

1. 5   15   30   10   45   60   15   75   ___   ___

    A.   80, 20
    B.   90, 20
    C.   20, 85
    D.   90, 30
    E.   85, 30

2. 2   4   6   6   9   12   12   16   ___   ___

    A.   16, 20
    B.   16, 16
    C.   20, 20
    D.   16, 18
    E.   18, 18

3. 9   26   13   7   13   26   5   26   13   3   13   ___   ___

    A.   26, 1
    B.   13, 26
    C.   26, 13
    D.   26, 3
    E.   26, 0

4. 5   10   10   9   15   20   8   7   ___   ___

    A.   6, 25
    B.   25, 6
    C.   25, 10
    D.   25, 30
    E.   6, 30

5. 33   26   28   30   23   34   ___   ___

    A.   17, 38
    B.   18, 37
    C.   20, 28
    D.   38, 18
    E.   18, 38

6. 27   1   1   30   1   2   34   1   3   39   1   ___   ___

    A.   45, 1
    B.   45, 4
    C.   44, 4
    D.   43, 4
    E.   4, 45

7. 1   2   2   3   4   4   8   5   ___   ___

    A.   12, 6
    B.   10, 4
    C.   16, 6
    D.   20, 4
    E.   12, 18

8.　　1　　1　　4　　5　　16　　25　　___　　___

    A.　64, 125
    B.　62, 120
    C.　54, 125
    D.　52, 120
    E.　74, 115

9.　　14　　3　　3　　12　　6　　6　　10　　9　　___　　___

    A.　9, 9
    B.　9, 8
    C.　8, 8
    D.　10, 10
    E.　9, 11

10.　41　　40　　39　　37　　40　　34　　30　　25　　39　　19　　___　　___

    A.　12, 4
    B.　12, 38
    C.　38, 12
    D.　13, 3
    E.　3, 13

11.　4　　6　　10　　12　　16　　18　　___　　___

    A.　20, 24
    B.　23, 23
    C.　20, 22
    D.　22, 24
    E.　22, 22

12.　32　　40　　1　　37　　39　　1　　42　　38　　1　　___　　___

    A.　47, 1
    B.　47, 37
    C.　1, 47
    D.　40, 1
    E.　40, 42

13.　22　　5　　6　　7　　23　　5　　6　　7　　24　　___　　___

    A.　6, 7
    B.　6, 25
    C.　5, 6
    D.　7, 25
    E.　5, 7

14.　60　　63　　55　　60　　46　　36　　60　　25　　___　　___

    A.　60, 13
    B.　12, 60
    C.　13, 60
    D.　14, 60
    E.　60, 14

15. 70   44   48   67   64   52   56   61   58   60   ___   ___

    A.   55, 60
    B.   64, 55
    C.   60, 55
    D.   62, 53
    E.   62, 55

16. 9   2   2   2   12   10   9   3   3   3   12   10   ___   ___

    A.   9, 3
    B.   8, 4
    C.   9, 5
    D.   9, 4
    E.   9, 10

17. 1   0   5   3   0   6   9   0   7   27   0   ___   ___

    A.   8, 72
    B.   81, 0
    C.   72, 0
    D.   8, 80
    E.   8, 81

18. 42   37   40   37   38   38   37   38   39   36   37   38   39   ___   ___

    A.   40, 34
    B.   39, 34
    C.   38, 33
    D.   38, 34
    E.   37, 36

19. 12   14   15   14   14   15   16   15   16   16   17   ___   ___

    A.   16, 17
    B.   17, 19
    C.   17, 20
    D.   16, 18
    E.   18, 16

20. 2   4   4   6   6   6   8   8   ___   ___

    A.   8, 8
    B.   8, 10
    C.   10, 8
    D.   8, 12
    E.   12, 12

21. 0   55   57   60   10   64   69   75   ___   ___

    A.   82, 89
    B.   89, 82
    C.   20, 82
    D.   82, 22
    E.   82, 84

22.   25   26   23   23   18   15   21   10   ___   ___

    A.   19, 7
    B.   7, 20
    C.   8, 19
    D.   8, 20
    E.   7, 19

23.   21   7   7   14   14   14   7   21   ___   ___

    A.   21, 7
    B.   20, 0
    C.   14, 0
    D.   14, 14
    E.   21, 0

24.   12   30   32   28   12   40   42   38   12   50   52   48   12   60   ___   ___

    A.   62, 58
    B.   62, 12
    C.   58, 12
    D.   12, 62
    E.   12, 58

ANSWER SHEET TO NUMBER SERIES/EXAM 2

1. Ⓐ Ⓑ Ⓒ Ⓓ Ⓔ   9. Ⓐ Ⓑ Ⓒ Ⓓ Ⓔ   17. Ⓐ Ⓑ Ⓒ Ⓓ Ⓔ
2. Ⓐ Ⓑ Ⓒ Ⓓ Ⓔ   10. Ⓐ Ⓑ Ⓒ Ⓓ Ⓔ   18. Ⓐ Ⓑ Ⓒ Ⓓ Ⓔ
3. Ⓐ Ⓑ Ⓒ Ⓓ Ⓔ   11. Ⓐ Ⓑ Ⓒ Ⓓ Ⓔ   19. Ⓐ Ⓑ Ⓒ Ⓓ Ⓔ
4. Ⓐ Ⓑ Ⓒ Ⓓ Ⓔ   12. Ⓐ Ⓑ Ⓒ Ⓓ Ⓔ   20. Ⓐ Ⓑ Ⓒ Ⓓ Ⓔ
5. Ⓐ Ⓑ Ⓒ Ⓓ Ⓔ   13. Ⓐ Ⓑ Ⓒ Ⓓ Ⓔ   21. Ⓐ Ⓑ Ⓒ Ⓓ Ⓔ
6. Ⓐ Ⓑ Ⓒ Ⓓ Ⓔ   14. Ⓐ Ⓑ Ⓒ Ⓓ Ⓔ   22. Ⓐ Ⓑ Ⓒ Ⓓ Ⓔ
7. Ⓐ Ⓑ Ⓒ Ⓓ Ⓔ   15. Ⓐ Ⓑ Ⓒ Ⓓ Ⓔ   23. Ⓐ Ⓑ Ⓒ Ⓓ Ⓔ
8. Ⓐ Ⓑ Ⓒ Ⓓ Ⓔ   16. Ⓐ Ⓑ Ⓒ Ⓓ Ⓔ   24. Ⓐ Ⓑ Ⓒ Ⓓ Ⓔ

[This page may be removed to mark answers.]

[This page is intentionally blank.]

FOLLOWING DIRECTIONS/EXAM 2

Note To Person Assisting In This Exam:

Remove from this test guide the pages of this exam that comprise the directions to be read out loud. The test applicant should be left with only the sample sheet and answer sheet. Read the following directions out loud at the suggested rate of 75-80 words per minutes, pausing only where indicated in parentheses. Speak as clearly as possible: Once a statement has been read, it cannot be repeated.

Examine Sample 1. (Pause 2-3 seconds.) If 14 is less than the sum of 7 plus 7, write the letter D, as in "dog," beside the number shown. (Pause 2 seconds.) If 14 is greater than or equal to the sum I just mentioned, write the letter E, as in "elephant," beside the number shown. (Pause 2 seconds.) Now, go to your answer sheet and darken the number-letter combination you have chosen for the question. (Pause 5 seconds.)

Examine Sample 2. (Pause 2-3 seconds.) Write the number 22 in the large box and number 23 in the smaller box if the letter C, as in "cat," is in the smaller of the two circles in the sample. (Pause 5 seconds.) Otherwise, write the number 8 in the smaller circle shown and the number 80 in the larger circle. (Pause 5 seconds.) Now, go to your answer sheet and mark both number-letter combinations selected. (Pause 10 seconds.)

Examine Sample 2 again. (Pause 2-3 seconds.) If the letter A, as in "apple," is in a smaller box than the letter B, as in "boy," is in, and the letter D, as in "dog," is in the smaller circle, go to number 72 on your answer sheet and darken the letter E, as in "elephant." (Pause 5 seconds.) Otherwise, go to number 71 on your answer sheet and darken the letter E, as in "elephant." (Pause 5 seconds.)

Examine Sample 3. (Pause 2-3 seconds.) If the third number in the sample is the second largest and the last number is the smallest, write the letter B, as in "boy," beside the number 2. (Pause 2 seconds.) If not, write the letter D, as in "dog," beside the number 2. (Pause 2 seconds.) Darken the number-letter combination selected on your answer sheet. (Pause 5 seconds.)

Examine Sample 3 again. (Pause 2-3 seconds.) If the three smallest numbers add up to be less than the first number shown, go to number 27 on your answer sheet and darken the letter B, as in "boy." (Pause 5 seconds.) Otherwise, go to that same number on your answer sheet and darken the letter A, as in "apple." (Pause 5 seconds.)

Examine Sample 3 one more time. (Pause 2-3 seconds.) Draw a circle, square, and triangle around the numbers 3, 30, and 1 respectively. (Pause 5 seconds.) Go to the same number that is within the square on your answer sheet and darken the letter C, as in "cat." (Pause 5 seconds.) Now, go to the same number that is within the triangle on your answer sheet and darken the letter D, as in "dog." (Pause 5 seconds.)

Examine Sample 4. (Pause 2-3 seconds.) Write the letter E, as in "elephant," beside the highest number shown if the fourth number is the lowest in the sample. (Pause 2 seconds.) Otherwise, write the letter A, as in "apple," beside the first number given. (Pause 2 seconds.) Now, go to your answer sheet and darken the number-letter combination chosen. (Pause 5 seconds.)

Examine Sample 5. (Pause 2-3 seconds.) Go to number 73 on your answer sheet and darken the only letter in this sample that is not enclosed in a geometric shapes. (Pause 5 seconds.)

Examine Sample 5 again. (Pause 2-3 seconds.) If the letters B, E, and A are enclosed by a square, triangle, and circle respectively, go to number 12 on your answer sheet and darken the letter A, as in "apple." (Pause 5 seconds.) Otherwise, go to number 19 on your answer sheet and darken the letter shown in the triangle. (Pause 5 seconds.)

Examine Sample 6. (Pause 2-3 seconds.) Write the letter B, as in "boy," beside the first and last numbers. (Pause 5 seconds.) Write the letter C, as in "cat," beside the middle number. (Pause 2 seconds.) Now, go to your answer sheet and darken the letter D, as in "dog," on number 63. (Pause 5 seconds.)

Examine Sample 6 again. (Pause 2-3 seconds.) If the letter E, as in "elephant," is the fifth letter in the alphabet, write the number 56 beside the letter D, as in "dog." (Pause 2 seconds.) Otherwise, write the number 55 beside the letter E, as in "elephant." (Pause 2 seconds.) Now, go to your answer sheet and darken the number-letter combination you just made. (Pause 5 seconds.)

Examine Sample 7. (Pause 2-3 seconds.) The first two digits of each number represents a given mail route. If the number is 50 or higher, it represents a city route; 49 or less represents rural delivery. (Pause 2 seconds.) The last three digits of each number designate the number of households served by each route. (Pause 2 seconds.) If there are more than two city routes in the sample, go to number 86 on your answer sheet and darken the letter D, as in "dog."

(Pause 5 seconds.) If there are only two rural routes shown in the sample, go to number 39 on your answer sheet and darken the letter B, as in "boy." (Pause 5 seconds.)

Examine Sample 7 again. (Pause 2-3 seconds.)Write the letters A, as in "apple," B, as in "boy," C, as in "cat," and E, as in "elephant," under the four numbers shown in the sample respectively. (Pause 5 seconds.) Go to number 38 on your answer sheet and darken the letter that corresponds to the route having the largest number of deliveries. (Pause 5 seconds.) Now, go to number 93 on your answer sheet and darken the letter that corresponds to the route having the second highest number of deliveries. (Pause 5 seconds.)

Examine Sample 8. (Pause 2-3 seconds.) Write the number 7 in the largest box that does not have an enclosed letter designation. (Pause 2 seconds.) Darken that number-letter combination on your answer sheet. (Pause 5 seconds.) Now, write the number 16 in the largest box and the number 91 in the smaller triangle. (Pause 2 seconds.) Darken both of these number-letter combinations on your answer sheet. (Pause 10 seconds.)

Examine Sample 9. (Pause 2-3 seconds.) Each of the figures shown represents the average time required by five different carriers to sort 1 foot of mail comprising both letters and flats. (Pause 2 seconds.) Go to number 88 on your answer sheet and darken the letter that corresponds to the most efficient carrier. (Pause 5 seconds.) Now, determine which carrier is the slowest and go to number 43 on your answer sheet and darken the corresponding letter. (Pause 5 seconds.)

Examine Sample 10. (Pause 2-3 seconds.) Write the letter A, as in "apple," beneath the second earliest time shown. (Pause 2 seconds.) Look at the minutes after the hour of the same selection, and go to the same number on your answer sheet and darken the same letter you wrote on your sample sheet. (Pause 5 seconds.)

Examine Sample 10 again. (Pause 2-3 seconds.) Write the letter D, as in "dog," beneath the latest time shown. (Pause 2 seconds.) If there is more than an hour's difference between this time and the second latest time given, go to number 61 on your answer sheet and darken the letter C, as in "cat." (Pause 5 seconds.) Otherwise, go to number 3 on your answer sheet and darken the same letter you wrote beneath the latest time sample. (Pause 5 seconds.)

If 13 is less than 12 and 3 is greater than 4, go to number 77 on your answer sheet and darken the letter A, as in "apple." (Pause 5 seconds.) If the preceding statement was only half-true, go to number 74 on your answer sheet and darken the letter D, as in "dog." (Pause 5 seconds.) Otherwise, go to number 77 on your answer sheet and darken the letter E, as in "elephant." (Pause 5 seconds.)

If Monday immediately precedes Sunday, and Tuesday immediately precedes Wednesday, go to number 46 on your answer sheet and darken the letter A, as in "apple." (Pause 5 seconds.) If the statement made was only half-true, go to number 47 on your answer sheet and darken the letter E, as in "elephant." (Pause 5 seconds.) Otherwise, go to number 46 on your answer sheet and darken the letter B, as in "boy." (Pause 5 seconds.)

-END OF TEST-

FOLLOWING DIRECTIONS/EXAM 2 SAMPLES

1.   13_____

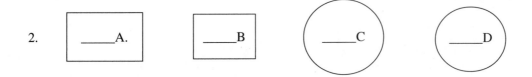

2.

3.   15_____   3_____   30_____   2_____   45_____   1_____

4.

5.

6.   47_____,   _____E,   53_____,   _____D,   62_____

7.   95723   10751   14210   87440

8.

9.   E   D   C   B   A
      18.25   15.72   9.67   24.03   12.60

10.   8:15 AM   9:10 PM   8:15 PM   7:40 PM   7:15 AM
      _____   _____   _____   _____   _____

[This page is intentionally blank.]

ANSWER SHEET TO FOLLOWING DIRECTIONS/EXAM 2

1. (A) (B) (C) (D) (E)   33. (A) (B) (C) (D) (E)   65. (A) (B) (C) (D) (E)
2. (A) (B) (C) (D) (E)   34. (A) (B) (C) (D) (E)   66. (A) (B) (C) (D) (E)
3. (A) (B) (C) (D) (E)   35. (A) (B) (C) (D) (E)   67. (A) (B) (C) (D) (E)
4. (A) (B) (C) (D) (E)   36. (A) (B) (C) (D) (E)   68. (A) (B) (C) (D) (E)
5. (A) (B) (C) (D) (E)   37. (A) (B) (C) (D) (E)   69. (A) (B) (C) (D) (E)
6. (A) (B) (C) (D) (E)   38. (A) (B) (C) (D) (E)   70. (A) (B) (C) (D) (E)
7. (A) (B) (C) (D) (E)   39. (A) (B) (C) (D) (E)   71. (A) (B) (C) (D) (E)
8. (A) (B) (C) (D) (E)   40. (A) (B) (C) (D) (E)   72. (A) (B) (C) (D) (E)
9. (A) (B) (C) (D) (E)   41. (A) (B) (C) (D) (E)   73. (A) (B) (C) (D) (E)
10. (A) (B) (C) (D) (E)   42. (A) (B) (C) (D) (E)   74. (A) (B) (C) (D) (E)
11. (A) (B) (C) (D) (E)   43. (A) (B) (C) (D) (E)   75. (A) (B) (C) (D) (E)
12. (A) (B) (C) (D) (E)   44. (A) (B) (C) (D) (E)   76. (A) (B) (C) (D) (E)
13. (A) (B) (C) (D) (E)   45. (A) (B) (C) (D) (E)   77. (A) (B) (C) (D) (E)
14. (A) (B) (C) (D) (E)   46. (A) (B) (C) (D) (E)   78. (A) (B) (C) (D) (E)
15. (A) (B) (C) (D) (E)   47. (A) (B) (C) (D) (E)   79. (A) (B) (C) (D) (E)
16. (A) (B) (C) (D) (E)   48. (A) (B) (C) (D) (E)   80. (A) (B) (C) (D) (E)
17. (A) (B) (C) (D) (E)   49. (A) (B) (C) (D) (E)   81. (A) (B) (C) (D) (E)
18. (A) (B) (C) (D) (E)   50. (A) (B) (C) (D) (E)   82. (A) (B) (C) (D) (E)
19. (A) (B) (C) (D) (E)   51. (A) (B) (C) (D) (E)   83. (A) (B) (C) (D) (E)
20. (A) (B) (C) (D) (E)   52. (A) (B) (C) (D) (E)   84. (A) (B) (C) (D) (E)
21. (A) (B) (C) (D) (E)   53. (A) (B) (C) (D) (E)   85. (A) (B) (C) (D) (E)
22. (A) (B) (C) (D) (E)   54. (A) (B) (C) (D) (E)   86. (A) (B) (C) (D) (E)
23. (A) (B) (C) (D) (E)   55. (A) (B) (C) (D) (E)   87. (A) (B) (C) (D) (E)
24. (A) (B) (C) (D) (E)   56. (A) (B) (C) (D) (E)   88. (A) (B) (C) (D) (E)
25. (A) (B) (C) (D) (E)   57. (A) (B) (C) (D) (E)   89. (A) (B) (C) (D) (E)
26. (A) (B) (C) (D) (E)   58. (A) (B) (C) (D) (E)   90. (A) (B) (C) (D) (E)
27. (A) (B) (C) (D) (E)   59. (A) (B) (C) (D) (E)   91. (A) (B) (C) (D) (E)
28. (A) (B) (C) (D) (E)   60. (A) (B) (C) (D) (E)   92. (A) (B) (C) (D) (E)
29. (A) (B) (C) (D) (E)   61. (A) (B) (C) (D) (E)   93. (A) (B) (C) (D) (E)
30. (A) (B) (C) (D) (E)   62. (A) (B) (C) (D) (E)   94. (A) (B) (C) (D) (E)
31. (A) (B) (C) (D) (E)   63. (A) (B) (C) (D) (E)   95. (A) (B) (C) (D) (E)
32. (A) (B) (C) (D) (E)   64. (A) (B) (C) (D) (E)

[This page may be removed to mark answers.]

[This page is intentionally blank.]

ANSWERS TO ADDRESS CROSS COMPARISON/EXAM 2

1.	D	33.	A	65.	D
2.	D	34.	A	66.	D
3.	A	35.	D	67.	D
4.	D	36.	A	68.	D
5.	D	37.	D	69.	A
6.	A	38.	D	70.	D
7.	D	39.	D	71.	A
8.	D	40.	D	72.	D
9.	A	41.	D	73.	D
10.	D	42.	D	74.	D
11.	D	43.	D	75.	A
12.	D	44.	D	76.	D
13.	D	45.	A	77.	D
14.	D	46.	D	78.	D
15.	D	47.	D	79.	D
16.	A	48.	D	80.	D
17.	D	49.	D	81.	A
18.	D	50.	D	82.	D
19.	A	51.	A	83.	D
20.	D	52.	D	84.	D
21.	D	53.	D	85.	A
22.	A	54.	D	86.	D
23.	D	55.	D	87.	D
24.	A	56.	D	88.	D
25.	A	57.	D	89.	A
26.	D	58.	A	90.	D
27.	D	59.	A	91.	A
28.	A	60.	D	92.	D
29.	D	61.	A	93.	D
30.	D	62.	D	94.	A
31.	A	63.	D	95.	D
32.	D	64.	A		

ANSWERS TO MEMORIZATION/EXAM 2

1.	E	31.	E	61.	C
2.	D	32.	B	62.	E
3.	C	33.	A	63.	A
4.	B	34.	A	64.	A
5.	D	35.	C	65.	B
6.	A	36.	A	66.	A
7.	E	37.	E	67.	C
8.	C	38.	B	68.	E
9.	B	39.	E	69.	B
10.	D	40.	C	70.	B
11.	E	41.	D	71.	E
12.	A	42.	A	72.	D
13.	A	43.	D	73.	C
14.	E	44.	C	74.	D
15.	D	45.	E	75.	C
16.	B	46.	D	76.	B
17.	C	47.	E	77.	A
18.	C	48.	B	78.	B
19.	A	49.	A	79.	E
20.	D	50.	B	80.	D
21.	E	51.	D	81.	C
22.	C	52.	E	82.	A
23.	B	53.	E	83.	B
24.	B	54.	C	84.	A
25.	A	55.	B	85.	E
26.	C	56.	B	86.	D
27.	D	57.	D	87.	D
28.	D	58.	D	88.	C
29.	B	59.	A		
30.	C	60.	A		

ANSWERS TO NUMBER SERIES/EXAM 2

1. B.

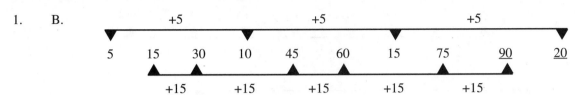

2. C.

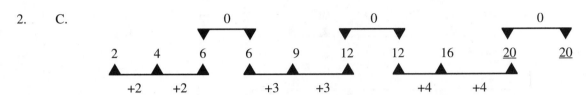

3. A.

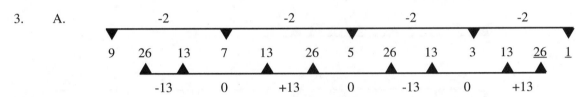

4. D.

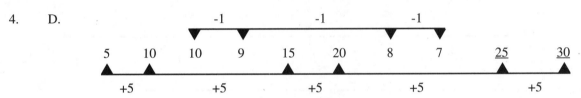

5. E.

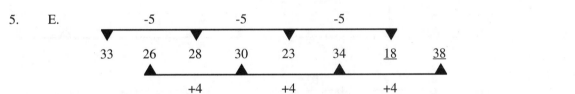

6. E.

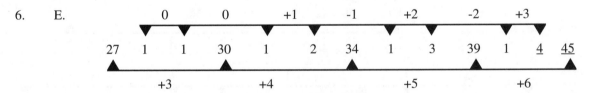

7. C.

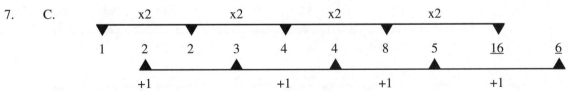

8. A.

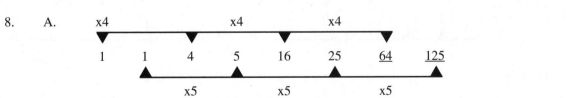

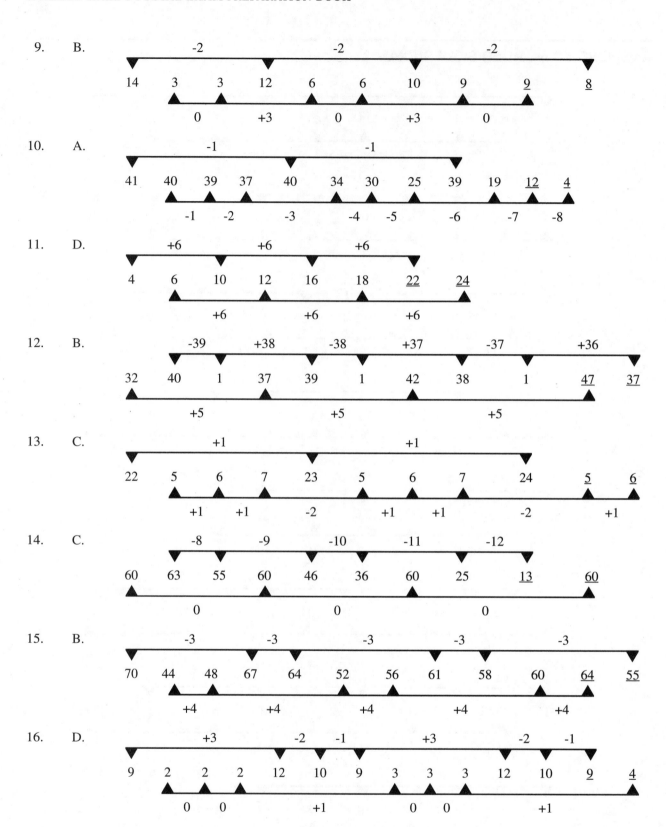

9.   B.

10.   A.

11.   D.

12.   B.

13.   C.

14.   C.

15.   B.

16.   D.

17. E.

x3   x3   x3   x3

1 0 5 3 0 6 9 0 7 27 0 8 81

+5 -5 +6 -6 +7 -7 +8

18. A.

-2   -2   -2   -2

42 37 40 37 38 38 37 38 39 36 37 38 39 40 34

0 (+1) -1 (+1 +1) -2 (+1 +1 +1)

19. D.

+1 -1 +1 +1 -1 +1 +1 -1

12 14 15 14 14 15 16 15 16 16 17 16 18

+2   +2   +2

20. A.

0   0 0   0 0 0

2 4 4 6 6 6 8 8 8 8

+2   +2   +2

21. C.

+2 +3 +4 +5 +6 +7

0 55 57 60 10 64 69 75 20 82

+10   +10

22. E.

-3 -5 -3 -5 -3

25 26 23 23 18 15 21 10 7 19

-2   -2   -2

23. E.

-7   -7   -7

21 7 7 14 14 14 7 21 21 0

0 +7 0 +7 0

24. A.

0   0   0

12 30 32 28 12 40 42 38 12 50 52 48 12 60 62 58

+2 -4 +12 +2 -4 +12 +2 -4 +12 +2 -4

ANSWERS TO FOLLOWING DIRECTIONS/EXAM 2

1.	13 E	10.	73 C	19.	91 B
2.	8 D	11.	19 A	20.	88 C
3.	80 C	12.	63 D	21.	43 B
4.	71 E	13.	56 D	22.	15 A
5.	2 B	14.	39 B	23.	3 D
6.	27 B	15.	38 B	24.	77 E
7.	30 C	16.	93 A	25.	47 E
8.	1 D	17.	7 C		
9.	69 E	18.	16 E		

To determine your performance on this exam, add the number of correct answers from each of the four sections of the test. Subtract from this total the number of incorrect answers from the Address Cross Comparison section. Ratings have been provided below to determine your overall standing.

225–232 correct, you have an excellent score.
208–224 correct, you have a good score.
207 or fewer correct requires more practice.

PART II
Examination 473

[This page is intentionally blank.]

Examination 473

The Postal Service, just like any other employer, desires to hire the best qualified applicants that are available in the current job market. Up until recently, the 470 test was offered to applicants. If a high enough test score was achieved, an oral interview would follow. Employment consideration was conditional on the outcome of the two (2) part screening process. That system was successfully used for many years; however, intra-agency studies indicated that personality profiling offered helpful insight toward an individual's potential work performance. Consequently, Exam 470 was replaced by Exam 473. This new exam is now how applicants apply for the positions of city carrier; mail handler; mail processing clerk; and sales, services, and distribution associate. For the time being, exam 460 will continue to be used for rural carrier associate testing.

Exam 473 is a five-part test that bears similarity to its predecessor (e.g., sections on address cross comparison and memory.) The distinctive differences involve forms completion, coding, and personality profiling. With the exception of personality profiling, the remaining four test sections will be elaborated on and followed by full-length practice exercises. Tips and effective short cuts to help you achieve high-test scores for each of these areas will be discussed. To give you a true sense of how the actual exam is submitted, practice exams have been provided along with applicable timetables. Be sure to abide by the time allowances given for proper test preparation.

Personality profiling, which addresses your work experience and personal character, has been purposefully set apart from the practice exercises. It is not for the lack of importance that this section has been left as a closing chapter to this book. Quite the contrary: over half the test questions on test 473 focus on this area. A representative sample consisting of 100 questions should provide a thorough picture of what to expect. These types of questions can be thought-provoking about how you see yourself interact with co-workers or react to various situations. Truthful responses are required on your behalf to lend credible insight into who you are as an individual. Because each of us has different backgrounds and personalities, responses to these questions will be quite varied. Therefore, it is a misnomer to think there are absolute right or wrong answers on this section. The composite of your responses, however, will be assessed and used in determining your potential for being hired by the Postal Service. See the chapter under Personality Profiling for further information about this aspect of the exam.

Address Cross Comparison

The first section of this exam involves comparing two lists of various street addresses and zip codes. If the combination of street address and zip codes were identical, selection A for NO ERRORS would be marked on the answer sheet. If the street addresses on both lists differ but the zip codes are identical selection B for STREET ADDRESS ONLY would be marked on the answer sheet. If the street addresses are identical on both lists, but the zip codes are different, then selection C for ZIP CODE ONLY would be marked on the answer sheet. If neither street address nor zip codes on both lists reconcile, then option D for BOTH would be marked accordingly. Below are sample exercises of what to expect on the examination.

ANSWER KEY:

A) NO ERRORS
B) STREET ADDRESS ONLY
C) ZIP CODE ONLY
D) BOTH

1. 1619 W. 40TH AVE.
    SAN DIEGO, CA   99721   1619 W. 40TH AVE.
                                                    SAN DIEGO, CA   99721

2. 9592 S. TRICIA LN.
    AKRON, OH   39582   9529 S. TRICIA LN.
                                                    AKRON, OH   39852

3. 205-C EDGEMONT PL.
    SPARKS, NV   80721-3721   205-C EDGEMONT DR.
                                                    SPARKS, NV   80721-3721

4. 38019 E. BUCKTHORNE CT.
    DES MOINES, IA   50075   38019 E. BUCKTHORNE CT.
                                                    DES MOINES, IA   50705

Question 1 shows that both address and zip codes are identical; therefore, selection **A NO ERRORS** would be marked on number 1 of your answer sheet.

Question 2 on the other hand, shows that both the street address and zip codes are different. Answer **D BOTH** would be marked on the answer sheet.

Question 3 shows a difference in the street addresses only but the zip codes are identical. In this case, Answer **B STREET ADDRESS ONLY** would be marked for question 3 on the answer sheet.

Question 4 has identical street addresses but different zip codes. Therefore, selection **C ZIP CODE ONLY** would be marked on the answer sheet.

Sample answer sheet with the correct answers filled in.

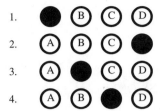

On the actual examination, you will have 11 minutes to compare sixty sets of addresses and zip codes. At first appearance this may seem like a simple exercise; however, many people will have a difficult time finishing this test because of time constraints. One way to save significant time is to become very familiar with the layout of the answer key. By thoroughly knowing what selections A-D represent you will not have to keep referring back to the key to select the answer and then find the corresponding answer blank on your answer sheet. With enough practice, you should be able to decide quickly the correct answer without the need to review the answer key. This is a proven technique that does save time and minimizes the prospect of incorrectly marked answers.

Another bit of helpful advice is to compare small blocks of information at a time. Rapid eye movement between limited bits of information allows for instantaneous comparisons and quick recognition of any differences. For example, you would break down the following comparisons accordingly:

1619 W. 40TH AVE.   1619 W. 40TH AVE.

SAN DIEGO, CA   99721   SAN DIEGO, CA   99721

1619 W. --- 1619 W.
40TH AVE. --- 40TH AVE.
SAN DIEGO, CA ---------------------------------- SAN DIEGO, CA
997 --- 997
21--- 21

The simplicity of this system should prevent you from inadvertently overlooking transposed numbers or subtle misspellings. Along these same lines, you need to train yourself to stop immediately from further comparing the street address if a difference becomes apparent. Let us say, for example, 1619 W. does not match 1691 W. At this point, there is little point in even looking at the rest of the street address. You should immediately switch your attention to the zip code and move on. This automatic response can be refined with practice. Without doubt, it will save you precious time.

As you work through each of the exercises provided, be careful not to lose your place on the answer sheet. If you do, you will inadvertently mark your answer for the wrong question, and your answers will be off for the remainder of the exam. Stay focused on the correct question and answer you are working on. It will help to use your index finger and little finger as points of references. Move them in unison down the address lists as you work through the questions. That way you will have less of a chance to lose your place as you are working through the exam. One last note of caution: All too often, people tend to guess at some answers if they feel there will not be enough time to complete the test. Accuracy is very important because you are penalized for wrong answers. One third of the incorrect answers are subtracted from your correct selection. The bottom line is that guessing is not advantageous. Below is an abbreviated work sheet to give you a general idea of how these exams are conducted. Give yourself 4 minutes to compare the twenty-five addresses and zip codes provided and mark your answers accordingly. To check your accuracy, the correct answers are at the end of the exercise.

ADDRESS CROSS COMPARISON SAMPLE

ANSWER KEY:

A) NO ERRORS
B) STREET ADDRESS ONLY
C) ZIP CODE ONLY
D) BOTH

1. 2121 SOUTH HAMPTON   2112 SOUTH HAMPTON
    COLUMBUS, OH   43185   COLUMBUS, OH   43185

2. 18-C BLACK HAWK CT.   18-C BLACK HAWK CT.
    STATESVILLE, NY   28561   STATESVILLE, NM   28561

3. 9021 FLAMINGO DR.   9021 FLAMINGO DR.
    HENDERSON, NV   89701-1611 HENDERSON, NV   89701-1611

4. 3312 ABBEYVILLE BLVD   3312 ABBOTSVILLE BLVD
    BUFFALO, NY   41521-1378 BUFFALO, NY   14512-1378

5. A-149 BIRCH BLVD   A-149 BIRCH BLVD
    NASHVILLE, TN   38714   NASHVILLE, KY   38741

6. 10371 BRIDLBROOK WAY   10317 BRIDELBROOK WAY
    FORT WORTH, TX   71625-4038 FORT WORTH, TX   71625-4038

7. 5751 GREEN WILLOW TRAIL   5751 GREEN WILLOW TRAIL
    LEESBURG, VA   12006   LEESBURG, VA   12060

8. BOX 162, STATE HWY 29   BOX 162, STATE RT 29
    PLANO, TX   76419   PLANO, TX   71694

9. 1313 SALIDA LN   1313 SALIDA LN
    FLORENCE, SC   29057-3500 FLORENCE, SC   29057-3500

10. 12 MONTROSE AVE   12 MONTROSE AVE
    WOODSTOCK, OH   44497   WOODSTOCK, OH   44497

11. 9307 ROSESMITH DR   9307 ROSESMITH DR
    NEWARK, NJ   09712-0571 NEWARK, NE   09217-0571

12. 902 DEERBLUFF PLACE   902 DEERBLUFF PLACE
    ROCHESTER, NY   16497-5608 ROTHCHESTER, NY   16497-5608

13. D-705 FERGUSON CR.   D-705 FERGUSON CR.
    LEESBURG, NM   84071   LEESBURG, NM   80471

14.	6161 HAVENCREST RD. BEAVERTON, OR 82617	6161 HAVENCREST RD. BEAVERTON, OR 82167
15.	50 ELDRIDGE PLACE ABINGDON, VA 24412	50 ELDRIDGE PLACE ABINGTON, VA 24412
16.	30117 GRANDSVILLE PL. GREENWICH, CT 08157-7997	30117 GRANDSVILLE PL. GREENWICH, CT 08157-7997
17.	4072 PATRICK ST. APT 101 SAN MATEO, CA 95409-0302	4027 PATRICK ST. APT 101 SAN MATEO, CA 95490-0302
18.	91 ERICSON WAY BELLA VISTA, AR 77214	91 ERIKSON WAY BELLA VISTA, AR 77214
19.	2000 PATRICK CIRCLE TUSCALOOSA, AL 34571	2000 PATRICK CIRCLE N. TUSCALOOSA, AL 34571-6219
20.	4949 S. FAIRMONT DR. WICHITA, KS 67018-1300	4949 S. FAIRMONT CT. WICHITA, KS 67018-3100
21.	700-L CLARE ST. INDIANAPOLIS, IN 42671-1584	700-L S. CLEAR ST. INDIANAPOLIS, IN 42671-1584
22.	14 CEDAR PARK DR. VALDOSTA, GA 37159	14 CEDAR PARK DR. VALDOSTA, GA 37519
23.	13599 NELLIS BLVD CHICAGO, IL 60069-1409	13599 NELLIS BLVD CHICAGO, IL 60069-1409
24.	3060 RAINBOW DR. IDAHO FALLS, ID 83715	3060 RAINBOW CR IDAHO FALL, ID 83715
25.	12792 CENTRAL AVE. BALTIMORE, MD 12257-6789	12792 CENTRAL AVE. BALTIMORE, MD 22157-6789

SAMPLE ANSWER SHEET

1. Ⓐ Ⓑ Ⓒ Ⓓ 9. Ⓐ Ⓑ Ⓒ Ⓓ 17. Ⓐ Ⓑ Ⓒ Ⓓ
2. Ⓐ Ⓑ Ⓒ Ⓓ 10. Ⓐ Ⓑ Ⓒ Ⓓ 18. Ⓐ Ⓑ Ⓒ Ⓓ
3. Ⓐ Ⓑ Ⓒ Ⓓ 11. Ⓐ Ⓑ Ⓒ Ⓓ 19. Ⓐ Ⓑ Ⓒ Ⓓ
4. Ⓐ Ⓑ Ⓒ Ⓓ 12. Ⓐ Ⓑ Ⓒ Ⓓ 20. Ⓐ Ⓑ Ⓒ Ⓓ
5. Ⓐ Ⓑ Ⓒ Ⓓ 13. Ⓐ Ⓑ Ⓒ Ⓓ 21. Ⓐ Ⓑ Ⓒ Ⓓ
6. Ⓐ Ⓑ Ⓒ Ⓓ 14. Ⓐ Ⓑ Ⓒ Ⓓ 22. Ⓐ Ⓑ Ⓒ Ⓓ
7. Ⓐ Ⓑ Ⓒ Ⓓ 15. Ⓐ Ⓑ Ⓒ Ⓓ 23. Ⓐ Ⓑ Ⓒ Ⓓ
8. Ⓐ Ⓑ Ⓒ Ⓓ 16. Ⓐ Ⓑ Ⓒ Ⓓ 24. Ⓐ Ⓑ Ⓒ Ⓓ
                              25. Ⓐ Ⓑ Ⓒ Ⓓ

ANSWERS FOR THE ABOVE EXERCISE ARE AS FOLLOWS:

1. B   14. C
2. B   15. B
3. A   16. A
4. D   17. D
5. D   18. B
6. B   19. D
7. C   20. D
8. D   21. B
9. A   22. C
10. A   23. A
11. D   24. B
12. B   25. C
13. C

If you scored:
23 or more correct answers, you have an excellent score.
19–22 correct answers, you have a good score.
18 or fewer correct answers, you need more practice.

ADDRESS CROSS COMPARISON EXERCISE 1   TIME: 11 MINUTES

ANSWER KEY:

(A) NO ERRORS
(B) STREET ADDRESS ONLY
(C) ZIP CODE ONLY
(D) BOTH

#					
1.	167801 DECATUR RD. COLUMBIA, SC	22901	16801 DECATUR RD. COLUMBIA, SC	22901	
2.	147 REGATTA DRIVE KNOXVILLE, TN	31729-1442	147 REGATTA DRIVE KNOXVILLE, TN	31729-1442	
3.	1580 N.W. MCKENZIE LN. HERSHEY, PA	16909-1609	1580 N.W. MCKENZIE LN. HERSHEY, PA	16909-1906	
4.	109 SW HWY 198 COLBY, NY	14712	198 NW HWY 198 COLBY, NY	14712	
5.	1708 MENDENHALL DR COLUMBUS, OH	52218-1506	1807 MENDENHALL DR COLUMBUS, SC	52281-1506	
6.	99 CHEROKEE RD APT 130-B SCOTTSBLUFF, NE	61046	99 CHEROKEE RD APT 130-B SCOTTSDALE, AZ	61046	
7.	5000 DEAVERMONT AVE. NASHUA, NH	30062	5000 DEVERMONT AVE. NASHUA, NH	30062	
8.	1612 CENTER POINT WAY OMAHA, NE	63812-1621	1621 CENTER POINT WAY OMAHA, NE	63182-1621	
9.	2600 N. MONTE CRISTO WAY WEST CHESTER, PA	24160-1005	2600 N. MONTE CRISTO WAY WEST CHESTER, PA	24106-1005	
10.	4000 E. BONANZA RD. LAS VEGAS, NV	91285	4000 E. BONANZA RD. LAS VEGAS, NV	91285	
11.	1777 S. 7TH ST. TUSCALOOSA, AL	37051-1222	1777 S. 7TH DR. TUSCALOOSA, AL	37051-1222	
12.	12 KINGSPARK CT SAN JOSE, CA	92516	12 KINGSPARK CT SAN JOSE, CA	92056	
13.	14455 E. WISTERIA PLACE NAMPA, ID	86720-1544	14455 E. WISTERIA PLACE NAMPA, ID	87620-1544	

14. 18 W. FORT APACHE
CARMEL, IN   40360

    18 W. FORT APACHE
    CARMEL, IN   40360

15. 2020 CUNNINGHAM RD.
BRUNSWICK, GA   28014

    2020 CUNNINGHAM RD.
    BRUNSWICK, GA   28041

16. 921 S. DECATOR BLVD.
SAINT CHARLES, IL   64035-1115

    921 N. DECATOR BLVD
    SAINT CHARLES, IL   64305-1115

17. 22536 VALLEY CREST BLVD.
TAMPA. FL   37362-1217

    22536 VALLEY CREST BLVD.
    TAMPA, FL   37362-1217

18. 16-C ABBOTSTON ST.
BALTIMORE, MD   12300

    16-C ABBOTSTON ST.
    BALTIMORE, MD   23100

19. 3554 VIEW SPRING DR.
MERIDIAN, ID   84712-5521

    3354 VIEW SPRING DR.
    MERIDIAN, ID   84712-5521

20. 10-F PINEWOOD CT
DURHAM, NC   21856-6677

    10-F PINEWOOD CT
    DURHAM, NC   21856-7766

21. 2007 MIRABELLE CIRCLE
CANTON, OH   40023

    3007 MIRABELLE CIRCLE
    CANTON, OH   40203

22. 8 SHELLY HURST RD.
GREENWOOD, IN   47200-5888

    8 SHELLEY HURST RD.
    GREENWOOD, IN   47200-5888

23. 1089 SE SAHARA PL
PALM SPRINGS, FL   30127-1089

    1089 SE SAHARA PL
    PALM SPRINGS, FL   30127-1089

24. 155 BALLANTYNE AVE
PHOENIX, AZ   85211

    155 BAILANTYNE AVE
    PHOENIX, AZ   85211

25. 11 SILVERMOON TRAIL
PUEBLO, CO   81113

    11 SILVERMAN TRAIL
    PUEBLO, CO   83113

26. 14761 S. HILDAGO POINT
TERRE HAUTE, IN   48777

    14761 S. HILDAGO POINT
    TERRE HAUTE, IN   48766

27. 32 YORKSHIRE CT APT C-35
ANNAPOLIS, MD   20051-6035

    32 YORKSHIRE CT APT C-35
    ANNAPOLIS, MD   20051-6035

28. 270 HARBOR VIEW TERRACE
FAYETTEVILLE, AR   46632-2071

    270 HARBOR VIEW TERRACE
    FAYETTEVILLE, AR   46632-2017

29. 3999 W. POLARIS ST.
SELMA, AL   37605

    3399 W. POLARES ST.
    SELMA, AL   37605

30. 15-A SHUQUALAK BLVD
PANAMA CITY, FL   31241-7815

    15-A SUEQUALAK BLVD
    PANAMA CITY, FL   31241-7815

31.	21541 DERBY ROAD TROY, NY 13805-1600	21541 DERBY ROAD. TROY, KY 13850-1600
32.	805 UNDERWOOD DR. SYRACUSE, NY 15868-2310	805 UNDERWOOD DR. SYRACUSE, NY 15886-2310
33.	1600 COUNTRY LANE WARREN, OH 45413	1600 COUNTRY LANE WARREN, OH 45413
34.	1813 W. HORIZON RIDGE SALEM, NC 20705	1813 W. HORIZON RIDGE SALEM, NC 20705
35.	15016 E. MINTER ROAD DES MOINES, IA 97617-4521	15106 E. MINTER ROAD DES MOINES, IA 97617-4521
36.	430 N. WASATCH DR. WICHITA FALLS, TX 69477	430 N. WASATCH DR. WICHITA FALLS, TX 64977
37.	10-E FORKS VISTA BLVD SALT LAKE CITY, UT 80214	10-E FORKS VIEW BLVD SALE LAKE CITY, UT 80241
38.	1670 CHERRY BLOSSOM LN CLEVELAND, OH 45971-4000	1670 CHERRY BLOSSOM LN CLEVELAND, OH 45971-4000
39.	147 SW PASSPORT AVE READING, PA 28471-4511	147 SE PASPORT AVE READING, PA 45411-1937
40.	1580 HINSON CENTER A-103 HAMPTON, NC 22657	1580 HINSON CENTER A-103 HAMPTON, NC 22657
41.	157 NW TOWNE CENTER MISSOURI CITY, TX 71749	157 NW TOWN CENTRE MISSOURI CITY, MO 71749
42.	18552 ARROWHEAD WAY GLEN ALLEN, WV 23157-1510	18552 ARROWHEAD WAY GLEN ALLYN, WV 23157-1510
43.	17805 NE HWY 257 JACKSON HOLE, WY 52715	17805 NE HWY 257 JACKSON HOLE, WY 52715
44.	123 N 9TH STREET MARYVILLE, TN 38712-1105	123 N 90TH STREET MARYVILLE, TN 38712-1015
45.	17-A MOUNTAIN VIEW RD PITTSBURGH, PA 15299-4012	17-A MOUNTAIN VIEW CT PITTSBURGH, PA 15299-4012
46.	911 RIO GRANDE AVE HENDERSONVILLE, NC	911 RIO GRANDE AVE 28610 HENDERSONVILLE, NC 26810
47.	189-D NW INDUSTRIAL RD ALANTIC CITY, NJ 04801	198-D NW INDUSTRIAL RD ATLANTIC CITY, NJ 04801

48.	1219 SW MANCHESTER BLVD STATEN ISLAND, NY 13051-1021	1219 SW MANCHESTER BLVD STATEN ISLAND, NY 13051-1021
49.	14701 S. CYPRESS DR. ALBANY, NY 10001-1472	14701 S. CYPRESS DR. STATEN ISLAND, NY 10001-1472
50.	1850 PRINCETON BLVD LARAMIE, WY 65156	1850 PRINCETON BLVD LARAMIE, WY 65165
51.	13 S. MADISON AVE LA CROSSE, WI 33551	13 S. MADISON AVE LA CROSSE, WI 32551
52.	4444 N. WATER ST. RICHMOND, VA 22398	4444 N. WATER ST. RICHMOND, VA 22398
53.	170 PECOS RD. EL CAJON, CA 94015-6711	170 PECOS RD. EL CAJON, CA 94015-6711
54.	1810 CHATEAU AVE WALNUT CREEK, CA 90571	18100 CHATEAU AVE WALNUT CREEK, CA 09571
55.	D-4091 CALLESTOGA PKWY DELRAY BEACH, FL 37215	D-4091 CALESTOGA BLVD DELRAY BEACH, FL 30251
56.	697 GARDENIA LANE OAK PARK, IL 60937-4017	692 GARDENIA LANE OAK PARK, IL 90637-4017
57.	4710 W. SYCAMORE DR. COMMERCE, GA 39157	4710 W. SYCAMORE DR. COMMERCE, GA 39157
58.	168-R HACIENDA DR. PALM DESERT, CA 91215	168-R HACIENDA DR. PALM SPRINGS, CA 91215
59.	18300 NW 8TH AVE APT C LONGMONT, CO 81023-3001	381800 NW 8TH AVE APT C LONGMONT, CO 81123-3001
60.	7-B CYPRESS LN ATLANTA, GA 30511-7102	708 CYPRESS LN ATLANTA, GA 50311-7102

ANSWER SHEET TO ADDRESS CROSS COMPARISON EXERCISE 1

1. Ⓐ Ⓑ Ⓒ Ⓓ   21. Ⓐ Ⓑ Ⓒ Ⓓ   41. Ⓐ Ⓑ Ⓒ Ⓓ
2. Ⓐ Ⓑ Ⓒ Ⓓ   22. Ⓐ Ⓑ Ⓒ Ⓓ   42. Ⓐ Ⓑ Ⓒ Ⓓ
3. Ⓐ Ⓑ Ⓒ Ⓓ   23. Ⓐ Ⓑ Ⓒ Ⓓ   43. Ⓐ Ⓑ Ⓒ Ⓓ
4. Ⓐ Ⓑ Ⓒ Ⓓ   24. Ⓐ Ⓑ Ⓒ Ⓓ   44. Ⓐ Ⓑ Ⓒ Ⓓ
5. Ⓐ Ⓑ Ⓒ Ⓓ   25. Ⓐ Ⓑ Ⓒ Ⓓ   45. Ⓐ Ⓑ Ⓒ Ⓓ
6. Ⓐ Ⓑ Ⓒ Ⓓ   26. Ⓐ Ⓑ Ⓒ Ⓓ   46. Ⓐ Ⓑ Ⓒ Ⓓ
7. Ⓐ Ⓑ Ⓒ Ⓓ   27. Ⓐ Ⓑ Ⓒ Ⓓ   47. Ⓐ Ⓑ Ⓒ Ⓓ
8. Ⓐ Ⓑ Ⓒ Ⓓ   28. Ⓐ Ⓑ Ⓒ Ⓓ   48. Ⓐ Ⓑ Ⓒ Ⓓ
9. Ⓐ Ⓑ Ⓒ Ⓓ   29. Ⓐ Ⓑ Ⓒ Ⓓ   49. Ⓐ Ⓑ Ⓒ Ⓓ
10. Ⓐ Ⓑ Ⓒ Ⓓ   30. Ⓐ Ⓑ Ⓒ Ⓓ   50. Ⓐ Ⓑ Ⓒ Ⓓ
11. Ⓐ Ⓑ Ⓒ Ⓓ   31. Ⓐ Ⓑ Ⓒ Ⓓ   51. Ⓐ Ⓑ Ⓒ Ⓓ
12. Ⓐ Ⓑ Ⓒ Ⓓ   32. Ⓐ Ⓑ Ⓒ Ⓓ   52. Ⓐ Ⓑ Ⓒ Ⓓ
13. Ⓐ Ⓑ Ⓒ Ⓓ   33. Ⓐ Ⓑ Ⓒ Ⓓ   53. Ⓐ Ⓑ Ⓒ Ⓓ
14. Ⓐ Ⓑ Ⓒ Ⓓ   34. Ⓐ Ⓑ Ⓒ Ⓓ   54. Ⓐ Ⓑ Ⓒ Ⓓ
15. Ⓐ Ⓑ Ⓒ Ⓓ   35. Ⓐ Ⓑ Ⓒ Ⓓ   55. Ⓐ Ⓑ Ⓒ Ⓓ
16. Ⓐ Ⓑ Ⓒ Ⓓ   36. Ⓐ Ⓑ Ⓒ Ⓓ   56. Ⓐ Ⓑ Ⓒ Ⓓ
17. Ⓐ Ⓑ Ⓒ Ⓓ   37. Ⓐ Ⓑ Ⓒ Ⓓ   57. Ⓐ Ⓑ Ⓒ Ⓓ
18. Ⓐ Ⓑ Ⓒ Ⓓ   38. Ⓐ Ⓑ Ⓒ Ⓓ   58. Ⓐ Ⓑ Ⓒ Ⓓ
19. Ⓐ Ⓑ Ⓒ Ⓓ   39. Ⓐ Ⓑ Ⓒ Ⓓ   59. Ⓐ Ⓑ Ⓒ Ⓓ
20. Ⓐ Ⓑ Ⓒ Ⓓ   40. Ⓐ Ⓑ Ⓒ Ⓓ   60. Ⓐ Ⓑ Ⓒ Ⓓ

[This page may be removed to mark answers.]

ANSWERS TO ADDRESS CROSS COMPARISON EXERCISE 1

1.	B	21.	D	41.	B
2.	A	22.	B	42.	B
3.	C	23.	A	43.	A
4.	B	24.	B	44.	D
5.	D	25.	D	45.	B
6.	B	26.	C	46.	C
7.	B	27.	A	47.	B
8.	D	28.	C	48.	A
9.	C	29.	B	49.	B
10.	A	30.	B	50.	C
11.	B	31.	D	51.	C
12.	C	32.	C	52.	A
13.	C	33.	A	53.	A
14.	A	34.	A	54.	D
15.	C	35.	B	55.	D
16.	D	36.	C	56.	D
17.	A	37.	D	57.	A
18.	C	38.	A	58.	B
19.	B	39.	D	59.	D
20.	C	40.	A	60.	D

If you scored:
56–60 correct, you have an excellent score.
52–55 correct answers, you have a good score.
51 or fewer, more practice is needed.

ADDRESS CROSS COMPARISON EXERCISE 2   TIME: 11 MINUTES

ANSWER KEY:

A) NO ERRORS
B) STREET ADDRESS ONLY
C) ZIP CODE ONLY
D) BOTH

1.	157 HERSTAD BLVD IDAHO FALLS, ID 84301	157 HERSTEAD AVE IDAHO FALLS, ID 84301
2.	1672 PASEO DEL PRADO PANAMA CITY, FL 34201	1672 PASEO DEL PRADO PANAMA CITY, FL 34201
3.	47-C FREMONT PL. TALLAHASSEE, FL 34562-1719	47-C FREMONT PL. TALLAHASSEE, FL 34562-1719
4.	4101 CAPITAL MEDICAL BLDG AURORA, CO 81105-0180	4101 CAPITOL MEDICAL BLDG AURORA, CO 81105-0180
5.	16057 BRADFORD CT SILVER SPRINGS, MD 20342-7152	16057 BRADFORD CT SILVER SPINGS, MD 20324-7152
6.	705 NASSAU RD LEXINGTON, KY 45051	705 NASSAU RD APT 3 LEXINGTON, KY 40551
7.	623 PRAIRIE KNOLL RD. LONGMONT, CO 81527	623 PRAIRIE KNOLL ST. LONGMONT, CO 81527
8.	1845 HARMON AVE. CHICAGO, IL 66215-4712	1845 HARMAN AVE. CHICAGO, IL 66215-4312
9.	14399 NW 73RD AVE MIAMI, FL 34852-1439	14399 NW 73RD AVE MIAMI, FL 38451-1493
10.	16590 SPRING MOUNTAIN RD. WATERBURY, CT 07176	16590 SPRING MOUNTAIN RD. WATERBURY, CT 07176
11.	170 LAKE MEAD BLVD VISTA, CA 92184-0171	170 LAKE MEADE ST VISTA, CA 92184-0171
12.	C-1450 DURANGO RIDGE MESA, AZ 85712	C-1540 DURANGO RIDGE SE MESA, AZ 80712
13.	14032 WHITE PASS RD COEUR D'ALENE, ID 84210	14032 WHITE PASS RD COEUR D'ALENE, ID 84210

14.	71 SE MONTANA AVE HOMESTEAD, FL	30317-4432	71 SE MONTANA AVE HOMESTEAD, FL	30317-4342	
15.	597 N. SIERRA VISTA REDWOOD CITY, CA	93651-4114	597 N. SERRA VISTA REDWOOD CITY, CA	93654-4114	
16.	4732 GREYSTONE MEADOW ATHENS, AL	36711-4732	4372 GRAYSTONE MEADOW ATHENS, AL	36711-4732	
17.	27-D E. HALIFAX ST. CHANDLER, AZ	84621	27-D E. HALIFAX ST. CHANDLER, AZ	84621	
18.	25712 44TH AVE APT 4 SAN ANTONIO, TX	78562	25712 4TH AVE APT 44 SAN ANTONIO, TX	77856	
19.	12400 56TH PLACE GAFFNEY, SC	23911-7215	21400 56TH PLACE GAFFNEY, SC	32911-7215	
20.	11-A CLINTON RD. MCGREGOR, ND	57832	11-A CLINTON RD. MCCREAGOR, ND	57832	
21.	27620 STATE HWY 2 FALLS CHURCH, NC	20241-0002	27620 STATE HWY 2 FALLS CHURCH, NC	20201-0002	
22.	124 DESSERT INN PLANO, TX	75718-1233	124 DESERT INN PLANO, TX	70718-1233	
23.	A-232 VIEWMONT CT. SIOUX FALLS, SD	58260	A-232 VIEWMONT CT. SIOUX FALLS, SD	52860	
24.	16 NW BLACKBERRY RD. CHESAPEAKE, VA	22099	16 NW BLACKBERRY RD. CHESAPEAKE, VA	22099	
25.	20701 NE 102ND ST NASHVILLE, TN	37021	70201 NE 102ND ST NASHVILLE, TN	37021	
26.	7000 BRIDLEBROOK AVE PITTSBURGH, PA	12513-4210	7000 BRIDLEBROOK AVE PITTSBURGH, PA	12153-4210	
27.	18180 CHARLESTON BLVD. SCRANTON, PA	18052-1507	81818 CHARLESTON BLVD. SCRANTON, PA	10852-1507	
28.	31 GREEN VALLEY DR. PROVIDENCE, RI	02095-7211	13 GREEN VALLEY RD PROVIDENCE, RI	20950-7211	
29.	285 AMBER WAVES HAMILTON, OH	40513	285 AMBER WAVES HAMILTON, OH	40513	
30.	C-109 COLONY CT. BUFFALO, NY	12478-0109	D-109 COLONY CT. BUFFALO, NY	12478-0109	

31.	1670 WOODLEAF LN PORTLAND, OR 97012-5001	1670 WOODLEAF LN PORTLAND, OR 17012-5001	
32.	4040 ZIMMERMAN DR. YOUNGSTOWN, OH 40451	4040 SIMMERMAN DR. YOUNGSTOWN, OH 40451	
33.	703 UNIVERSITY WAY EVANSTON, IL 60211-5712	703 UNIVERSITY WAY EVANSTON, IL 60221-5712	
34.	49 BURMINGHAM DR. MACON, GA 32115	49 BURMINGHAM DR. MACON, GA 32115	
35.	506 CHIPPEWA AVE SAN BERNARDINO, CA 94233	506 CHIPPEWA BLVD SAN BERNARDINO, CA 94233	
36.	731-F BAYBERRY BLVD AURORA, CO 81033	731-F BAYBERRY BLVD AURORA, CA 81033	
37.	123 VAN GUARD WAY COCOA, FL 39211-4710	321 VAN GUARD WAY COCOA, FL 11293-4710	
38.	29914 GOLDEN OAK PKWY STRATFORD, CT 60012	29914 GOLDEN OAK PKWY STRATFORD, CT 60001	
39.	9-L RUSSIAN RIVER AVE. GRAND JUNCTION, CO 85102	9-L RUSHING RIVER AVE. GRAND JUNCTION, CO 85102	
40.	17007 NW 9TH AVE SAN JOSE, CA 91588-4200	17007 NW 10TH AVE SAN JOSE, CA 91588-4200	
41.	17 MILLSTONE WAY LITTLEROCK, AR 72015-0017	71 MILLSTONE WAY LITTLEROCK, AR 72051-0017	
42.	N. BONITO PLAZA D-14 FLAGSTAFF, AZ 80651-4201	N. BONITO PLACE D-14 FLAGSTAFF, AZ 80561-4201	
43.	43 E. CHESAPEAKE BAY ANCHORAGE, AK 99555	43 E. CHESAPEAKE BAY ANCHORAGE, AK 99555	
44.	4015 MOUNT WILSON CT. GARY, IN 46052-1109	4015 MOUNT WILSON ST. GARY, IN 46025-1109	
45.	80 W 24TH PLACE BOLINGBROOK, IL 64044	808 W. 24ND AVE BOLINGBROOK, IL 64044	
46.	3462 FLORENCE BLVD. HUDSON, FL 36451-0714	3462 FLORENCE BLVD. HUDSON, FL 33451-0714	
47.	16-E EMPIRE MESA TORRANCE, CA 95001-6719	16-E EMPRES MESA TORRANCE, CA 95011-6719	

48.	4480 JONES BLVD. ALBERTSVILLE, AL 35900-4017	4480 JONES BLVD. ALBERTSVILLE, AL 35900-4017
49.	290-A GIBSON PLACE OSHKOSH, WI 54099	209-A GIBSON PLACE OSHKOSH, WI 50499
50.	19000 TEXAS STAR DR. CORPUS CHRISTI, TX 73510	1900 TEXAS STAR DR. CORPUS CHRISTI, TX 73510
51.	104 OLD TOWN CENTER RD POTTSTOWN, PA 19564	104 NEW TOWN CENTER RD POTTSTOWN, PA 19564
52.	1503 SW YARNELL PL PORTLAND, OR 97200-1521	15030 SW YARNELL PL PORTLAND, OR 97200-1521
53.	13299 SE 43RD ST. MEMPHIS, TN 38110-2999	13299 SE 43RD ST. MEMPHIS, TN 38111-2999
54.	249 SPANISH RIDGE ARLINGTON, TX 76605	249 SPANISH RIDGE ARLINGTON, TX 76605
55.	15690 GARDEN PL. PROVIDENCE, RI 02900	16590 GARDEN PL. PROVIDENCE, RI 02900
56.	F-157 ASPENDALE CT. NEW CASTLE, PA 16002	F-157 ASPANDALE CT. NEW CASTLE, PA 16002
57.	8160 WALLINGFORD SQ LEXINGTON, SC 27092-1105	8160 WALLINGFORD SQ LEXINGTON, SC 27092-1105
58.	43690-E W. GREYMONT DR. GREENSBORO, NC 27409-1100	43690-E W. GRAYMONT DR. GREENSBORO, NC 27409-1100
59.	357 PERRY AVE SEATTLE, WA 98383	357 PERRY AVE SEATTLE, WA 98393
60.	732 S. 6TH ST EAU CLAIRE, WI 57401	732 S 60TH ST EAU CLAIRE, WI 57401-5501

ANSWERS TO ADDRESS CROSS COMPARISON EXERCISE 2

#					#					#				
1.	Ⓐ	Ⓑ	Ⓒ	Ⓓ	21.	Ⓐ	Ⓑ	Ⓒ	Ⓓ	41.	Ⓐ	Ⓑ	Ⓒ	Ⓓ
2.	Ⓐ	Ⓑ	Ⓒ	Ⓓ	22.	Ⓐ	Ⓑ	Ⓒ	Ⓓ	42.	Ⓐ	Ⓑ	Ⓒ	Ⓓ
3.	Ⓐ	Ⓑ	Ⓒ	Ⓓ	23.	Ⓐ	Ⓑ	Ⓒ	Ⓓ	43.	Ⓐ	Ⓑ	Ⓒ	Ⓓ
4.	Ⓐ	Ⓑ	Ⓒ	Ⓓ	24.	Ⓐ	Ⓑ	Ⓒ	Ⓓ	44.	Ⓐ	Ⓑ	Ⓒ	Ⓓ
5.	Ⓐ	Ⓑ	Ⓒ	Ⓓ	25.	Ⓐ	Ⓑ	Ⓒ	Ⓓ	45.	Ⓐ	Ⓑ	Ⓒ	Ⓓ
6.	Ⓐ	Ⓑ	Ⓒ	Ⓓ	26.	Ⓐ	Ⓑ	Ⓒ	Ⓓ	46.	Ⓐ	Ⓑ	Ⓒ	Ⓓ
7.	Ⓐ	Ⓑ	Ⓒ	Ⓓ	27.	Ⓐ	Ⓑ	Ⓒ	Ⓓ	47.	Ⓐ	Ⓑ	Ⓒ	Ⓓ
8.	Ⓐ	Ⓑ	Ⓒ	Ⓓ	28.	Ⓐ	Ⓑ	Ⓒ	Ⓓ	48.	Ⓐ	Ⓑ	Ⓒ	Ⓓ
9.	Ⓐ	Ⓑ	Ⓒ	Ⓓ	29.	Ⓐ	Ⓑ	Ⓒ	Ⓓ	49.	Ⓐ	Ⓑ	Ⓒ	Ⓓ
10.	Ⓐ	Ⓑ	Ⓒ	Ⓓ	30.	Ⓐ	Ⓑ	Ⓒ	Ⓓ	50.	Ⓐ	Ⓑ	Ⓒ	Ⓓ
11.	Ⓐ	Ⓑ	Ⓒ	Ⓓ	31.	Ⓐ	Ⓑ	Ⓒ	Ⓓ	51.	Ⓐ	Ⓑ	Ⓒ	Ⓓ
12.	Ⓐ	Ⓑ	Ⓒ	Ⓓ	32.	Ⓐ	Ⓑ	Ⓒ	Ⓓ	52.	Ⓐ	Ⓑ	Ⓒ	Ⓓ
13.	Ⓐ	Ⓑ	Ⓒ	Ⓓ	33.	Ⓐ	Ⓑ	Ⓒ	Ⓓ	53.	Ⓐ	Ⓑ	Ⓒ	Ⓓ
14.	Ⓐ	Ⓑ	Ⓒ	Ⓓ	34.	Ⓐ	Ⓑ	Ⓒ	Ⓓ	54.	Ⓐ	Ⓑ	Ⓒ	Ⓓ
15.	Ⓐ	Ⓑ	Ⓒ	Ⓓ	35.	Ⓐ	Ⓑ	Ⓒ	Ⓓ	55.	Ⓐ	Ⓑ	Ⓒ	Ⓓ
16.	Ⓐ	Ⓑ	Ⓒ	Ⓓ	36.	Ⓐ	Ⓑ	Ⓒ	Ⓓ	56.	Ⓐ	Ⓑ	Ⓒ	Ⓓ
17.	Ⓐ	Ⓑ	Ⓒ	Ⓓ	37.	Ⓐ	Ⓑ	Ⓒ	Ⓓ	57.	Ⓐ	Ⓑ	Ⓒ	Ⓓ
18.	Ⓐ	Ⓑ	Ⓒ	Ⓓ	38.	Ⓐ	Ⓑ	Ⓒ	Ⓓ	58.	Ⓐ	Ⓑ	Ⓒ	Ⓓ
19.	Ⓐ	Ⓑ	Ⓒ	Ⓓ	39.	Ⓐ	Ⓑ	Ⓒ	Ⓓ	59.	Ⓐ	Ⓑ	Ⓒ	Ⓓ
20.	Ⓐ	Ⓑ	Ⓒ	Ⓓ	40.	Ⓐ	Ⓑ	Ⓒ	Ⓓ	60.	Ⓐ	Ⓑ	Ⓒ	Ⓓ

[This page may be removed to mark answers.]

ANSWERS TO ADDRESS CROSS COMPARISON EXERCISE 2

1.	B	21.	C	41.	D
2.	A	22.	D	42.	D
3.	A	23.	C	43.	A
4.	B	24.	A	44.	D
5.	C	25.	B	45.	B
6.	D	26.	C	46.	C
7.	B	27.	D	47.	D
8.	D	28.	D	48.	A
9.	C	29.	A	49.	D
10.	A	30.	B	50.	B
11.	B	31.	C	51.	B
12.	D	32.	B	52.	B
13.	A	33.	C	53.	C
14.	C	34.	A	54.	A
15.	D	35.	B	55.	B
16.	B	36.	B	56.	B
17.	A	37.	D	57.	A
18.	D	38.	C	58.	B
19.	D	39.	B	59.	C
20.	B	40.	B	60.	D

If you scored:
56–60 correct, you have an excellent test score.
52–55 correct, you have a good test score.
51 or fewer correct, more practice is needed.

Forms Completion

The second part of this examination involves reviewing forms that are similar to those typically used in the Postal Service. Some forms apply to specific customer service requests while others are used to detail various retail sales transactions or document the delivery status of a given mail piece. You will need to review the forms provided on the test and obtain an understanding as to their basic purpose. From the information given in the question, you will either have to choose the proper endorsement to mark on the forms or determine what information is pertinent to the line item given. As an example, look over the return receipt form below and answer the sample questions that follow.

RETURN RECEIPT

(1) RECIPIENT'S PRINTED NAME
_____

(2) RECIPIENT'S SIGNATURE
_____

(3) (Check applicable ID)
     A) ____ ADDRESSEE
     B) ____ AGENT

(4) A) DATE OF DELIVERY
     _____

     B) TIME OF DELIVERY
     _____

(5) ARTICLE TRACKING NUMBER
_____

(6) REQUESTED SERVICE
    (Check appropriate box)

    A) ____ INSURED
    B) ____ CERTIFIED
    C) ____ REGISTERED
    D) ____ EXPRESS
    E) ____ MERCHANDISE
           RETURN RECEIPT

1. Where on the form would you enter the tracking number for a certified letter?

    A) Box 4
    B) Box 5
    C) Box 6B
    D) Box 6E

2. Which of these would be a correct entry for Box 4A?

    A) A check mark
    B) The addressee's signature
    C) 8-17-05
    D) 3:20 P.M.

3.   If the article being signed for is a registered letter which of the following should be checked?

    A)   Box 5
    B)   Box 6B
    C)   Box 6C
    D)   Box 6E

4.   Where would you enter the printed name of the person who sent this mailing?

    A)   Box 1
    B)   Box 2
    C)   Box 3A
    D)   None of the above

5.   An overnight express mail parcel was delivered to Mr. Smith at 8:45 A.M. on June 10, 2005. How would you correctly enter this information on the return receipt shown?

    A)   6-10-05 and 8:45 A.M. would be entered in boxes 4A and 4B respectively.
    B)   Box 6D would be checked
    C)   Both A and B
    D)   None of the above

SAMPLE ANSWER SHEET

1. (A) (B) (C) (D)
2. (A) (B) (C) (D)
3. (A) (B) (C) (D)
4. (A) (B) (C) (D)
5. (A) (B) (C) (D)

THE CORRECT ANSWERS FOR THE ABOVE EXERCISE ARE:

1. B
2. C
3. C
4. D
5. C

As you can see by this example, some of the questions can be straightforward line items to mark on your answer sheet. Other questions may be purposefully misleading such as question number 4. Note that it asks for the printed name of the person who sent the article instead of who the recipient was. In this case, option D would apply because the return receipt, as shown, does not include the sender's information. Sample question number 5 highlights another point to be aware of. There will be questions on the actual exam that offer multiple correct answers. All too often, applicants find the first right option that appears and then incorrectly mark that on the answer sheet because they have not taken the time to review the remaining options to determine if there is a more correct answer. All options (answers) should be closely reviewed before determining the correct answer.

You will have 15 minutes to complete 30 questions for this portion of the exam. Simply answering two questions per minute will guarantee your completion of this exercise. If you are unsure of a particular answer, skip it, and move on to the next question. Be careful not to spend excessive time on any one particular question. If time permits, you can come back to that question and again look at the answers provided. If you are still unsure of an answer, mark your answer sheet with your best guess. Wrong answers will not be penalized on this part of the exam.

FORMS COMPLETION PRACTICE EXERCISE 1

ANSWER QUESTIONS 1–14 BASED ON THE FOLLOWING INFORMATION.
DELIVERY NOTICE RECEIPT

1) DATE OF NOTICE

_____

2) ARTICLE AVAILABLE FOR PICKUP
AFTER
TIME   DATE
2A)   2B)

3) _____ IF THIS BOX IS CHECKED A SIGNATURE IS REQUIRED AT THE TIME OF DELIVERY.

4) NAME OF SENDER

_____

5) ADDRESS OF SENDER

_____

6) CHECK APPLICABLE BOX FOR NOTICE LEFT OR INDICATE TOTAL NUMBER OF ARTICLES DELIVERED.

    A) INSURED _____
    B) CERTIFIED _____
    C) REGISTERED _____
    D) EXPRESS _____
    E) DELIVERY CONFIRMATION _____
    F) SIGNATURE CONFIRMATION _____

7) ARTICLE DESCRIPTION
(Check appropriate box)

    A) ____ PARCEL
    B) ____ MAGAZINE
    C) ____ LETTER
    D) ____ OVERSIZED ENVELOPE

8) PAYMENT REQUIRED FOR ITEM MAILED.
    A) _____ COD
    B) _____ CUSTOMS
    C) _____ POSTAGE DUE
    D) $_____ AMOUNT REQUIRED

9) ITEM NUMBER

_____

_____

_____

_____

10) LEFT NOTICE
A) RECIPIENT'S NAME

_____

B) RECIPIENT'S ADDRESS

_____

C) ARTICLE DELIVERY DATE

_____

D) DELIVERED BY

_____

1.   Which of the following would be an appropriate entry for Box 1?

A)   4-12-05
B)   Bill Thompson
C) $13.75
D)   4:30 P.M.

2.   Where would you enter the sender's address on the above form?

A)   Box 2B
B)   Box 4
C)   Box 5
D)   Box 7C

3.   If an article that was mailed had insufficient postage, which of the following would apply?

A)   Box 9
B)   Box 8C would be checked and the balance due would be given in Box 8D
C)   Box 3
D)   Box 8A would be checked and the balance due would be given in Box 9

4.   7-14-05 could be entered where on this delivery notice?

A)   Box 1
B)   Box 2B
C)   Box 10C
D)   All of the above

5.   Letter carrier C. Williams delivers a registered letter to a business address on his route. Which of the following endorsements would be a correct entry on the form?

A)   Both Box 6C and Box 7C would be checked.
B)   Both Box 6F and 7D would be checked.
C)   Box 6C would be marked with the number 1 and Box 7C would be checked.
D)   Both Box 3 and Box 7B would be checked.

6.   From the information provided in question 5, the letter carrier's name would be entered where?

A)   Box 10A
B)   Box 10D
C)   Box 6E
D)   Box 4

7.   Where would you correctly enter the item number for an insured parcel?

A)   Box 9
B)   Box 7A
C)   Box 6A
D)   None of the above

8.   Letter carrier Jenkins attempted to deliver an overnight express letter to the Gordon family on 4-02-05; however, no one was home at the time to sign for the article. If Ms. Jenkins expected to finish the remainder of

her deliveries and return to the post office no later than 3:30 P.M., how should the attempted delivery notice be marked?

A)   4-02-05 and 3:30 P.M. should be entered for Boxes 2A and 2B respectively
B)   Box 3 should be checked
C)   3:30 P.M. and 4-02-05 should be entered for Boxes 10C and 10D respectively
D)   3:30 P.M. and 4-02-05 should be entered for Boxes 2A and 2B respectively

9.   Which of the following endorsements correctly identify the article referred to in question 8?

A)   Enter the number 1 in Box 6D and check Box 7C
B)   Check Boxes 6D and 7C
C)   Check Box 6D and enter the number 1 in Box 7C
D)   None of the above

10. If circumstances require leaving notice for an attempted delivery, where would you enter the recipient's address on the form?

A)   Box 5
B)   Box 10A
C)   Box 10B
D)   Box 10D

11.   Assuming a small international packet had a $15 customs charge that needed to be collected, the amount owed would be entered where on the delivery notice?

A)   Box 7A
B)   Box 8B
C)   Box 8C
D)   Box 8D

12.   05171 43712 13972 represents a signature confirmation item number for a package mailed by a law firm. Where on the delivery receipt would this information be entered?

A)   Box 6D
B)   Box 6E
C)   Box 7A
D)   Box 9

13.   In reference to question 12, a signature by the recipient would be required at the time of delivery. Which of the following would be a proper endorsement for an attempted delivery notice?

A)   Check Box 6F
B)   Check Box 3
C)   Check Box 7A
D)   All of the above

14.   Bruce Smith sent a certified letter to Ben Averly but the Averly family was away on vacation until the end of the week. Which of the following should be entered in Box 10A on the delivery notice?

A)   Ben Averly
B)   Bruce Smith
C)   A check mark
D)   None of the above

ANSWER QUESTIONS 15–30 BASED ON THE FOLLOWING INFORMATION.
CUSTOMER AUTHORIZATION TO HOLD MAIL

1) CUSTOMER'S NAME
_____

2) ADDRESS
_____

3) SIGNATURE
_____

====================================
NOTE: Mail can be held for a minimum of 5 days or a maximum of 40 days.
====================================

4) PERSONS AUTHORIZED ON BEHALF OF CUSTOMER TO PICK UP MAIL. (If more than 2 individuals are authorized to pick up mail, another HOLD MAIL form must be filled out.)
_____

RECEIVED BY:

8) WINDOW SERVICES CLERK
_____

9) CARRIER
_____

10) CITY/RURAL ROUTE NUMBER
_____

11) DATE HOLD ORDER RECEIVED
_____

5) START DATE
_____

6) ENDING DATE
_____

7) CHECK ONE OF THE FOLLOWING OPTIONS FOR RESUMPTION OF MAIL SERVICE.

A) ____ ALL MAIL HELD WILL BE PICKED UP BY THE CUSTOMER, AT WHICH POINT REGULAR DELIVERY SERVICE WILL BE RESUMED.

B) ____ ALL MAIL HELD FOR THE PERIOD SPECIFIED WOULD BE DELIVERED ON THE END DATE SHOWN AND REGULAR DELIVERY SERVICE SHALL BE RESUMED THEREAFTER.

C) ____ CHANGE OF ADDRESS FORMS WILL BE SUBMITTED WITHIN THE REQUIRED 40 DAY PERIOD AT WHICH POINT MAIL WILL BE FORWARDED.

====================================
If customer elects option 7A the window services clerk must check the box indicating that all mail held has been picked up, date the resumed delivery order, and initial the form.
====================================

12) A) DATE OF RESUMED DELIVERY REQUESTED: _____
    B) _____ ALL MAIL HELD HAS BEEN RECEIVED BY CUSTOMER

    C) _____ WINDOW SERVICE CLERK INITIALS

Elaine Hollbrook was leaving college for two weeks during spring break to visit her parents. Ms. Hollbrook went to the post office and filed a request to have her mail held beginning March 27, 2005 through April 10, 2005. She was relatively sure she would return to campus by April 10th. In the event something changed, however, she thought it best that she should not have her delivery service resumed until she picked up her mail from the post office. Window clerk Melanie Patterson received the authorization order to hold Ms. Hollbrook's mail on March 23, 2005. Elaine Hollbrook's address is 2020 E. 15th Street, Apt 5, Ames, IA 50070, which is on city route 1027. She has authorized Ken Holmes, Barb Hendricks, and Chris Medford to pick up her mail in the interim. As it turned out, Ms. Hollbrook actually returned on April 7th and picked up her accumulated mail from window service clerk Jerry Conway. Ms. Hollbrook also requested to have her delivery service resumed the next day.

15.   Where would you correctly enter Elaine Hollbrook's name on the form?

A)   Line item 1
B)   Line item 4
C)   Line item 10
D)   Box 7C

16.   What would be the correct information placed on line item 5?

A)   3-22-05
B)   3-27-05
C)   4-10-05
D)   4-27-05

17.   What would be the correct information placed on line item 11?

A)   3-23-05
B)   3-27-05
C)   4-10-05
D)   4-27-05

18.   Where should the number 1027 be entered on this form?

A)   Line item 6
B)   Line item 8
C)   Line item 9
D)   Line item 10

19.   Chris Medford, Barb Hendricks, and Ken Holmes are names that should be entered where?

A)   Line item 1
B)   Line item 2
C)   Line item 4
D)   Two of the names listed should be placed under line item 4 and the third name should be placed on another Authorization to Hold Mail form.

20.   Which of the following alternatives would be the correct information entered on line item 12C?

A)   Melanie Patterson
B)   Kim Holmes
C)   J. C.
D)   M. P.

21.   According to the information provided, line item 6 would be correctly filled in with which of the following?

A)   3-27-05
B)   3-29-05
C)   4-07-05
D)   4-10-05

22.   Line item 9 would be filled in correctly with which of the following?

A)   Elaine Hollbrook
B)   Melanie Patterson
C)   Barb Hendricks
D)   None of the above

23.   2020 E. 15th Street, Apt 5, Ames, IA, 50070, should be entered where on the Authorization to Hold Mail form?

A)   Line item 1
B)   Line item 2
C)   Line item 10
D)   Line item 7B

24.   According to Elaine Hollbrook's request to hold mail, which of the following should be checked by the receiving clerk?

A)   Box 7A
B)   Box 7B
C)   Box 7C
D)   Box 12B

25.   Window service clerk Jerry Conway would correctly enter which of the following dates on line item 12A pursuant to Ms. Hollbrook's instructions?

A)   3-27-05
B)   4-08-05
C)   4-10-05
D)   4-11-05

26.   What other information should be entered on this form by Mr. Conway at the time Ms. Hollbrook collects her accumulated mail?

A)   Box 12B should be checked
B)   Box 12B should be checked and Jerry Conway's name entered on line item 12C
C)   Both Box 12B and line item 12C should be checked
D)   Box 12B should be checked and initials J. C. should be entered on line time 12C

27.   Where would Ms. Hollbrook need to sign on the forms to formalize her request to have her mail held?

A)   Line item 1
B)   Line item 3
C)   Line item 8
D)   Line item 12C

28.   If Ms. Hollbrook elected to check option 7B on her Hold Mail request, which of the following dates would her regular delivery service be resumed?

A)   3-27-05
B)   4-07-05
C)   4-10-05
D)   4-13-05

29.   Which of the following selections would be correctly entered on line item 8?

A)   Jerry Conway
B)   Melanie Patterson
C)   4-10-05
D)   4-13-05

30.   On the Hold Mail form, which of the following would be a proper endorsement for a customer who wanted his or her mail held for a period of 45 days prior to submitting a change of address order?

A)   Check Box 7A
B)   Check Box 7B
C)   Check Box 7C
D)   None of the above

FORMS COMPLETION EXERCISE 1 ANSWER SHEET

1. A B C D
2. A B C D
3. A B C D
4. A B C D
5. A B C D
6. A B C D
7. A B C D
8. A B C D
9. A B C D
10. A B C D

11. A B C D
12. A B C D
13. A B C D
14. A B C D
15. A B C D
16. A B C D
17. A B C D
18. A B C D
19. A B C D
20. A B C D

21. A B C D
22. A B C D
23. A B C D
24. A B C D
25. A B C D
26. A B C D
27. A B C D
28. A B C D
29. A B C D
30. A B C D

[This page may be removed to mark answers.]

ANSWERS TO FORMS COMPLETION EXERCISE 1

1.	A		16.	B
2.	C		17.	A
3.	B		18.	D
4.	D		19.	D
5.	C		20.	C
6.	B		21.	D
7.	A		22.	D
8.	D		23.	B
9.	B		24.	A
10.	C		25.	B
11.	D		26.	D
12.	D		27.	B
13.	D		28.	C
14.	A		29.	B
15.	A		30.	D

(NOTE: 45 days exceeds the maximum amount of time that mail can be held.)

If you scored:
27–30 correct, you have an excellent score.
24–26 correct, you have a good score.
23 or fewer, more practice is needed.

FORMS COMPLETION EXERCISE 2

ANSWER QUESTIONS 1–9 BASED ON THE FOLLOWING INFORMATION.
DELIVERY REQUEST FOR RURAL CUSTOMERS

1) CUSTOMER'S NAME

_____

2) RURAL BOX NUMBER

_____

3) STREET NAME

_____

4) LOCATION OF POST OFFICE SERVING AREA (ZIP +4 ONLY)

_____

5) A) HOME TELEPHONE NO

_____

B) BUSINESS TELEPHONE NO

_____

6) RURAL ROUTE ID NUMBER

_____

7) PRINT THE FULL NAMES OF ALL INDIVIDUALS WHO WILL RECEIVE MAIL AT THIS ADDRESS

_____
_____
_____
_____
_____

8) IF A PACKAGE DOES NOT REQUIRE A SIGNATURE, BUT IS TOO LARGE TO PLACE IN THE MAIL BOX, INDICATE WHICH OF THE FOLLOWING SERVICES WOULD BE PREFERRED BY CHECKING THE CORRESPONDING BOX.

A) _____ LEAVE NOTICE FOR PICK-UP AT THE POST OFFICE
B) _____ LEAVE ON STEPS OR PORCH OF RESIDENCE
C) _____ LEAVE ITEM NEXT TO THE MAILBOX UNLESS INCLEMENT WEATHER IS A FACTOR.

NOTE: Rural Customers understand if either 8B or 8C is checked the Postal Service is not liable for potential damage or theft.

9) CUSTOMER'S SIGNATURE

_____

10) DATE SUBMITTED FOR RURAL CARRIER RECORD

_____

1.   (404) 491-1705 would be a correct entry for which of the following?

A)   Line item 4
B)   Line item 5A
C)   Line item 6
D)   Line item 10

2.   If a rural customer preferred not to have oversized packages left in an unsecured location, which of the following boxes would be appropriately checked?

A)   Box 8A
B)   Box 8B
C)   Box 8C
D)   None of the above

3.   Referring to question 2, where on the form does the rural customer confirm that he or she understands postal policies on oversized package delivery?

A)   Line item 1
B)   Line item 7
C)   Box 8C
D)   Line item 9

4.   98370-5550 would be a correct entry for which of the following?

A)   Line item 2
B)   Line item 3
C)   Line item 4
D)   Line item 6

5.   10/05/05 is information that would be entered where on the form?

A)   Line item 3
B)   Line item 6
C)   Line item 8A
D)   Line item 10

6.   If the Hansen family rural box number is 540 and they currently receive delivery service from rural carrier Mike Dorsett on route 12, how would this information be correctly entered on the form?

A)   540 and Mike Dorsett would be entered on line item 2 and 6 respectively
B)   540 and 12 would be entered on line item 2 and 6 respectively
C)   540 and 12 would be entered on line item 3 and 10 respectively
D)   540 and Mike Dorsett would be entered on line item 3 and 7 respectively

7.   Which of the following names conform to what is requested in line item 7?

A)   J.B.D.
B)   J.B. Dobbs
C)   James Decker
D)   James B. Decker

8. Where would you correctly enter the rural customer's name on the delivery request form?

A) Line item 6
B) Line item 3
C) Line item 2
D) Line item 1

9. If rural customer Barbara Day had a home-based business that required the use of a cell phone, where would this information be included on the delivery request form?

A) Line item 2
B) Line item 5A
C) Line item 5B
D) Box 8A

ANSWER QUESTIONS 10–18 BASED ON THE FOLLOWING INFORMATION.
UNDELIVERABLE PERIODICAL NOTICE

1) LAST KNOWN FORWARDING ADDRESS

A) Post Office Box Number

_____

B) Street Number

_____

C) Street Name

_____

D) Apartment Number

_____

E) Suite Number

_____

F) City

_____

G) State

_____

H) Zip Code +4

_____

2) REASON FOR NON-DELIVERY OTHER THAN FORWARD EXPIRATION (CHECK APPLICABLE BOX)

A) _____ Insufficient Address

B) _____ Customer unknown

C) _____ No such street number

D) _____ No such street

E) _____ Customer refused mailing

F) _____ Article unclaimed

3) INITIALS OF DISPATCH CLERK

_____

4) DATE

_____

5) ZIP CODE +4 OF OFFICE RETURNING PERIODICAL TO MAILER

_____

6) CHECK APPROPRIATE BOX
A) _____ Charge to mailer required
(If checked specify amount)
$_____

B) _____ No Charge

10.   If a magazine was to be returned to the mailer because the address label lacked a street name, which of the following boxes would be checked?

A)   Box 2A
B)   Box 2C
C)   Box 2D
D)   Box 6A

11.   Samantha Keys received an adult magazine in the mail that she neither ordered nor wanted. She promptly gave the article back to the carrier and requested that it be returned to the mailer. Considering the circumstances, which of the following entries would be checked on the Undeliverable Periodical Notice?

A)   Line item 1A
B)   Box 2E
C)   Box 2F
D)   Box 6A

12.   Where would 11-15-05 be correctly entered on the notice?

A)   Line item 1B
B)   Line item 1H
C)   Line item 4
D)   Line item 5

13.   P.C. is information that is appropriate to enter where on the form?

A)   Line item 1D
B)   Line item 1F
C)   Line item 3
D)   Line item 5

14.   If a mailer is charged a processing fee for a returned periodical, how is this information properly marked on the notice?

A)   Box 6A would be checked
B)   Box 6A would be checked in addition to specifying the amount charged to the mailer
C)   Box 6B would be checked
D)   Box 6B would be checked in addition to specifying the amount charged to the mailer

15.   57211-5721 would be an appropriate entry for which of the following?

A)   Line item 1B
B)   Line item 1H
C)   Line item 5
D)   Both line item 1H and 5

16.   If the last known forwarding address for a given business is 2705 Kessler Street, Suite 5-A Tacoma, WA, 98005-4172, all of the following are correct entries on the Undeliverable Periodical Notice except:

A)   Suite 5-A on line item 1D
B)   Kessler Street on line item 1C
C)   Tacoma, WA on line items 1F and 1G respectively
D)   All of the above are correct

17.   Assume a magazine addressed to a postal customer for general delivery was not picked up from window services over the course of ten days. Consequently, the article was returned to the mailer. What would be a proper endorsement on the Undeliverable Periodical Notice given the circumstances?

A)   Check box 2A
B)   Check box 2E
C)   Check box 2F
D)   Check box 6A

18.   A box holder returned a periodical sorted to their post office box to a window service clerk. Although the current box holder has had the same P.O. Box for a number of years, they did not recognize the addressee's name on the periodical. Which of the following would be a proper form endorsement for returning the article?

A)   Check box 2A
B)   Check box 2B
C)   Check box 2C
D)   Check box 2F

ANSWER QUESTIONS 19–30 BASED ON THE FOLLOWING INFORMATION.

CUSTOMS DECLARATION AND MAILING NOTICE

1. EXPORTER'S (SENDER'S) NAME
    _____

2. BUSINESS ADDRESS   HOME ADDRESS
    A) P.O. BOX OR SUITE #   D) P.O. BOX OR SUITE #
    _____   _____

    B) STREET ADDRESS   E) STREET ADDRESS
    _____   _____

    C) CITY/STATE/ZIP   F) CITY/STATE/ZIP
    _____   _____

        G) COUNTRY
        _____

3. IMPORTER'S (RECIPIENT'S) NAME
    _____

4. A) P.O. BOX OR SUITE #   B) STREET ADDRESS
    _____   _____

    C) CITY/COUNTRY/POST CODE
    _____

5. OFFICE OF ORIGINATION
    TRACKING CODE
    _____

6. A) INSURANCE NUMBER
    _____

    B) INSURANCE COVERAGE
    $ _____

7. IMPORTER'S (RECIPIENT'S)
    A) PHONE NUMBER
    _____

    B) E-MAIL ADDRESS
    _____

    C) FAX NUMBER
    _____

    D) TAX CODE (IF APPLICABLE)
    _____

8.

A) DESCRIPTION OF ARTICLES	B) QUANTITY SENT	ITEM WT C) LBS	D) OZ	ARTICLE VALUATION E) IN US CURRENCY

9. THE ARTICLES LISTED ARE CONSIDERED (CHECK APPLICABLE BOX)

    A) _____ RETURNED MERCHANDISE   B) _____ GIFT
    C) _____ PERSONAL/BUSINESS DOCUMENTS   D) _____ COMMERCIAL PURCHASE

10. SERVICE TYPE REQUESTED (CHECK APPLICABLE BOX)
    A) _____ INTERNATIONAL EXPRESS
    B) _____ PRIORITY AIR MAIL
    C) _____ SURFACE STANDARD

11. CUSTOM'S INVOICE NUMBER
    _____

12. CUSTOM'S CERTIFICATE NUMBER
    _____

13. CUSTOM'S LICENSE NUMBER
    _____

14. IN THE EVENT OF NON-DELIVERY CHECK ONE FOR PREFERRED DISPOSTION OF ARTICLE SENT.
    A) _____ DO NOT RETURN   B) _____ RETURN AT MAILER'S
    C) _____ FORWARD TO ADDRESS SHOWN BELOW   EXPENSE

15. POSTAGE AND FEES TOTAL
    $ _____

16. A) OFFICE OF ORIGINATION DATE
    STAMP _____

    B) INITIALS OF RECEIVING CLERK
    _____

17. A) EXPORTER'S (SENDER'S)
    SIGNATURE
    _____

    B) DATE SIGNED _____

19. The name of the person who will be receiving the mailed article would be correctly entered where on the Customs Declaration form?

A) Line item 1
B) Line item 2A
C) Line item 3
D) Line item 16B

20. If the mailed articles were described as clothing being returned to a retailer, which of the following form endorsements would be correct?

A) Box 9A would be checked
B) Box 9B would be checked
C) Box 9C would be checked
D) Box 9D would be checked

21. Where would klm@dlyca.com appropriately be entered on the form?

A) Line item 2A
B) Line item 7B
C) Line item 8D
D) Line item 13

22. If a package going through customs weighs 9½ pounds, how would this information be properly entered on the Customs Declaration form?

A) 9.5 would be entered under line item 8C
B) 9 and .5 would be entered under 8C and 8D respectively
C) 9 and 8 would be entered under 8C and 8D respectively
D) 9.5 would be entered under line item 8E

23. Where on the form does the mailer sign his or her name to confirm liability for the article being sent?

A) Line item 1
B) Line item 3
C) Line item 16B
D) Line item 17A

24. If fees and postage total $23.78 to mail a given item, where would this information be properly entered on the customs form?

A) Line item 6B
B) Line item 7D
C) Line item 8E
D) Line item 15

25. Assume a postal customer was in a hurry to get a small gift packet to a relative who lived overseas. If express mail was the chosen service to get it there, where on the customs form would this information be noted?

A) Box 9B would be checked
B) Box 9C would be checked
C) Box 10A would be checked
D) Box 10C would be checked

26.   If a mailer is willing to cover the cost of return postage for an undeliverable article, that information is indicated where on the form?

A)   Box 9A would be checked
B)   Box 14B would be checked
C)   Line item 6B would stipulate the amount covered
D)   None of the above

27.   A detailed description of package contents intended to go through customs would be listed under which of the following?

A)   Line item 8A
B)   Line item 8B
C)   Line item 8E
D)   Line item 9A

28.   If 567-X represents a certificate number for a customs mailing, where would this information be entered on the Customs Declaration form?

A)   Line item 5
B)   Line item 11
C)   Line item 12
D)   Line item 13

29.   Office of destination date stamp would be under which of the following line items?

A)   4C
B)   5
C)   16
D)   None of the above

30.   Assume a package is to be mailed from a resident living in Seattle, WA to an address in Edmonton, Alberta, Canada. Which of the following are accurate endorsements needed on the Customs Declaration Form?

A)   Seattle, WA and Edmonton, Alberta, Canada would be written in on line items 2C and 4C respectively
B)   Edmonton, Alberta, Canada and Seattle, WA would be written in on line items 2C and 4C respectively
C)   Seattle, WA and Edmonton, Alberta, Canada would be written in on line items 2F and 4C respectively
D)   None of the above

FORMS COMPLETION EXERCISE 2 ANSWER SHEET

1. (A) (B) (C) (D)   11. (A) (B) (C) (D)   21. (A) (B) (C) (D)
2. (A) (B) (C) (D)   12. (A) (B) (C) (D)   22. (A) (B) (C) (D)
3. (A) (B) (C) (D)   13. (A) (B) (C) (D)   23. (A) (B) (C) (D)
4. (A) (B) (C) (D)   14. (A) (B) (C) (D)   24. (A) (B) (C) (D)
5. (A) (B) (C) (D)   15. (A) (B) (C) (D)   25. (A) (B) (C) (D)
6. (A) (B) (C) (D)   16. (A) (B) (C) (D)   26. (A) (B) (C) (D)
7. (A) (B) (C) (D)   17. (A) (B) (C) (D)   27. (A) (B) (C) (D)
8. (A) (B) (C) (D)   18. (A) (B) (C) (D)   28. (A) (B) (C) (D)
9. (A) (B) (C) (D)   19. (A) (B) (C) (D)   29. (A) (B) (C) (D)
10. (A) (B) (C) (D)   20. (A) (B) (C) (D)   30. (A) (B) (C) (D)

[This page may be removed to mark answers.]

ANSWERS TO FORM COMPLETION EXERCISE 2

1.	B	16.	A
2.	A	17.	C
3.	D	18.	B
4.	C	19.	C
5.	D	20.	A
6.	B	21.	B
7.	D	22.	C (8 ounces = ½ pound)
8.	D	23.	D
9.	C	24.	D
10.	A	25.	C
11.	B	26.	B
12.	C	27.	A
13.	C	28.	C
14.	B	29.	D
15.	D	30.	C

If you scored:
27–30 correct, you have an excellent score.
24–26 correct, you have a good score.
23 or fewer, more practice is needed.

CODING

The third part of this test involves address coding. A guide is provided that lists various address ranges that are specific to four different routes. Look at the examples below:

SERVICE RANGE	ROUTE ID
700-900 NE 13th ST. 1200-4999 DELANEY RD.	ROUTE A
6700-8999 WESTMONT PKWY 1350-1800 SW 42ND AVE. 0100-1199 DELANEY RD.	ROUTE B
901 1599 NE 13TH ST. 5200-9999 COLLINS BLVD. 5000-6900 DELANEY RD.	ROUTE C
ALL OTHER ADDRESSES THAT ARE NOT INCLUDED IN THE ABOVE RANGES	ROUTE D

(NOTE: For test purposes assume all street numbers run in progressive order from low to high.)

Delivery route A is responsible for any address that falls between 700 and 900 NE 13th St. and 1200-4999 Delaney Rd. Therefore, 812 NE 13th St. and 1362 Delaney Rd. would be two examples of street addresses that are served by Route A. One aspect to pay particular attention to is that some concurrent numbers for the same street can belong to different routes. For instance, 1199 Delaney Rd. belongs to route B while 1200 Delaney Rd. belongs to route A. On the actual test, there will be one or two streets common to two or more routes. Understanding how these street addresses are segregated is, without doubt, a prerequisite to scoring high on the exam. All addresses that are not included in routes A, B, and C are, by default, served by route D.

This section of the test consists of 36 street addresses that require coding. You will have 6 minutes to complete the exercise. As you work through each of the practice exercises provided, your proficiency will improve. It is realistic to complete this exercise in less than 5 minutes. What is important to note here is the memory section that immediately follows utilizes the same coding guide. Therefore, if there is any extra time remaining, you can get a head start over others in memorizing some of the addresses given.

Look at the coding guide provided below and take 2 minutes to code as many of the 12 sample addresses as possible. You can check your accuracy with the answers that follow.

SERVICE RANGE	ROUTE ID
300–499 NW COLCHESTER 1399–1999 MANZANITA AVE.	ROUTE A
275–499 SHERMAN HEIGHTS BLVD. 2000–2399 MANZANITA AVE. 500–999 NW COLCHESTER	ROUTE B
17000–29999 HWY 99 500–975 SHERMAN HEIGHTS BLVD.	ROUTE C
ALL OTHER ADDRESSES NOT SERVED BY THE ABOVE ROUTES	ROUTE D

STREET ADDRESSES	ROUTE CODE
1. 325 MANZANITA AVE.	Ⓐ Ⓑ Ⓒ Ⓓ
2. 900 SHERMAN HEIGHTS BLVD.	Ⓐ Ⓑ Ⓒ Ⓓ
3. 501 NW COLCHESTER	Ⓐ Ⓑ Ⓒ Ⓓ
4. 16999 HWY 99	Ⓐ Ⓑ Ⓒ Ⓓ
5. 2117 MANZANITA AVE.	Ⓐ Ⓑ Ⓒ Ⓓ
6. 403 NW COLCHESTER	Ⓐ Ⓑ Ⓒ Ⓓ
7. 1379 MANZANITA AVE.	Ⓐ Ⓑ Ⓒ Ⓓ
8. 612 SHERMAN HEIGHTS BLVD.	Ⓐ Ⓑ Ⓒ Ⓓ
9. 274 SHERMAN HEIGHTS BLVD.	Ⓐ Ⓑ Ⓒ Ⓓ
10. 301 NW COLCHESTER	Ⓐ Ⓑ Ⓒ Ⓓ
11. 2389 MANZANITA AVE.	Ⓐ Ⓑ Ⓒ Ⓓ
12. 25676 HWY 99	Ⓐ Ⓑ Ⓒ Ⓓ

THE CORRECT ANSWERS FOR THIS SAMPLE-CODING TEST ARE AS FOLLOWS:

1.	D	5.	B	9.	D
2.	C	6.	A	10.	A
3.	B	7.	D	11.	B
4.	D	8.	C	12.	C

NOTE: If you find you are running out of time trying to complete these types of exercises, do not attempt to guess the answer. One third of the number of incorrect answers will be subtracted from those that were answered correctly.

CODING EXERCISE 1   **TIME: 6 MINUTES**

SERVICE RANGE   ROUTE ID

0–199 NE JEFFERSON PT.   ROUTE A
700–2399 147TH AVE.
500–1999 WINTERS RD.

2400–2999 147TH AVE.   ROUTE B
350–1975 PIONEER HILL
200–999 NE JEFFERSON PT.

0–349 PIONEER HILL   ROUTE C
2000–4999 WINTERS RD.
325–675 SW 15TH ST.

ALL OTHER ADDRESSES NOT SERVED   ROUTE D
BY THE ABOVE ROUTES

STREET ADDRESS   ROUTE CODE

1.   219 NE JEFFERSON PT.   Ⓐ Ⓑ Ⓒ Ⓓ

2.   349 PIONEER HILL   Ⓐ Ⓑ Ⓒ Ⓓ

3.   5012 WINTERS RD.   Ⓐ Ⓑ Ⓒ Ⓓ

4.   670 SW 16TH ST.   Ⓐ Ⓑ Ⓒ Ⓓ

5.   23 NE JEFFERSON PT.   Ⓐ Ⓑ Ⓒ Ⓓ

6.   1913 PIONEER HILL   Ⓐ Ⓑ Ⓒ Ⓓ

7.   420 SW 15TH ST.   Ⓐ Ⓑ Ⓒ Ⓓ

8.   659 147TH AVE.   Ⓐ Ⓑ Ⓒ Ⓓ

9.   52 NE JEFFERSON PT.   Ⓐ Ⓑ Ⓒ Ⓓ

10. 1950 PIONEER HILL   Ⓐ Ⓑ Ⓒ Ⓓ

11. 2397 149TH AVE.   Ⓐ Ⓑ Ⓒ Ⓓ

12. 4301 WINTERS RD.   Ⓐ Ⓑ Ⓒ Ⓓ

13. 817 147TH AVE.   Ⓐ Ⓑ Ⓒ Ⓓ

14. 611 SW 15TH ST.   Ⓐ Ⓑ Ⓒ Ⓓ

	STREET ADDRESS		ROUTE CODE

15. 12031 PARKER PLACE — Ⓐ Ⓑ Ⓒ Ⓓ

16. 419 PIONEER HILL — Ⓐ Ⓑ Ⓒ Ⓓ

17. 600 WINTERS RD. — Ⓐ Ⓑ Ⓒ Ⓓ

18. 333 SW 15TH ST. — Ⓐ Ⓑ Ⓒ Ⓓ

19. 2357 PIONEER HILL — Ⓐ Ⓑ Ⓒ Ⓓ

20. 16-C NE JEFFERSON PT. — Ⓐ Ⓑ Ⓒ Ⓓ

21. 2020 SEDONA BLVD. — Ⓐ Ⓑ Ⓒ Ⓓ

22. 1899 PIONEER HILL — Ⓐ Ⓑ Ⓒ Ⓓ

23. 12-B PIONEER HILL — Ⓐ Ⓑ Ⓒ Ⓓ

24. 701 147TH AVE. — Ⓐ Ⓑ Ⓒ Ⓓ

25. 325 NE 15TH ST. — Ⓐ Ⓑ Ⓒ Ⓓ

26. 901 NE JEFFERSON PT. — Ⓐ Ⓑ Ⓒ Ⓓ

27. 613 SW 15TH ST. — Ⓐ Ⓑ Ⓒ Ⓓ

28. 1414 WINTERS RD. — Ⓐ Ⓑ Ⓒ Ⓓ

29. 50070 PIONEER HILL — Ⓐ Ⓑ Ⓒ Ⓓ

30. 2425 147TH AVE. — Ⓐ Ⓑ Ⓒ Ⓓ

31. 4903 WINTERS RD. — Ⓐ Ⓑ Ⓒ Ⓓ

32. 19 NE JEFFERSON PT. — Ⓐ Ⓑ Ⓒ Ⓓ

33. 632 WINTERS RD. — Ⓐ Ⓑ Ⓒ Ⓓ

34. 149-D 13TH ST. SW — Ⓐ Ⓑ Ⓒ Ⓓ

35. 207 NE JEFFERSON PT. — Ⓐ Ⓑ Ⓒ Ⓓ

36. 2590 147TH AVE. — Ⓐ Ⓑ Ⓒ Ⓓ

ANSWERS TO CODING EXERCISE 1

1.	B	13.	A	25.	D
2.	C	14.	C	26.	B
3.	D	15.	D	27.	C
4.	D	16.	B	28.	A
5.	A	17.	A	29.	D
6.	B	18.	C	30.	B
7.	C	19.	D	31.	C
8.	D	20.	A	32.	A
9.	A	21.	D	33.	A
10.	B	22.	B	34.	D
11.	D	23.	C	35.	B
12.	C	24.	A	36.	B

If you scored:
34–36 correct, you have an excellent score.
32–33 correct, you have a good score.
31 or fewer, more practice is needed.

CODING EXERCISE 2   TIME: 6 MINUTES

SERVICE RANGE	ROUTE ID
1500-3599 S. BEACH DR. 45-575 SW 10TH AVE.	ROUTE A
2300-6999 KENWORTH PLACE 75-1499 S. BEACH DR. 576-1975 SW 10TH AVE.	ROUTE B
17-99 MORRIS CREEK LN. 1690-2790 HWY 120 375-2299 KENWORTH PLACE	ROUTE C
ALL OTHER ADDRESSES NOT SERVED BY THE ABOVE ROUTES	ROUTE D

	STREET ADDRESS	ROUTE CODE
1.	3099 HWY 120	Ⓐ Ⓑ Ⓒ Ⓓ
2.	1677 S. BEACH DR.	Ⓐ Ⓑ Ⓒ Ⓓ
3.	2301 KENWORTH PLACE	Ⓐ Ⓑ Ⓒ Ⓓ
4.	82 MORRIS CREEK LN	Ⓐ Ⓑ Ⓒ Ⓓ
5.	2017 HAWTHORNE BLVD.	Ⓐ Ⓑ Ⓒ Ⓓ
6.	79 SW 10TH AVE.	Ⓐ Ⓑ Ⓒ Ⓓ
7.	1579 S. BEACH DR.	Ⓐ Ⓑ Ⓒ Ⓓ
8.	5031 KENWORTH PLACE	Ⓐ Ⓑ Ⓒ Ⓓ
9.	576 SE 10TH AVE.	Ⓐ Ⓑ Ⓒ Ⓓ
10.	67-C MORRIS CREEK LN.	Ⓐ Ⓑ Ⓒ Ⓓ
11.	2107 KENWORTH PLACE	Ⓐ Ⓑ Ⓒ Ⓓ
12.	49 SW 10TH AVE.	Ⓐ Ⓑ Ⓒ Ⓓ
13.	1449 S. BEACH DR.	Ⓐ Ⓑ Ⓒ Ⓓ
14.	6907 KENWORTH PLACE	Ⓐ Ⓑ Ⓒ Ⓓ
15.	1699 HWY 120	Ⓐ Ⓑ Ⓒ Ⓓ

16.   1709 KINSTON PLACE   (A) (B) (C) (D)

17.   37-D SW 9TH ST.   (A) (B) (C) (D)

18.   3411 S. BEACH DR.   (A) (B) (C) (D)

19.   1499 MORRIS CREEK LN.   (A) (B) (C) (D)

20.   2600 HWY 120   (A) (B) (C) (D)

21.   1919 SW 10TH AVE.   (A) (B) (C) (D)

22.   1817 S. BEACH DR.   (A) (B) (C) (D)

23.   2790 120TH AVE.   (A) (B) (C) (D)

24.   2111 KENWORTH PLACE   (A) (B) (C) (D)

25.   596 SW 10TH AVE.   (A) (B) (C) (D)

26.   49 SW 10TH AVE.   (A) (B) (C) (D)

27.   1690 HWY 102   (A) (B) (C) (D)

28.   102 MORRIS CREEK LN.   (A) (B) (C) (D)

29.   99 S. BEACH DR.   (A) (B) (C) (D)

30.   27 MORRIS CREEK LN.   (A) (B) (C) (D)

31.   1976 KENWORTH PLACE   (A) (B) (C) (D)

32.   3519 S. BEACH DR.   (A) (B) (C) (D)

33.   573 SW 10TH AVE.   (A) (B) (C) (D)

34.   577 SW 10TH AVE.   (A) (B) (C) (D)

35.   800 KENWORTH BLVD.   (A) (B) (C) (D)

36.   39 MORRIS CREEK LN.   (A) (B) (C) (D)

ANSWERS TO CODING EXERCISE 2

1.	D	13.	B	25.	B
2.	A	14.	B	26.	A
3.	B	15.	C	27.	D
4.	C	16.	D	28.	D
5.	D	17.	D	29.	B
6.	A	18.	A	30.	C
7.	A	19.	D	31.	C
8.	B	20.	C	32.	A
9.	D	21.	B	33.	A
10.	C	22.	A	34.	B
11.	C	23.	D	35.	D
12.	A	24.	C	36.	C

If you scored:
34–36 correct, you have an excellent score.
32–33 correct, you have a good score.
31 or fewer, more practice is needed.

Memory

Before going any further into this test section, you will need to refer back to the section of this book on Examination 460 on memory (pages 35-40) to get a basic understanding of imaging and association techniques and number-letter transpositions. The memorization test format between EXAM 460 and EXAM 473 is comparable with few exceptions. A somewhat different approach, however, will be discussed for EXAM 473 that will positively give you a distinct advantage over other applicants. Principally, the difference that exists between the two exams is that EXAM 460 requires the memorization of various address ranges and what letter designated (i.e., A-E) column they fall under. For example, 2300 - 2399 KING STREET belongs under column A and the answer sheet would be marked accordingly. EXAM 473, on the other hand, will take the same address range and ask about a specific address that falls within those address parameters. For example, 2319 KING STREET is an address that falls under which column, or in this case, is served by which letter designated route. For some people, it may not be a difficult task to use the memory skills explained in this book to assess quickly and accurately letter designations for addresses randomly picked. There is another way, however, to do the exercise that should make things easier. The very same coding guide that was worked on in the previous exercises is the same guide that is expected to be memorized for this portion of the exam. You will still need to memorize the entire coding guide verbatim; but, at the close of your study time when you are instructed to start the actual test, write out the entire code in the TEST BOOKLET-and NOT on your answer sheet. You are permitted to do this, and it should not take you longer than one minute to do so. Since you are given 7 minutes to complete 36 test questions, you will be left with 6 minutes to complete the exercise. This now becomes a basic coding exercise that is exactly like what was worked on in the previous test section.

On the actual exam, you will be provided 3 minutes to study this coding guide in tandem with a practice work sheet. Then you will be given another 5 minutes to study another page in the test booklet that shows only the coding guide. At the completion of that study, you will then be told to start the test. It is very important to use your study time wisely. Concentrate on your story fabrications. It is strongly suggested to ignore the practice worksheet entirely. If you have good story lines worked out, you undoubtedly have the key for achieving a high-test score.

NOTE: If, for whatever reason, you find you are running out of time to complete the exercise, do not attempt to guess the answers. One third of the number of incorrect answers will be subtracted from those that were answered correctly.

MEMORIZATION EXERCISE 1   TIME: 3 MINUTES

SERVICE RANGE	ROUTE ID
1500-4999 GARRISON BLVD. 750-1890 NW 32ND AVE.	ROUTE A
375-1499 GARRISON BLVD. 590-1325 DECATUR AVE. 1891-1975 NW 32ND AVE.	ROUTE B
50-1899 PEREGRINE CT. 1326-4350 DECATUR AVE. 3275-5799 E. BENDER WAY	ROUTE C
ALL OTHER ADDRESSES NOT SERVED BY THE ABOVE ROUTES	ROUTE D

OPTIONAL WORKSHEET PROVIDED BELOW

	STREET ADDRESSES	ROUTE CODE
1.	398 GARRISON BLVD.	Ⓐ Ⓑ Ⓒ Ⓓ
2.	1399 DECATUR AVE.	Ⓐ Ⓑ Ⓒ Ⓓ
3.	1801 PROGRESSIVE CT.	Ⓐ Ⓑ Ⓒ Ⓓ
4.	4205 E. BENDER WAY	Ⓐ Ⓑ Ⓒ Ⓓ
5.	791 NW 32ND AVE.	Ⓐ Ⓑ Ⓒ Ⓓ
6.	1902 NW 33RD AVE.	Ⓐ Ⓑ Ⓒ Ⓓ
7.	1607 GARRISON BLVD.	Ⓐ Ⓑ Ⓒ Ⓓ
8.	888 DECATUR AVE.	Ⓐ Ⓑ Ⓒ Ⓓ
9.	1320 NW 32ND AVE.	Ⓐ Ⓑ Ⓒ Ⓓ
10.	6209 E. BENDER WAY	Ⓐ Ⓑ Ⓒ Ⓓ
11.	679 PEREGRINE CT.	Ⓐ Ⓑ Ⓒ Ⓓ
12.	1933 NW 32ND ST.	Ⓐ Ⓑ Ⓒ Ⓓ
13.	582 GARRISON BLVD.	Ⓐ Ⓑ Ⓒ Ⓓ
14.	760 NW 32ND AVE.	Ⓐ Ⓑ Ⓒ Ⓓ
15.	2020 DECATUR ST.	Ⓐ Ⓑ Ⓒ Ⓓ

SERVICE RANGE	ROUTE ID
1500-4999 GARRISON BLVD. 750-1890 NW 32ND AVE.	ROUTE A
375-1499 GARRISON BLVD. 590-1325 DECATUR AVE. 1891-1975 NW 32ND AVE.	ROUTE B
50-1899 PEREGRINE CT. 1326-4350 DECATUR AVE. 3275-5799 E. BENDER WAY	ROUTE C
ALL OTHER ADDRESSES NOT SERVED BY THE ABOVE ROUTES	ROUTE D

MEMORIZATION EXERCISE 1   TIME: 7 MINUTES

1.   4900 GARRISON BLVD.

2.   16790 JOHNSON ST.

3.   1917 NW 32ND AVE.

4.   4311 DECATUR AVE.

5.   16 FRANKFORT LN.

6.   757 NW 32ND AVE.

7.   1470 NW 37TH AVE.

8.   1312 DECATUR AVE.

9.   90 HADLOCK ST.

10. 342 PEREGRINE CT.

11. 5342 E. BENDER WAY

12. 1501 GARRISON BLVD.

13. 1899 NW 32ND AVE.

14. 402 CHESTER PKWY.

15. 3799 DECATUR AVE.

16. 1212 PEREGRINE CT.

17. 14-C AUSTIN ST.

18. 1515 GARRISON BLVD.

19. 590 NW 32ND AVE.

20. 3844 DECATUR AVE.

21. 4999 E. BENDER WAY

22. 170 PEREGRINE CT.

23. 1670 NW 32ND AVE.

24. 500 GARRISON BLVD.

25. 1902 NW 72ND AVE.

26. 1118 DECATIR AVE.

27. 807 NW 32ND AVE.

28. 4209 E. BENDER WAY

29. 1616 FIRCREST

30. 387 GARRISON BLVD.

31. 4987 GARRISON BLVD.

32. 1313 PEREGRINE ST.

33. 1379 DECATUR BLVD.

34. 3775 E. BENDER ST.

35. 1900 NW 32ND AVE.

36. 20015 FAIRMONT LN.

ANSWER SHEET TO MEMORIZATION EXERCISE 1 ROUTE CODES

1. Ⓐ Ⓑ Ⓒ Ⓓ
2. Ⓐ Ⓑ Ⓒ Ⓓ
3. Ⓐ Ⓑ Ⓒ Ⓓ
4. Ⓐ Ⓑ Ⓒ Ⓓ
5. Ⓐ Ⓑ Ⓒ Ⓓ
6. Ⓐ Ⓑ Ⓒ Ⓓ
7. Ⓐ Ⓑ Ⓒ Ⓓ
8. Ⓐ Ⓑ Ⓒ Ⓓ
9. Ⓐ Ⓑ Ⓒ Ⓓ
10. Ⓐ Ⓑ Ⓒ Ⓓ
11. Ⓐ Ⓑ Ⓒ Ⓓ
12. Ⓐ Ⓑ Ⓒ Ⓓ

13. Ⓐ Ⓑ Ⓒ Ⓓ
14. Ⓐ Ⓑ Ⓒ Ⓓ
15. Ⓐ Ⓑ Ⓒ Ⓓ
16. Ⓐ Ⓑ Ⓒ Ⓓ
17. Ⓐ Ⓑ Ⓒ Ⓓ
18. Ⓐ Ⓑ Ⓒ Ⓓ
19. Ⓐ Ⓑ Ⓒ Ⓓ
20. Ⓐ Ⓑ Ⓒ Ⓓ
21. Ⓐ Ⓑ Ⓒ Ⓓ
22. Ⓐ Ⓑ Ⓒ Ⓓ
23. Ⓐ Ⓑ Ⓒ Ⓓ
24. Ⓐ Ⓑ Ⓒ Ⓓ

25. Ⓐ Ⓑ Ⓒ Ⓓ
26. Ⓐ Ⓑ Ⓒ Ⓓ
27. Ⓐ Ⓑ Ⓒ Ⓓ
28. Ⓐ Ⓑ Ⓒ Ⓓ
29. Ⓐ Ⓑ Ⓒ Ⓓ
30. Ⓐ Ⓑ Ⓒ Ⓓ
31. Ⓐ Ⓑ Ⓒ Ⓓ
32. Ⓐ Ⓑ Ⓒ Ⓓ
33. Ⓐ Ⓑ Ⓒ Ⓓ
34. Ⓐ Ⓑ Ⓒ Ⓓ
35. Ⓐ Ⓑ Ⓒ Ⓓ
36. Ⓐ Ⓑ Ⓒ Ⓓ

ANSWERS TO MEMORIZATION EXERCISE 1

1.	A	13.	B	25.	D
2.	D	14.	D	26.	B
3.	B	15.	C	27.	A
4.	C	16.	C	28.	C
5.	D	17.	D	29.	D
6.	A	18.	A	30.	B
7.	D	19.	D	31.	A
8.	B	20.	C	32.	D
9.	D	21.	C	33.	D
10.	C	22.	C	34.	D
11.	C	23.	A	35.	B
12.	A	24.	B	36.	D

If you scored:
34–36 correct, you have an excellent score.
32–33 correct, you have a good score.
31 or fewer, more practice is needed.

MEMORIZATION EXERCISE 2   **TIME: 3 MINUTES**

SERVICE RANGE	ROUTE ID
3000-7999 WASHINGTON AVE. 45-960 W. 33RD AVE.	ROUTE A
961-1450 W. 33RD AVE. 1780-4675 PALMER LN. 790-2999 WASHINGTON AVE.	ROUTE B
2399-5099 BURNHAM DR. 300-1779 PALMER LN. 150-925 CAMINO BLVD.	ROUTE C
ALL OTHER ADDRESSES NOT SERVED BY THE ABOVE ROUTES	ROUTE D

OPTIONAL WORKSHEET PROVIDED BELOW

	STREET ADDRESSES	ROUTE CODE
1.	4312 WASHINGTON AVE.	Ⓐ Ⓑ Ⓒ Ⓓ
2.	317 PALMER LN.	Ⓐ Ⓑ Ⓒ Ⓓ
3.	1812 VICTORIA PL.	Ⓐ Ⓑ Ⓒ Ⓓ
4.	913 CAMINO BLVD.	Ⓐ Ⓑ Ⓒ Ⓓ
5.	701 W. 33RD AVE.	Ⓐ Ⓑ Ⓒ Ⓓ
6.	4320 PALMER LN.	Ⓐ Ⓑ Ⓒ Ⓓ
7.	3745 BURNHAM DR.	Ⓐ Ⓑ Ⓒ Ⓓ
8.	50713 W. 33RD AVE.	Ⓐ Ⓑ Ⓒ Ⓓ
9.	899 WASHINGTON AVE.	Ⓐ Ⓑ Ⓒ Ⓓ
10.	191 CAMINO BLVD.	Ⓐ Ⓑ Ⓒ Ⓓ
11.	1700 PALMER LN.	Ⓐ Ⓑ Ⓒ Ⓓ
12.	80 W. KENMORE ST.	Ⓐ Ⓑ Ⓒ Ⓓ
13.	1233 W. 33RD AVE.	Ⓐ Ⓑ Ⓒ Ⓓ
14.	3035 BURNHAM DR.	Ⓐ Ⓑ Ⓒ Ⓓ
15.	791 WASHINGTON AVE.	Ⓐ Ⓑ Ⓒ Ⓓ

STUDY TIME: 5 MINUTES

SERVICE RANGE	ROUTE ID
3000-7999 WASHINGTON AVE. 45-960 W. 33RD AVE.	ROUTE A
961-1450 W. 33RD AVE. 1780-4675 PALMER LN. 790-2999 WASHINGTON AVE.	ROUTE B
2399-5099 BURNHAM DR. 300-1779 PALMER LN. 150-925 CAMINO BLVD.	ROUTE C
ALL OTHER ADDRESSES NOT SERVED BY THE ABOVE ROUTES	ROUTE D

MEMORIZATION EXERCISE 2   **TIME: 7 MINUTES**

1. 1375 W. 32ND ST.

2. 1799 WASHINGTON AVE.

3. 5003 BURNHAM DR.

4. 55 W. 33RD AVE.

5. 7900 WASHINGTON AVE.

6. 416 PALMER LN.

7. 4099 RIDGEMONT DR.

8. 901 CAMINO BLVD.

9. 962 W. 33RD AVE.

10. 4380 PALMER LN.

11. 49 W. 32ND AVE.

12. 3007 WASHINGTON AVE.

13. 238 CAMINO BLVD.

14. 48 N. HIGHLAND CT.

15. 2403 PALMER LN.

16. 555 W. 33RD AVE.

17. 52 W. 33RD AVE.

18. 4444 BURNHAM DR.

19. 1899 PALMER LN.

20. 140 CHESTNUT DR.

21. 833 CAMINO BLVD.

22. 3300 WASHINGTON AVE.

23. 4692 NW 33RD ST.

24. 4218 PALMER LN.

25. 2400 BURNHAM DR.

26. 158 CAMINO BLVD.

27. 5090 DEVONVILLE

28. 49 W. 33RD AVE.

29. 3990 WASHINGTON AVE.

30. 1203 W. 3RD ST.

31. 2050 PALMER LN.

32. 1617 BURNHAM DR.

33. 902 CAMINO BLVD.

34. 4020 WASHINGTON AVE.

35. 1895 W. 30TH ST.

36. 999 W. 33RD AVE.

ANSWER SHEET TO MEMORIZATION EXERCISE 2 ROUTE CODES

1. A B C D   13. A B C D   25. A B C D
2. A B C D   14. A B C D   26. A B C D
3. A B C D   15. A B C D   27. A B C D
4. A B C D   16. A B C D   28. A B C D
5. A B C D   17. A B C D   29. A B C D
6. A B C D   18. A B C D   30. A B C D
7. A B C D   19. A B C D   31. A B C D
8. A B C D   20. A B C D   32. A B C D
9. A B C D   21. A B C D   33. A B C D
10. A B C D   22. A B C D   34. A B C D
11. A B C D   23. A B C D   35. A B C D
12. A B C D   24. A B C D   36. A B C D

ANSWERS TO MEMORIZATION EXERCISE 2

1.	D	13.	C	25.	C
2.	B	14.	D	26.	C
3.	C	15.	B	27.	D
4.	A	16.	A	28.	A
5.	A	17.	A	29.	A
6.	C	18.	C	30.	D
7.	D	19.	B	31.	B
8.	C	20.	D	32.	D
9.	B	21.	C	33.	C
10.	B	22.	A	34.	A
11.	D	23.	D	35.	D
12.	A	24.	B	36.	B

If you scored:
34–36 correct, you have an excellent score.
32–33 correct, you have a good score.
31 or fewer, more practice is needed.

Exam 1

**DO NOT OPEN THIS TEST BOOKLET UNTIL
YOU ARE TOLD TO START BY THE INDIVIDUAL
ASSISTING YOU IN THIS EXERCISE**

[This page is intentionally blank.]

ADDRESS CROSS COMPARISON

TIME: 11 MINUTES

ANSWER KEY:

A) NO ERRORS
B) STREET ADDRESS ONLY
C) ZIP CODE ONLY
D) BOTH

1.	901 COLEMAN AVE. LAKELAND, FL 38319		901 COLEMAN AVE. LAKELAND, FL 38319	
2.	1199 S MARIETTA CT SANTA BARBARA, CA 93001		1199 S ARISVILLE CT SANTA BARBARA, CA 93001	
3.	105 SW HWY 99 BOX 102 MELBOURNE, AR 74205		501 SW HWY 99 BOX 102 MELBOURNE, AR 72405	
4.	16700 GARLAND WAY WATERFORD, MI 43820-5710		16700 GRACELAND WAY WATERFORD, MI 42380-5710	
5.	889 PERSHING SQUARE ROCKVILLE, MD 28051-0222		889 PEARSHING SQUARE ROCKVILLE, MD 28051-0222	
6.	30107 MOCCASIN TRAIL ANN ARBOR, MI 41850-6650		30107 MOCCASIN TRAIL ANN ARBOR, MI 41850-5066	
7.	2016 MEADFORD COVE SHREVEPORT, LA 71052		2016 MEADFORD COVE SHREVEPORT, LA 71052	
8.	6913 SW 24TH ST MARION, IN 49705		6013 SW 24TH ST MARION, IN 49705	
9.	1144 N. INDUSTRIAL RD MCDONOUGH, GA 30162		1144 N. INDUSTRIAL RD MCDONOUGH, GA 30172	
10.	35-A WARM SPRINGS DR SAINT PETERSBURG, FL 37311-9970		35-A WARM SPRINGS RD SAINT PETERSBURG, FL 37711-9970	
11.	7744 EMBARCADERO ST. GREELY, CO 80197		7744 EMBARCADERO ST. GREELY, CO 80197	
12.	2020 S. IROQUOIS RD VAN NUYS, CA 94156		20202 S. IROQUOIS RD VAN NUYS, CA 94156	
13.	700 MILL POND CR HALL RIVER, MD 27051		700 MILL POND CR HALL RIVER, MI 27501	

14.	46464 CAMBRIDGE TERRACE BOSTON, MA 01257-1616	46464 CAMBRIDGE TERRACE BOSTON, MA 01257-1616
15.	15703 WINDEMERE PKWY LAKE CHARLES, LA 76051	15703 WINDEMERE PKWY LAKE CHARLES, AL 76051
16.	40 S. SPRINGFELD DR. NAPA, CA 93678	40 S. SPRINGFIELD DR. NAPA, CA 93678
17.	2020-C RENAISSANCE BLVD URBANA, IL 68152-7100	2020-C RENAISSANCE BLVD URBANA, IL 08152-7100
18.	26379 E OXFORD PLACE MACON, GA 32117	26379 E OXFORD PLACE MACON, LA 32217
19.	8031 ARLINGTON DR ORLANDO, FL 38221-6053	8031 ARLING DR ORLANDO, FL 38221-6503
20.	60012 SW 13TH PL PETALUMA, CA 95271	60012 SW 13TH PL PETALUMA, CA 95271
21.	10 SW MARCO VALLEY CIRCLE ROCKWALL, TX 70521	10 SW MARCO VALLEY CIRCLE ROCKWALL, TX 75210
22.	414-B SUNSET BLVD NASHVILLE, TN 37952-1116	414-B SUNSET BLVD NASHVILLE, TN 37952-1116
23.	8000 BRENTWOOD OAKS W PROVIDENCE, RI 09207-0575	8000 BRENTWOOD OAKS W. PROVIDENCE, MI 09207-0575
24.	11117 PACIFIC PLACE NW BEAVERTON, OR 90775-1422	1117 PACIFIC PLACE SW BEAVERTON, OR 90775-1424
25.	403-A GREENBRIAR PKWY MIDLAND, TX 77907	403-A GREENBRIAR PKWY MIDLAND, TX 77907
26.	123 SAWDUST HILL HOUSTON, TX 77152	123 SAWDUST HILL HOUSTON, TX 71752
27.	999 PLYMOUTH LN APT 210 OREM, UT 80423	999 PLYMOUTH LN APT 210 OREM, UT 80243
28.	2795 SW 240TH ST. FORT MILL, SC 21750-2395	2795 SW 240TH ST. FORT MILL, SC 21750-2395
29.	2347 HARPERS FERRY LANDING FRANKLIN, TN 37169	2374 HARPERS FERRY LANDING FRANKLIN, TN 37169
30.	3030 BAYVALLEY DR GROTON, CT 03650-0555	3030 BAYVALLEY DR GROTON, CT 36500-0555

31. 912 JACKSON PLACE E.
SAN JOSE, CA   91572-2222

    912 JACKSON PLACE E.
    SAN JOSE, CA   91572-2222

32. 5050 SW SANTA FE LANE
PUEBLO, CO   80155-1201

    550 SE SANTA FE LANE
    PUEBLO, CO   80055-1201

33. 77-D ARCADIA COURT
HAMDEN, CT   05671

    77-D ARCADIA COURT
    HAMDEN, VT   05771

34. 6829 BROKEN ARROW LN
MONTGOMERY, AL   31652-1004

    6829 BROKEN ARROW LN
    MONTGOMERY, AL   31652-1004

35. 5980 CARMICHAEL PKWY
LOS ANGELES, CA   92349-1222

    5980 CARMICHAEL PKWY
    LOS ANGELES, CA   92319-1222

36. 2027 WOODEN BRIDGE CT
BILLINGS, MT   59001

    7022 WOODEN BRIDGE CT
    BILLINGS, MT   59001

37. 6677 BLUE GROUSE PT
SAINT CLOUD, MN   53671

    7766 BLUE GROUSE PT
    SAINT CLOUD, MN   53691

38. A-160 EASTERN AVE
SAINT LOUIS, MO   63004-1236

    A-160 EASTERN AVE
    SAINT LOUIS, MO   63004-1236

39. 901 STATE ROUTE 3 BOX 15
DULUTH, MN   58411

    901 STATE ROUTE 3 BOX 15
    DULUTH, MN   58411

40. 66715 S. HARTHVIEW LN
SOUTH BEND, IN   40611-1307

    66715 S. HARTHVIEW LN
    SOUTH BEND, IN   40671-1307

41. 80-C SOUTH LONDON CT
ALPHARETTA, GA   30152

    8-C SOUTH LONDON CT
    ALPHARETTA, GA   30152

42. 371 BOX CANYON RD
MILTON, AK   32577

    371 BOX CANYON RD
    MILTON, AL   32577

43. 3574 W. 186TH DR.
TOPEKA, KS   66601-5711

    3574 W. 136TH DR
    TOPEKA, KS   66601-5711

44. 399 PATRICK AVE E.
SAINT CHARLES, MO   64405

    390 PATRICK AVE E.
    SAINT CHARLES, MO   64405

45. 4040 CRANBERRY LAKE DR.
CANTON, OH   48817-7778

    4040 CRANBERRY LAKE DR
    CANTON, OH   48817-7778

46. 8889 BECKFORD PLACE
WEYMOUTH, MA   01289-8001

    3339 BECKFORD PLACE
    WEYMOUTH, MA   01289-8101

47. C-211 MYLANDER LN NW
BALTIMORE, MD   21150-0051

    C-211 MYLANDER CT NW
    BALTIMORE, MD   01150-0051

48. 2710 YAROBOUGH BLVD
GREENWOOD, IN   41671

    2710 YAROBOUGH BLVD
GREENWOOD, IN   41671

49. 13342-M BRIDGE LAKE RD
SMYRNA, GA   30155

    13342-M BRIDGE LAKE RD
SMYRNA, GA   30144

50. 1781 N 30TH ST
KANSAS CITY, KS   60612-4099

    1781 N 30TH ST
KANSAS CITY, MO   60612-4099

51. 16 N HAYDAN MEADOW RD
DURHAM, NC   27134-5000

    16 N HAYDEN MEADOW RD
DURHAM, NC   27134-5000

52. 5050 SENATE AVE E
HAMILTON, OH   41475

    5050 SENATE AVE E
HAMILTON, OH   41475

53. 27233 LA SHAMBRA PKWY
CHATTANOOGA, TN   34785-6281

    27223 LA SHAMBRA PKWY
CHATTANOOGA, TN   43785-6281

54. 140 CONSTITUTION DR
DAYTON, OH   44501-7013

    140 CONSTITUTION DR
DAYTON, OH   44501-7013

55. A-1716 NW PATTERSON WAY
ASHEVILLE, NC   28110

    A-1716 NW PATTERSON WAY
ASHEVILLE, NC   78110

56. 108 EMERALD ST W
VALLEY STREAM, NY 11180

    108 EMERALD ST W
VALLER RIVER, NY   11180

57. 1461 E. RUBY LAKE
BROOKLYN, NY   12105-7700

    1461 E. RUBY LAKE
BROOKLYN, NY   12105-7700

58. 87051 E. HWY 80 BOX 44
ODESSA, TX   76701

    87051 E. HWY 44 BOX 80
ODESSA, TX   76701

59. 2027-A DEER ISLAND RD
JOHNS ISLAND, SC   23976

    2027-A DEER ISLAND RD
JOHNS ISLAND, SC   23796

60. A-1515 VAN LAWRENCE RD
PITTSBURGH, PA   12535-7011

    A-1515 VAN LAWRENCE RD
PITTSBURGH, PA   10535-7099

ANSWER SHEET TO EXAMINATION 1 ADDRESS CROSS COMPARISON

1. Ⓐ Ⓑ Ⓒ Ⓓ
2. Ⓐ Ⓑ Ⓒ Ⓓ
3. Ⓐ Ⓑ Ⓒ Ⓓ
4. Ⓐ Ⓑ Ⓒ Ⓓ
5. Ⓐ Ⓑ Ⓒ Ⓓ
6. Ⓐ Ⓑ Ⓒ Ⓓ
7. Ⓐ Ⓑ Ⓒ Ⓓ
8. Ⓐ Ⓑ Ⓒ Ⓓ
9. Ⓐ Ⓑ Ⓒ Ⓓ
10. Ⓐ Ⓑ Ⓒ Ⓓ
11. Ⓐ Ⓑ Ⓒ Ⓓ
12. Ⓐ Ⓑ Ⓒ Ⓓ
13. Ⓐ Ⓑ Ⓒ Ⓓ
14. Ⓐ Ⓑ Ⓒ Ⓓ
15. Ⓐ Ⓑ Ⓒ Ⓓ
16. Ⓐ Ⓑ Ⓒ Ⓓ
17. Ⓐ Ⓑ Ⓒ Ⓓ
18. Ⓐ Ⓑ Ⓒ Ⓓ
19. Ⓐ Ⓑ Ⓒ Ⓓ
20. Ⓐ Ⓑ Ⓒ Ⓓ

21. Ⓐ Ⓑ Ⓒ Ⓓ
22. Ⓐ Ⓑ Ⓒ Ⓓ
23. Ⓐ Ⓑ Ⓒ Ⓓ
24. Ⓐ Ⓑ Ⓒ Ⓓ
25. Ⓐ Ⓑ Ⓒ Ⓓ
26. Ⓐ Ⓑ Ⓒ Ⓓ
27. Ⓐ Ⓑ Ⓒ Ⓓ
28. Ⓐ Ⓑ Ⓒ Ⓓ
29. Ⓐ Ⓑ Ⓒ Ⓓ
30. Ⓐ Ⓑ Ⓒ Ⓓ
31. Ⓐ Ⓑ Ⓒ Ⓓ
32. Ⓐ Ⓑ Ⓒ Ⓓ
33. Ⓐ Ⓑ Ⓒ Ⓓ
34. Ⓐ Ⓑ Ⓒ Ⓓ
35. Ⓐ Ⓑ Ⓒ Ⓓ
36. Ⓐ Ⓑ Ⓒ Ⓓ
37. Ⓐ Ⓑ Ⓒ Ⓓ
38. Ⓐ Ⓑ Ⓒ Ⓓ
39. Ⓐ Ⓑ Ⓒ Ⓓ
40. Ⓐ Ⓑ Ⓒ Ⓓ

41. Ⓐ Ⓑ Ⓒ Ⓓ
42. Ⓐ Ⓑ Ⓒ Ⓓ
43. Ⓐ Ⓑ Ⓒ Ⓓ
44. Ⓐ Ⓑ Ⓒ Ⓓ
45. Ⓐ Ⓑ Ⓒ Ⓓ
46. Ⓐ Ⓑ Ⓒ Ⓓ
47. Ⓐ Ⓑ Ⓒ Ⓓ
48. Ⓐ Ⓑ Ⓒ Ⓓ
49. Ⓐ Ⓑ Ⓒ Ⓓ
50. Ⓐ Ⓑ Ⓒ Ⓓ
51. Ⓐ Ⓑ Ⓒ Ⓓ
52. Ⓐ Ⓑ Ⓒ Ⓓ
53. Ⓐ Ⓑ Ⓒ Ⓓ
54. Ⓐ Ⓑ Ⓒ Ⓓ
55. Ⓐ Ⓑ Ⓒ Ⓓ
56. Ⓐ Ⓑ Ⓒ Ⓓ
57. Ⓐ Ⓑ Ⓒ Ⓓ
58. Ⓐ Ⓑ Ⓒ Ⓓ
59. Ⓐ Ⓑ Ⓒ Ⓓ
60. Ⓐ Ⓑ Ⓒ Ⓓ

FORMS COMPLETION

TIME: 15 MINUTES

ANSWER QUESTIONS 1–15 BASED ON THE FOLLOWING INFORMATION.

EXPRESS MAIL RECEIPT

POSTAL CLERICAL ENTRY ONLY:

1. OFFICE OF ORIGINATION ZIP CODE +4

   _____

2. RECEIVING CLERK'S INITIALS

   _____

3. DATE ARTICLE ACCEPTED FOR MAILING

   _____

4. TIME ARTICLE WAS ACCEPTED

   _____

5. WEIGHT A) _____ LBS B) _____ OZ

6. A) POSTAGE FEE $_____
   B) INSURANCE FEE $_____
   C) RETURN RECEIPT FEE $_____
   D) FEES TOTAL: $_____
   E) CORPORATE ACCOUNT NO: _____

7. CHECK ONE
   A) _____ OVERNIGHT
   B) _____ 2ND DAY

8. A) SCHEDULED DELIVERY TIME

   _____

   B) SCHEDULED DELIVERY DATE

   _____

9. A) SENDER'S PHONE NUMBER

   _____

   B) SENDER'S NAME

   _____

   C) SENDER'S ADDRESS

   _____

10. ATTEMPTED DELIVERY DATE

    _____

11. TIME OF ATTEMPT

    _____

12. SIGNATURE OF EMPLOYEE

    _____

13. ARTICLE DELIVERY DATE

    _____

14. TIME OF DELIVERY

    _____

15. SIGNATURE OF EMPLOYEE

    _____

16. _____ SIGNATURE WAIVER
    If checked, sender must sign waiver request (item 17)

17. WAIVER REQUEST

    _____

18. A) RECIPIENT'S PHONE NUMBER

    _____

    B) RECIPIENT'S NAME

    _____

    C) RECIPIENT'S ADDRESS

    _____

1.   If an article were sent express mail from a Chicago, IL, post office, where would that information be correctly entered on the Express Mailing Receipt?

A)   Line item 1
B)   Line item 9C
C)   Line item 18C
D)   None of the above

2.   If 56032 represented an express mail corporate account number, where on the form would this information be placed?

A)   Line item 1
B)   Line item 6E
C)   Line item 9A
D)   Line item 10

3.   If the combined postage, insurance, and return receipt fees came to $47.27, where on the form would this information be entered?

A)   Line item 5A and B
B)   Line item 6A
C)   Line item 6D
D)   Line item 17

4.   If an express mailing was accepted by the post office on 10-13-05 and handled as a second day air with a scheduled delivery date of 10-15-05, how would that information be correctly entered on the form?

A)   10-13-05 and 10-15-05 would be entered on line items 3 and 8B respectively
B)   10-15-05 and 10-13-05 would be entered on line item 3 and 10 respectively
C)   Box 7B would be checked
D)   Both A and C

5.   Where would a person sign on this form to request a signature waiver?

A)   Line item 9B
B)   Line item 17
C)   Line item 18
D)   None of the above

6.   Where on this form would the sender's phone number be entered?

A)   Line item 9A
B)   Line item 11
C)   Line item 18A
D)   Line item 18C

7.   If city carrier Ron Nelson attempted to deliver an express pouch to a business that was closed for the weekend, which of the following represents a correct endorsement on the mailing receipt?

A)   Ron Nelson's signature would be entered on line item 2
B)   Ron Nelson's signature would be entered on line item 12
C)   Ron Nelson's signature would be entered on line item 15
D)   None of the above

8.   If window service clerk Adrian Miller accepted an express mailing from a customer at 2:00 P.M. on 8-17-05, how would this information correctly be entered on the form?

A)   Adrian Miller's name, 2:00 P.M., and 8-17-05 would be entered on line items 2, 4, and 3 respectively.
B)   Adrian Miller's name, 2:00 P.M., and 8-17-05 would be entered on line items 2, 3, and 4 respectively.
C)   A.M., 2:00 P.M., and 8-17-05 would be entered on line item 2, 4, and 3 respectively.
D)   A.M., 2:00 P.M., and 8-17-05 would be entered on line items 12, 14, and 13 respectively.

9.   If the addressee on an express mailing had to be immediately contacted for whatever reason, where on the mailing receipt can that information can be found?

A)   Line item 6E
B)   Line item 9A
C)   Line item 18A
D)   Line item 18C

10.   Where are return receipt fees itemized on the form?

A)   Line item 6A
B)   Line item 6B
C)   Line item 6C
D)   Line item 6D

11.   A customer wanted to express mail a small packet that weighted 10 ounces. Where on this form would that information be entered?

A)   Line item 5B
B)   Line item 5A
C)   Line item 6A
D)   Line item 6B

12.   If the post office accepted an express mailed article on 12-20-05 and box 7B was checked, line item 8B should have which of the following entered?

A)   3:00 P.M.
B)   12-22-05
C)   12-23-05
D)   Cannot be determined

13.   Which of the following is true if the sender fills in line item 17?

A)   Box 16 must be checked
B)   Line items 8A and 8B need to be endorsed by the sender
C)   Line items 3, 4, and 5 need to be endorsed by the sender
D)   None of the above

14.   47568-5555 would be a correct entry for which of the following?

A)   Line item 1
B)   Line item 9A
C)   Line item 18A
D)   None of the above

15. Sales Services and Distribution Associate Denise Marlowe handled a customer pick up of an express mailing. Where on the mailing receipt would she be required to sign?

A) Line item 2
B) Line item 15
C) Line item 17
D) Line item 18B

ANSWER QUESTIONS 16–30 BASED ON THE FOLLOWING INFORMATION.
CHANGE OF ADDRESS FORWARDING ORDER

POSTAL USE ONLY

1. NUMBER RT DESIGNATION
    _____

2. DATE ENTERED INTO SYSTEM
    _____

3   EXPIRATION DATE IF TEMPORARY
    _____

4. CLERK OR CARRIER INITIALS
    _____

(ONE CUSTOMER NAME PER FORM)
8. A) CUSTOMER'S FIRST NAME
    _____

    B) CUSTOMER'S LAST NAME
    _____

    C) MIDDLE INITIAL
    _____

11. A) CUSTOMER'S PRINTED NAME
    _____

    B) CUSTOMER'S SIGNATURE
    _____

12. DATE FORWARDING ORDER SIGNED
    _____

5. CHANGE OF ADDRESS
    REQUESTED FOR (Check one)
    A) _____ FAMILY
    B) _____ INDIVIDUAL
    C) _____ BUSINESS

6. IS THIS FORWARDING REQUEST
    FOR A TEMPORARY MOVE?
    (Check one)
    A) _____ YES
    B) _____ NO

7. IF 6A IS CHECKED ENTER THE
    NUMERICAL DATE WHEN TO
    DISCONTINUE THE FORWARDING
    ORDER. _____

9. FORMER MAILING ADDRESS
    A) STREET OR P.O. BOX NUMBER
    _____
    B) SUITE OR APT NUMBER
    _____
    C) CITY
    _____
    D) STATE
    _____
    E) ZIP CODE
    _____

10. NEW ADDRESS
    A) STREET OR P.O. BOX NUMBER
    _____
    B) SUITE OR APT NUMBER
    _____
    C) CITY
    _____
    D) STATE
    _____
    E) ZIP CODE
    _____

16. The date August 16, 2005, as written, could be entered where on this form?

A) Line item 2, 3, 7, and 12
B) Line item 2 and 3
C) Line item 12
D) Both B and C

17. The number 1023 would be a proper entry for which of the following?

A) Line item 1
B) Line item 4
C) Line item 7
D) None of the above

18. If window service clerk Ken Patterson accepted a forwarding order request from a customer on June 10, 2005, which of the following form endorsements would be correct?

A) 6-10-05 and K. Patterson would be entered on line items 3 and 4 respectively
B) 6-10-05 and K.P. would be entered on line items 2 and 4 respectively
C) 6-10-05 and K.P. would be entered on line items 3 and 4 respectively
D) None of the above

19. Jane Wilson filed an address forwarding order for her family because they were heading south for the winter. They intended to return on March 14, 2006. How would this information be properly entered on the Change of Address form?

A) Box 5A would be checked and March 14, 2006 would be written on line item 7
B) Box 5A would be checked and 03-04-06 would be entered on line item 7
C) Boxes 5A and 6A would be checked and 03-14-06 would be entered on line item 7
D) Boxes 5A and 6B would be checked and 03-14-06 would be entered on line item 7

ANSWER QUESTIONS 20–30 BASED ON THE FOLLOWING INFORMATION:

Windows Sales Associate Tim McBride accepted a Change of Address request on August 18, 2005, from customers John and Marie Ellington. They were both planning to move from their parent's address to attend the University of Washington. Their current address is 1570 E. Jackson Ave., Tacoma, WA 98472, and their new address on the university campus will be 172 Roosevelt Dr. Apt. 2E, Seattle, WA 98499. The forwarding order would go into effect immediately. Both customers, however, would be back for summer vacation on May 15, 2006. Mail delivery should then resume to their former address. Letter carrier Diane Foster (route 1027) was informed of the request and given a copy of the change order to place on file.

20.   What name(s) would be entered on line item 8A of the forwarding order request?

A)   Ellington
B)   Time
C)   Both John and Marie
D)   Either Marie or John

21.   What information should be entered on line item 12?

A)   The same information entered on line item 2
B)   05-15-06
C)   08-28-06
D)   Can't be determined

22.   What information would be the correct entry for line item 10C?

A)   University of Washington
B)   Tacoma
C)   Seattle
D)   Washington

23.   Line item 4 should be endorsed with which of the following?

A)   A check mark
B)   T.M.
C)   J.E.
D)   Tina McBride

24.   Which of the following represents a correct entry for line item 9B?

A)   Roosevelt Dr.
B)   Suite 2-E
C)   Apt. 2-E
D)   Does not apply; therefore, it should be left blank

25.   Where would either John or Marie Ellington sign on the form to authorize the forwarding order request?

A)   Line item 4
B)   Line item 11A
C)   Line item 11B
D)   Line item 12

26. What information properly applies to line item 1?

A) 1027
B) Diane Foster
C) Tina McBride
D) 98742

27. Which of the following would be the correct entry for line item 9E?

A) 172
B) 1027
C) 98472
D) 98499

28. What information represents the correct form entry for line items 3 and 7?

A) 08-28-05
B) 08-28-06
C) 05-15-06
D) It was not provided

29. Which of the following form endorsements would apply under the circumstances given?

A) Boxes 5B and 6A would be checked
B) Boxes 5A and 6B would be checked
C) Boxes 5B and 6B would be checked
D) Boxes 5C and 6A would be checked

30. All of the following are correct entries on the Change of Address Order except?

A) 1570 E. Jackson Ave entered on line item 9A
B) WA would be entered only on line item 9D
C) Apt number 2-E entered on line item 10B
D) Either John or Marie Ellington's printed name would be entered on line item 11A

ANSWER SHEET EXAMINATION 1 FORMS COMPLETION

1. (A) (B) (C) (D)   11. (A) (B) (C) (D)   21. (A) (B) (C) (D)
2. (A) (B) (C) (D)   12. (A) (B) (C) (D)   22. (A) (B) (C) (D)
3. (A) (B) (C) (D)   13. (A) (B) (C) (D)   23. (A) (B) (C) (D)
4. (A) (B) (C) (D)   14. (A) (B) (C) (D)   24. (A) (B) (C) (D)
5. (A) (B) (C) (D)   15. (A) (B) (C) (D)   25. (A) (B) (C) (D)
6. (A) (B) (C) (D)   16. (A) (B) (C) (D)   26. (A) (B) (C) (D)
7. (A) (B) (C) (D)   17. (A) (B) (C) (D)   27. (A) (B) (C) (D)
8. (A) (B) (C) (D)   18. (A) (B) (C) (D)   28. (A) (B) (C) (D)
9. (A) (B) (C) (D)   19. (A) (B) (C) (D)   29. (A) (B) (C) (D)
10. (A) (B) (C) (D)   20. (A) (B) (C) (D)   30. (A) (B) (C) (D)

CODING   **TIME: 6 MINUTES**

SERVICE RANGE	ROUTE ID
1300-6399 HORSTMAN RD. 890-2300 NE 23RD ST. 350-1199 STERLING AVE.	ROUTE A
600-1299 HORSTMAN RD. 36100-54099 HWY 151 1200-1575 STERLING AVE.	ROUTE B
54100-62399 HWY 151 180-599 HORSTMAN RD.	ROUTE C
ALL OTHER ADDRESSES THAT ARE NOT INCLUDED IN THE ABOVE RANGES	ROUTE D

STREET ADDRESSES	ROUTE CODE ANSWERS
1. 1317 NE 23RD ST.	Ⓐ Ⓑ Ⓒ Ⓓ
2. 59727 HWY 151	Ⓐ Ⓑ Ⓒ Ⓓ
3. 125 HORSTMAN RD.	Ⓐ Ⓑ Ⓒ Ⓓ
4. 1299 STERLING AVE.	Ⓐ Ⓑ Ⓒ Ⓓ
5. 678 HORSTMAN RD.	Ⓐ Ⓑ Ⓒ Ⓓ
6. 2300 NE 13TH ST.	Ⓐ Ⓑ Ⓒ Ⓓ
7. 1001 STERLING AVE.	Ⓐ Ⓑ Ⓒ Ⓓ
8. 61309 HWY 151	Ⓐ Ⓑ Ⓒ Ⓓ
9. 895 NE 33RD AVE.	Ⓐ Ⓑ Ⓒ Ⓓ
10. 1399 STERLING AVE.	Ⓐ Ⓑ Ⓒ Ⓓ
11. 1000 STERLING AVE.	Ⓐ Ⓑ Ⓒ Ⓓ
12. 350 HORSTMAN AVE.	Ⓐ Ⓑ Ⓒ Ⓓ
13. 55033 HWY 151	Ⓐ Ⓑ Ⓒ Ⓓ
14. 6350 HORSTMAN RD.	Ⓐ Ⓑ Ⓒ Ⓓ
15. 37199 STERLING AVE.	Ⓐ Ⓑ Ⓒ Ⓓ

16. 53000 HWY 151   Ⓐ Ⓑ Ⓒ Ⓓ

17. 199 HORSTMAN RD.   Ⓐ Ⓑ Ⓒ Ⓓ

18. 603 FOSTER ST.   Ⓐ Ⓑ Ⓒ Ⓓ

19. 1680 HABNER BLVD.   Ⓐ Ⓑ Ⓒ Ⓓ

20. 475 STERLING AVE.   Ⓐ Ⓑ Ⓒ Ⓓ

21. 2205 NE 23RD ST.   Ⓐ Ⓑ Ⓒ Ⓓ

22. 1290 HORSTMAN RD.   Ⓐ Ⓑ Ⓒ Ⓓ

23. 61000 HWY 151   Ⓐ Ⓑ Ⓒ Ⓓ

24. 572 HORSTMAN RD.   Ⓐ Ⓑ Ⓒ Ⓓ

25. 1419 JUNIPER CT.   Ⓐ Ⓑ Ⓒ Ⓓ

26. 1100 STERLING AVE.   Ⓐ Ⓑ Ⓒ Ⓓ

27. 1208 STERLING AVE.   Ⓐ Ⓑ Ⓒ Ⓓ

28. 899 NE 23RD ST.   Ⓐ Ⓑ Ⓒ Ⓓ

29. 54299 HWY 151   Ⓐ Ⓑ Ⓒ Ⓓ

30. 1519-C CRESTVIEW   Ⓐ Ⓑ Ⓒ Ⓓ

31. 36111 HWY 151   Ⓐ Ⓑ Ⓒ Ⓓ

32. 1573 STERLING AVE.   Ⓐ Ⓑ Ⓒ Ⓓ

33. 1919 W 23RD ST.   Ⓐ Ⓑ Ⓒ Ⓓ

34. 63990 HORSTMAN RD.   Ⓐ Ⓑ Ⓒ Ⓓ

35. 2017 BELLPARK LN.   Ⓐ Ⓑ Ⓒ Ⓓ

36. 1090 STERLING AVE.   Ⓐ Ⓑ Ⓒ Ⓓ

MEMORY   **TIME: 3 MINUTES**

SERVICE RANGE	ROUTE ID
1300-6399 HORSTMAN RD. 890-2300 NE 23RD ST. 350-1199 STERLING AVE.	ROUTE A
600-1299 HORSTMAN RD 36100-54099 HWY 151 1200-1575 STERLING AVE.	.ROUTE B
54100-62399 HWY 151 180-599 HORSTMAN RD.	ROUTE C
ALL OTHER ADDRESSES NOT SERVED BY THE ABOVE ROUTES	ROUTE D

OPTIONAL WORKSHEET PROVIDED BELOW

	STREET ADDRESSES	ROUTE CODE
1.	1872 NE 23RD ST.	Ⓐ Ⓑ Ⓒ Ⓓ
2.	890 NE 23RD AVE.	Ⓐ Ⓑ Ⓒ Ⓓ
3.	1125 HORSTMAN RD.	Ⓐ Ⓑ Ⓒ Ⓓ
4.	57199 HWY 151	Ⓐ Ⓑ Ⓒ Ⓓ
5.	1315 STERLING AVE.	Ⓐ Ⓑ Ⓒ Ⓓ
6.	427 LAKEVIEW	Ⓐ Ⓑ Ⓒ Ⓓ
7.	677 HORSTMAN RD.	Ⓐ Ⓑ Ⓒ Ⓓ
8.	371 STERLING ST.	Ⓐ Ⓑ Ⓒ Ⓓ
9.	54080 HWY 151	Ⓐ Ⓑ Ⓒ Ⓓ
10.	188 HORSTMAN RD.	Ⓐ Ⓑ Ⓒ Ⓓ
11.	6399 STERLING AVE.	Ⓐ Ⓑ Ⓒ Ⓓ
12.	2399 NE 23RD ST.	Ⓐ Ⓑ Ⓒ Ⓓ
13.	61505 HWY 151	Ⓐ Ⓑ Ⓒ Ⓓ

14.   5000 HORSTMAN RD.   Ⓐ Ⓑ Ⓒ Ⓓ

15.   4025 NE 43ᴿᴰ ST.   Ⓐ Ⓑ Ⓒ Ⓓ

SERVICE RANGE	ROUTE ID
1300-6399 HORSTMAN RD. 890-2300 NE 23RD ST. 350-1199 STERLING AVE.	ROUTE A
600-1299 HORSTMAN RD. 36100-54099 HWY 151 1200-1575 STERLING AVE.	ROUTE B
54100-62399 HWY 151 180-599 HORSTMAN RD.	ROUTE C
ALL OTHER ADDRESSES NOT SERVED BY THE ABOVE ROUTES	ROUTE D

MEMORY

TIME: 7 MINUTES

1. 6390 HORSTMAN RD.
2. 1300 STERLING ST.
3. 50000 HWY 151
4. 329 HORSTMAN RD.
5. 1525 STERLING AVE.
6. 1900 NE 51ST ST.
7. 350 STERLING AVE.
8. 36077 HWY 15
9. 401 HORSTMAN RD.
10. 59999 HWY 151
11. 1204 STERLING AVE.
12. 1818 NE 23RD ST.
13. 207 E. CISCO BLVD.
14. 399 STERLING AVE.
15. 1501 STERLING ST.
16. 1750 NE 23RD ST.
17. 38500 HWY 151
18. 61500 HWY 151

19. 1377 HORSTMAN RD.
20. 1000 STERLING AVE.
21. 1313 STERLING BLVD.
22. 37-D COVINGTON DR.
23. 53000 HWY 151
24. 499 HORSTMAN RD.
25. 1515-F STERLING AVE.
26. 1401 NE 23RD ST.
27. 6200 HORSTMAN RD.
28. 1717 W. BAKER
29. 805-B ELLINGTON PL.
30. 37777 HWY 151
31. 413 HORSTMAN RD.
32. 2020 IVERNESS
33. 990 STERLING AVE.
34. 892 HORSTMAN RD.
35. 592 HORSTMAN AVE.
36. 5410 HWY 151

ANSWER SHEET FOR EXAMINATION 1 MEMORY QUESTIONS

1. Ⓐ Ⓑ Ⓒ Ⓓ
2. Ⓐ Ⓑ Ⓒ Ⓓ
3. Ⓐ Ⓑ Ⓒ Ⓓ
4. Ⓐ Ⓑ Ⓒ Ⓓ
5. Ⓐ Ⓑ Ⓒ Ⓓ
6. Ⓐ Ⓑ Ⓒ Ⓓ
7. Ⓐ Ⓑ Ⓒ Ⓓ
8. Ⓐ Ⓑ Ⓒ Ⓓ
9. Ⓐ Ⓑ Ⓒ Ⓓ
10. Ⓐ Ⓑ Ⓒ Ⓓ
11. Ⓐ Ⓑ Ⓒ Ⓓ
12. Ⓐ Ⓑ Ⓒ Ⓓ

13. Ⓐ Ⓑ Ⓒ Ⓓ
14. Ⓐ Ⓑ Ⓒ Ⓓ
15. Ⓐ Ⓑ Ⓒ Ⓓ
16. Ⓐ Ⓑ Ⓒ Ⓓ
17. Ⓐ Ⓑ Ⓒ Ⓓ
18. Ⓐ Ⓑ Ⓒ Ⓓ
19. Ⓐ Ⓑ Ⓒ Ⓓ
20. Ⓐ Ⓑ Ⓒ Ⓓ
21. Ⓐ Ⓑ Ⓒ Ⓓ
22. Ⓐ Ⓑ Ⓒ Ⓓ
23. Ⓐ Ⓑ Ⓒ Ⓓ
24. Ⓐ Ⓑ Ⓒ Ⓓ

25. Ⓐ Ⓑ Ⓒ Ⓓ
26. Ⓐ Ⓑ Ⓒ Ⓓ
27. Ⓐ Ⓑ Ⓒ Ⓓ
28. Ⓐ Ⓑ Ⓒ Ⓓ
29. Ⓐ Ⓑ Ⓒ Ⓓ
30. Ⓐ Ⓑ Ⓒ Ⓓ
31. Ⓐ Ⓑ Ⓒ Ⓓ
32. Ⓐ Ⓑ Ⓒ Ⓓ
33. Ⓐ Ⓑ Ⓒ Ⓓ
34. Ⓐ Ⓑ Ⓒ Ⓓ
35. Ⓐ Ⓑ Ⓒ Ⓓ
36. Ⓐ Ⓑ Ⓒ Ⓓ

ANSWERS TO EXAMINATION 1 ADDRESS CROSS COMPARISON

1.	A	21.	C	41.	B
2.	B	22.	A	42.	B
3.	D	23.	B	43.	B
4.	D	24.	D	44.	B
5.	B	25.	A	45.	A
6.	C	26.	C	46.	D
7.	A	27.	C	47.	D
8.	B	28.	A	48.	A
9.	C	29.	B	49.	C
10.	D	30.	C	50.	B
11.	A	31.	A	51.	B
12.	B	32.	D	52.	A
13.	D	33.	D	53.	D
14.	A	34.	A	54.	A
15.	B	35.	C	55.	C
16.	B	36.	B	56.	B
17.	C	37.	D	57.	A
18.	D	38.	A	58.	B
19.	D	39.	A	59.	C
20.	A	40.	C	60.	C

ANSWERS TO EXAMINATION 1 FORMS COMPLETION

1.	D	16.	D *
2.	B	17.	A
3.	C	18.	B
4.	D	19.	C
5.	B	20.	D
6.	A	21.	A
7.	B	22.	C
8.	C	23.	B
9.	C	24.	D
10.	C	25.	C
11.	A	26.	A
12.	B	27.	C
13.	A	28.	C
14.	A	29.	A
15.	B	30.	B

* NOTE: THE DATE CAN BE WRITTEN IN FOR ITEMS 2, 3, AND 12.
ITEM 7 REQUIRES A NUMERICAL ENTRY.

ANSWERS TO EXAMINATION 1 CODING

1.	A	13.	C	25.	D
2.	C	14.	A	26.	A
3.	D	15.	D	27.	B
4.	B	16.	B	28.	A
5.	B	17.	C	29.	C
6.	D	18.	D	30.	D
7.	A	19.	D	31.	B
8.	C	20.	A	32.	B
9.	D	21.	A	33.	D
10.	B	22.	B	34.	D
11.	A	23.	C	35.	D
12.	D	24.	C	36.	A

ANSWERS TO EXAMINATION 1 MEMORY

1.	A	19.	A
2.	D	20.	A
3.	B	21.	D
4.	C	22.	D
5.	B	23.	B
6.	D	24.	C
7.	A	25.	B
8.	D	26.	A
9.	C	27.	A
10.	C	28.	D
11.	B	29.	D
12.	A	30.	B
13.	D	31.	C
14.	A	32.	D
15.	D	33.	A
16.	A	34.	B
17.	B	35.	D
18.	C	36.	D

Add together your correct answer count for each of the four test sections given.
   If they total:
151–162 correct, you have an excellent score.
138–150 correct, you have a good score.
137 or less correct, you need additional practice.

[This page is intentionally blank.]

Exam 2

**DO NOT OPEN THIS TEST BOOKLET
UNTIL YOU ARE TOLD TO START
BY THE INDIVIDUAL ASSISTING
YOU IN THIS EXERCISE**

TIME: 11 MINUTES   **ADDRESS CROSS COMPARISON**

ANSWER KEY:

A) NO ERRORS
B) STREET ADDRESS ONLY
C) ZIP CODE ONLY
D) BOTH

1.   35 ZIRCON RIDGE   35 ZIRCON RIDGE
     ARLINGTON, VA   70655-1321   ARLINGTON, VA   70655-1321

2.   1857 SADLE RIDGE CT   1557 SADDLE RIDGE CT
     PHILADELPHIA, PA   19054   PHILADELPHIA, PA   19054

3.   122-B 52ND AVE S.   122-B 52ND AVE N.
     FAYETTEVILLE, NC   23184   FAYETTEVILLE, NC   23184

4.   44596 100TH ST. E   44596 104TH ST. E
     WISCONSIN RAPIDS, WI 50567   WISCONSIN RAPIDS, WI 55067

5.   A-160 WINE RIVER S.   A-160 WINE RIVER S.
     LYNWOOD, WA   94855-3712   LYNWOOD, WA   94835-3712

6.   80-560 STATE ROUTE 32   80-560 STATE ROUTE 32
     DANVILLE, WV   25431-0506   DANVILLE, WV   25431-5060

7.   2013 CROSS CREEK WAY   2013 CROSS CREEK WAY
     ADA, OK   72405   AGRA, OK   72405

8.   10999 E. CARRIAGE LANE   1099 E. CARRIAGE LANE
     GREENSBORO, NC   23740   GREENSBORO, NC   27240

9.   721 BEAR CREEK   721 BARE CREEK
     LAS VEGAS, NV   89005-1502   LAS VEGAS, NV   89005-1502

10. 7005 TAMERACK AVE   7005 TAMERACK AVE
     KEESPORT, PA   15071-1300   KEYSPORT, PA   15071-1300

11. A-1412 E WINDHAM HILLS   A-1412 E WINDHAM HILLS
     RALEIGH, NC   26715   RALEIGH, NC   26715

12. S. GALVESTON APTS A-1051   S. GALVESTON APTS A-1051
     WHITE FALLS, AR   76473-1019   WHITE FALLS, AR   47643-1019

13. 20991 CORLISTA LN   20991 CORLESTA LN
     FRESNO, CA   91255-1407   FRESNO, CA   91255-1407

14.	18-D BELVEDERE DOUGLAS, GA 30511	81-D BELVEDERE DOUGLAS, GA 30511
15.	203 MOUNT OGLETHORPE TRAIL TAMPA, FL 30619-1500	203 MOUNT OGLETHORPE TRAIL TAMPA, FL 30619-1500
16.	799 E. YUCCA BLOSSOM TUCSON, AZ 87582	997 E YUCCA BLOSSOM TUCSON, AZ 87528
17.	30 E. NESBIT FERRY RD NEW BEDFORD, MA 01855	30 E. NESBIT FERRY RD NEW BEDFORD, MA 18552
18.	1158 YOUNGSTON CT BRANDON, MS 35971-1201	1158 YOUNGSTON CT BRANDON, MS 35971-2101
19.	22809 NW 108TH AVE INDIANAPOLIS, IN 40266-2211	22809 SW 108TH AVE INDIANAPOLIS, IN 40266-2211
20.	280226 WHISPERING HILL LOUISVILLE, KY 41272-2801	280226 WHISPERING HILLS LOUISVILLE, KY 41272-2801
21.	13098 TANGERINE DR NEW ORLEANS, LA 71052	13098 TANGERINE DR NEW ORLEANS, LA 71052
22.	1401 W. WALNUT ST DES MOINES, WA 50399	1901 W. WALUT ST DES MOINES, WA 59039
23.	232 INGERSOL TERRACE BELLEVUE, WA 98065-2994	232 ENGERSOL TERRACE BELLEVUE, WA 98605-2994
24.	598-C 48TH AVE. N HONOLULU, HI 97814-2000	598-C 48TH AVE. N HONOLULU, HI 97814-2000
25.	BOX 89 ZORANO CIRCLE PALM COAST, FL 39022	BOX 98 ZORANO CIRCLE PALM COAST, FL 39022
26.	175 KAHIKOLU PLACE LAHAINA, HI 97655	175 KAHIKOLEY PLACE LAHAINA, HI 97655
27.	30905 LIKENS COURT MARTINEZ, CA 90851-3277	30905 LIKENS COURT MARTINEZ, CA 90851-7777
28.	C-103 DOGWOOD CT CANTON, GA 31107	C-103 DOGWOOD CT CANTON, GA 31107
29.	3030 OVERLOOK RIDGE AVE COLORADO SPRINGS, CO 89117	3030 OVERLOOK RIDGE AVE COLORADO SPRINGS, CO 81119
30.	27-G S. BIRKSHIRE WAY PRESCOTT, AZ 80512-7881	27-G S. BERKSHIRE WAY PRESCOTT, AZ 80012-7881

31.	1515 WALKER LN CROSSVILLE, TN	35811-7000		5151 WALKER LN CROSSVILLE, TN	35811-7000
32.	1-W CANYON ROAD PORTLAND, OR	92735-0001		1-W CANYON ROAD PORTLAND, OR	92735-0001
33.	4040 LYNBROOK DR ROLETTE, ND	56923		4040 LYNBROOK DR. ROLETTE, ND	52963
34.	678 BLUE HERON WAY ROCHESTER, NY	16472-5550		678 S. BLUE HERON WAY ROCHESTER, NY	96472-5550
35.	8012 N. UNION ST PLAINFIELD, NJ	06705		8012 N. UNION ST PLANEFIELD, NJ	06705
36.	9091 PRINCETON NW CONCORD, NH	00356-1870		90901 PRINCETON NW CONCORD, NH	03056-1807
37.	2175 TABOR HILLS OMAHA, NE	61852		2175 TABOR HILLS OMAHA, NE	61852
38.	2975 NW 129TH AVE CAMDEN, NJ	08755		2075 NW 129TH AVE CAMDEN, NJ	08755
39.	19499 E. INDIAN HILLS RD PHOENIX, AZ	85020-1113		19499 E. INDIAN HILLS RD PHOENIX, AZ	85020-1118
40.	1021 DARTMOUTH CT APT-12 WARREN, OH	43471-1129		1021 DARTMOUTH CT APT-12 WARREN, OH	43742-1129
41.	8370 BENTLEY PKWY HIGH POINT, NC	27104		8370 BENTLEY PKWY WINSTON-SALEM, NC	27104
42.	10000 CROSSWIND LINCOLN, NE	68215		10000 CROSSWIND LINCOLN, NE	68215
43.	18576 HWY 98 LOT-A CROSSVILLE, TN	35871		18576 HWY 98 LOT-A CROSSVILLE, TN	33871
44.	13590 WINSLOW LN EASLEY, SC	25971		13590 WINSLOW LN EASLEY, SC	25971
45.	777 E BEAUMONT SANDS READING, PA	16971-4445		111 E BEAUMONT SANDS READING, PA	61971-4445
46.	4039 W. 42TH AVE PHILADELPHIA, PA	19972-6650		4039 N. 42TH AVE PHILADELPHIA, PA	19972-6650
47.	6-F CHESTNUT VALLEY CLEVELAND, OH	40412-7033		6-F WALNUT VALLEY CLEVELAND, OH	40412-7033

48.	29738 SANCHEZ LN RIVERSIDE, CA 98402-7101	29738 SANCHEZ LN RIVERSIDE, CA 98402-7101
49.	507 QUAIL RUN BLVD WALNUT CREEK, CA 93702	507 QUAIL RUN BLVD PALMDALE, CA 92703
50.	58891 S. 11TH ST MESA, AZ 82571	59981 S. 11TH ST MESA, AZ 82571
51.	333 VICKSBURG WAY CANTON, MI 33581	333 VICKSBURG WAY CANTON, MI 35381
52.	7379 BLANCHARD BLVD PRESTON, MD 28157	7379 BLANCHARD BLVD PRESTON, MD 28157
53.	4980 S. BIANCA DR WEST PALM BEACH, FL 34371-5555	4980 S. BLANCA DR WEST PALM BEACH, FL 34371-6666
54.	163-A W. BRITTANY ST. GRAND JUNCTION, CO 85105	163-A W. BRITTANY ST. GRAND JUNCTION, CO 85105
55.	WINTERDALE BOX 741 TRACY, CA 95000	WINTERDALE BOX 174 TRACY, CA 95000
56.	3700 MOUNT SHONA RD LEESBURG, FL 37452-8877	3700 MOUNT SHASTA RD LEESBURG, FL 37542-8877
57.	2567 E. NAVAHO JCT PHOENIX, AZ 85701-2001	2567 E. NAVAHO JCT PHOENIX, AZ 85701-2001
58.	4000 MAGNOLIA CT SANTA MARIA, CA 94355	4040 MAGNOLIA CT SANTA MARIA, CA 94355
59.	80555 OZARK BAY MOBILE, AL 36075-1205	80555 OZARK BAY MOBILE, AL 36075-1205
60.	7-S PRICKLY PEAR AVE APT 13 SCOTTSDALE, AZ 80519-1400	7-E PRICKLY PEAR AVE APT 13 SCOTTSDALE, AZ 80511-1400

[This page is intentionally blank.]

ANSWER SHEET EXAMINATION 2 ADDRESS CROSS COMPARISON

1. Ⓐ Ⓑ Ⓒ Ⓓ   21. Ⓐ Ⓑ Ⓒ Ⓓ   41. Ⓐ Ⓑ Ⓒ Ⓓ
2. Ⓐ Ⓑ Ⓒ Ⓓ   22. Ⓐ Ⓑ Ⓒ Ⓓ   42. Ⓐ Ⓑ Ⓒ Ⓓ
3. Ⓐ Ⓑ Ⓒ Ⓓ   23. Ⓐ Ⓑ Ⓒ Ⓓ   43. Ⓐ Ⓑ Ⓒ Ⓓ
4. Ⓐ Ⓑ Ⓒ Ⓓ   24. Ⓐ Ⓑ Ⓒ Ⓓ   44. Ⓐ Ⓑ Ⓒ Ⓓ
5. Ⓐ Ⓑ Ⓒ Ⓓ   25. Ⓐ Ⓑ Ⓒ Ⓓ   45. Ⓐ Ⓑ Ⓒ Ⓓ
6. Ⓐ Ⓑ Ⓒ Ⓓ   26. Ⓐ Ⓑ Ⓒ Ⓓ   46. Ⓐ Ⓑ Ⓒ Ⓓ
7. Ⓐ Ⓑ Ⓒ Ⓓ   27. Ⓐ Ⓑ Ⓒ Ⓓ   47. Ⓐ Ⓑ Ⓒ Ⓓ
8. Ⓐ Ⓑ Ⓒ Ⓓ   28. Ⓐ Ⓑ Ⓒ Ⓓ   48. Ⓐ Ⓑ Ⓒ Ⓓ
9. Ⓐ Ⓑ Ⓒ Ⓓ   29. Ⓐ Ⓑ Ⓒ Ⓓ   49. Ⓐ Ⓑ Ⓒ Ⓓ
10. Ⓐ Ⓑ Ⓒ Ⓓ   30. Ⓐ Ⓑ Ⓒ Ⓓ   50. Ⓐ Ⓑ Ⓒ Ⓓ
11. Ⓐ Ⓑ Ⓒ Ⓓ   31. Ⓐ Ⓑ Ⓒ Ⓓ   51. Ⓐ Ⓑ Ⓒ Ⓓ
12. Ⓐ Ⓑ Ⓒ Ⓓ   32. Ⓐ Ⓑ Ⓒ Ⓓ   52. Ⓐ Ⓑ Ⓒ Ⓓ
13. Ⓐ Ⓑ Ⓒ Ⓓ   33. Ⓐ Ⓑ Ⓒ Ⓓ   53. Ⓐ Ⓑ Ⓒ Ⓓ
14. Ⓐ Ⓑ Ⓒ Ⓓ   34. Ⓐ Ⓑ Ⓒ Ⓓ   54. Ⓐ Ⓑ Ⓒ Ⓓ
15. Ⓐ Ⓑ Ⓒ Ⓓ   35. Ⓐ Ⓑ Ⓒ Ⓓ   55. Ⓐ Ⓑ Ⓒ Ⓓ
16. Ⓐ Ⓑ Ⓒ Ⓓ   36. Ⓐ Ⓑ Ⓒ Ⓓ   56. Ⓐ Ⓑ Ⓒ Ⓓ
17. Ⓐ Ⓑ Ⓒ Ⓓ   37. Ⓐ Ⓑ Ⓒ Ⓓ   57. Ⓐ Ⓑ Ⓒ Ⓓ
18. Ⓐ Ⓑ Ⓒ Ⓓ   38. Ⓐ Ⓑ Ⓒ Ⓓ   58. Ⓐ Ⓑ Ⓒ Ⓓ
19. Ⓐ Ⓑ Ⓒ Ⓓ   39. Ⓐ Ⓑ Ⓒ Ⓓ   59. Ⓐ Ⓑ Ⓒ Ⓓ
20. Ⓐ Ⓑ Ⓒ Ⓓ   40. Ⓐ Ⓑ Ⓒ Ⓓ   60. Ⓐ Ⓑ Ⓒ Ⓓ

FORMS COMPLETION   TIME: 15 MINUTES

ANSWER QUESTIONS 1–13 BASED ON THE FOLLOWING INFORMATION.
POSTAL VENDING MACHINE / REQUEST FOR REIMBURSEMENT

1. CUSTOMER'S PRINTED NAME
    _____

2. HOME ADDRESS
    A) STREET
    _____

    B) APT/SUITE NUMBER
    _____

    C) CITY/STATE
    _____

    D) ZIP CODE
    _____

3. CAN BE REACHED AT
    A) DAY TIME PHONE (AREA CODE)
    _____

    B) EVENING PHONE (AREA CODE)
    _____

> **NOTE:** Original copy of this form goes to customer; second copy is kept by sales and services associate; third copy goes to general service administration.

4. AMOUNT CLAIMED TO BE LOST
    $ _____

5. TIME LOSS OCCURRED _____ AM
    _____ PM (Check one)

6. DATE LOSS OCCURRED (NUMERICAL ENTRY ONLY) _____

7. MACHINE'S 8 DIGIT REFERENCE NUMBER
    (Posted directly above change dispenser)
    _____

10. A) DATE OF REIMBURSEMENT REQUEST
    _____

    B) CUSTOMER'S SIGNATURE
    _____

8. CHECK BOX THAT APPLIES TO CLAIM
    A) _____ NO CHANGE WAS PROVIDED
    B) _____ MACHINE BECAME JAMMED
    C) _____ DID NOT RECEIVE POSTAGE THAT WAS PAID FOR
    D) _____ INCORRECT CHANGE WAS PROVIDED
    E) _____ DEBIT/CREDIT CHARGE WAS INCORRECT

9. OPTIONAL CUSTOMER COMMENT

OFFICIAL USE ONLY

11. A) DATE CLAIM RECEIVED
    _____

    B) RECEIVED BY
    _____

    C) INITIALS OF ACTING SUPERVISOR FOR VERIFICATION _____

12. ATTEMPTED TO CONTACT CUSTOMER
    A) TIME _____ _____ AM
    _____ PM (check one)
    B) DATE (Numerical entry only) _____

13. CLAIM AMOUNT PAID
    $ _____

14. MEANS OF PAYMENT (Check one)
    A) _____ CASH REIMBURSEMENT
    B) _____ DEBIT/CREDIT REIMBURSEMENT
    C) _____ CORRECT POSTAGE PROVIDED
    D) _____ PAYMENT DENIED

15. SALES AND SERVICES ASSOCIATE
    SIGNATURE _____

1.	Where would the customer's written name be correctly entered on this form?

A)	Line item 1
B)	Line item 10B
C)	Line item 11B
D)	Line item 15

2.	If a customer wanted to convey to postal personnel that this was the second time this month the same problem occurred, where would this information be properly entered?

A)	Line item 7
B)	Line item 8A
C)	Line item 9
D)	Line item 10

3.	(460) 532-1451 would be a correct entry for which of the following?

A)	Line item 3A
B)	Line item 5A
C)	Line item 7
D)	Line item 13

4.	At 9:30 A.M., Sales and Services Associate Ted Galloway tried to reach Bob Anderson at home to get further specifics regarding a customer loss claim. How should this information be documented on the reimbursement form?

A)	Line item 12A should be marked 9:30
B)	Line item 12A should be marked 9:30 with A.M. checked
C)	Line item 12A should be marked 9:30 with P.M. checked
D)	Line item 12B should be marked 9:30 A.M.

5.	If a postal customer claimed to have lost change in a postage vending machine on Sunday, September 4, 2005, how is this information appropriately entered on the form?

A)	Tuesday would be entered on line item 6
B)	Tuesday, September 4, 2005 would be entered on line item 6
C)	Tuesday, 09-04-05 would be entered on line item 10A
D)	09-04-05 would be entered on line item 6

6.	For which of the following would 872624057 be a correct entry?

A)	Line item 4
B)	Line item 7
C)	Line item 3A
D)	None of the above

7.	If a customer discovered an improper vending machine charge for postage on their MasterCard, where is this correctly noted on the reimbursement request form?

A)	The MasterCard number would be entered on line item 7
B)	Box 8D would be checked
C)	Box 8E would be checked
D)	Box 14C would be checked

8.   If a claimant paid $37.00 for a roll of stamps she did not receive, where on this form would this be correctly documented?

A)   Line item 4
B)   Line item 13
C)   Line item 15
D)   Box 14C would be checked

9.   Referring to question 8, if the claimant had her MasterCard account credited accordingly, which of the following endorsement would be a correct entry on the form?

A)   Box 14B would be checked
B)   Box 14C would be checked
C)   Box 14D would be checked
D)   None of the above

10.   Station Manager Julia Parker agreed with Sales and Services Associate Karl Stone that a particular request for reimbursement should not be paid. Which of the following selections correctly document the action described?

A)   Box 14D would be checked and Karl Stone's signature would be entered on line item 15
B)   Karl Stone's name would be entered on line item 11B if he were the clerk who received the claim from the customer in question
C)   J. P. would be entered on line item 11C
D)   All of the above

11.   If a customer who filed a request for reimbursement resided at 1414 E. 29th St., Denver, CO, 50757, which of the following selections represent an incorrect form entry?

A)   50757 would be entered on line item 2D
B)   1414 E. 29th St. would be entered on line item 2B
C)   Denver, CO would be entered on line item 2C
D)   All of the above options are correct

12.   Which of the following options is incorrect with regard to reimbursement request forms?

A)   Line items 6 and 10A would both reflect the same date provided the customer immediately filed a loss claim with a window clerk during business hours
B)   The amount customers claim to have lost would be entered on line item 4
C)   Customers would receive the second copy of this form for their records
D)   All of the above are correct

13.   Assume a customer did not receive the correct change from a postal products vending machine purchase. Subsequent to filing a loss claim with the post office, the customer received a cash reimbursement. Which of the following form endorsements would apply?

A)   Box 8A would be checked
B)   Box 8D would be checked
C)   Box 14A would be checked
D)   Both boxes 8D and 14A would be checked

ANSWER QUESTIONS 14–21 BASED ON THE FOLLOWING INFORMATION.

RECEIPT FOR INSURED MAIL

1. POSTMARK PLACEMENT

    _____

2. FROM:
    A) NAME

    _____

    B) STREET / P.O. BOX NUMBER

    _____

    C) SUITE / APT NUMBER

    _____

    D) CITY / STATE / ZIP CODE

    _____

3. TO:
    A) NAME

    _____

    B) STREET / P.O. BOX NUMBER

    _____

    C) SUITE / APT NUMBER

    _____

    D) CITY / STATE / ZIP CODE

4. TRACKING/CONFIRMATION NUMBER

    _____

5. POSTAGE FEES $ _____

6. A) INSURANCE FEES $ _____
    B) INSURED AMOUNT $ _____

7. SPECIAL SERVICE FEES

    A) SPECIAL HANDLING $ _____
    B) RETURN RECEIPT $ _____
    C) RESTRICTED DELIVERY $ _____

    D) FEES TOTAL: $ _____

8. DESCRIPTION OF CONTENTS
    (Check applicable boxes)
    A) _____ LIQUID

    B) _____ PERISHABLES

    C) _____ FRAGILE

_____

14. Where is U.S. 4871 2254 1130 LE most likely to be entered on this form?

A) Line item 4
B) Line item 6B
C) Line item 7D
D) None of the above

15. If the insured amount for an article being mailed were $400, where on the insured mail receipt would this information be entered?

A) Line item 1
B) Line item 6B
C) Line item 7D
D) None of the above

NORMAN HALL'S POSTAL EXAM PREPARATION BOOK

16. If a customer requested that only one particular individual could sign for the article they were mailing, where on the receipt would such a request be accounted for?

A) Line item 6A
B) Line item 7B
C) Line item 7C
D) Cannot be determined from the information given

17. Where is the sender's name and street address entered on this form?

A) Line items 3A and B respectively
B) Line item 2A and B respectively
C) Line item 3B and C respectively
D) Line item 2B and C respectively

18. If the sum of itemized costs to mail an insured parcel came to $13.25, where is this information correctly entered?

A) Line item 5
B) Line item 6A
C) Line item 6B
D) Line item 7D

19. Assuming that a doctor's clinic needed to mail liquid serum contained in glass ampoules to a laboratory for analysis, which of the following endorsements would apply if the articles contents were insured?

A) Box 8A would be checked
B) Box 8B would be checked
C) Box 8C would be checked
D) All of the above

20. Where on the receipt would you find the date of mailing?

A) Line item 1
B) Line item 4
C) Line item 5
D) No such designation is shown

21. If a special handling fee was required on an insured article, where on the form would that be itemized?

A) Line item 6A
B) Line item 7A
C) Line item 7B
D) Line item 7C

ANSWER QUESTIONS 22–30 BASED ON THE FOLLOWING INFORMATION.
BUSINESS DELIVERY RECEIPT FOR ACCOUNTABLE ARTICLE(S)

1.   REFERENCE TRACKING NUMBER _____

2.   A) BUSINESS NAME _____
          B) STREET ADDRESS _____
          C) CITY/STATE/ZIP _____

3. ARTICLE DESIGNATION:

A) INSURED B) CERTIFIED C) REGISTERED D) OVERNIGHT EXPRESS E) 2ND DAY EXPRESS F) COD

4. ITEMIZED DESIGNATION	5. ARTICLE NUMBER	6. ASSIGNMENT CODE AR = ARTICLE REFUSED RRR = RETURN RECEIPT REQUESTED ADH = ARTICLE DAMAGED IN HANDLING U = ARTICLE UNCLAIMED

(IF MORE THAN 5 ARTICLES USE AN ADDITIONAL FORM)

7.   DATE OF DELIVERY _____

8.   DELIVERED BY _____

9.   BUSINESS BILLING NUMBER _____

22.   Where on this form is the date of delivery entered?

A)   Line item 1
B)   Line item 4
C)   Line item 7
D)   Line item 9

23.   Where is the business billing number correctly entered on the delivery receipt?

A)   Line item 2A
B)   Line item 6
C)   Line item 8
D)   Line item 9

24.   What would be the correct letter designation to place in column 4 to identify an insured article?

A)   A
B)   B
C)   C
D)   D

25.   What would be the correct letter designation to place in column 4 to identify a COD?

A)   C
B)   D
C)   E
D)   F

26.   If city carrier Kristi Patterson was responsible for delivering accountable articles to the XYZ Corporation, where would her name be properly entered on the form?

A)   Line item 2A
B)   Line item 7
C)   Line item 8
D)   Line item 9

27.   Assume a certified mailing was returned because the recipient never responded to the pick up notices left. Which of the following assignment codes represents a correct form entry?

A)   AR
B)   RRR
C)   ADH
D)   U

28.   A registered parcel (article number 457 381 005 210) had a return receipt that required a signature. Which of the following assignment codes would be a proper entry on the delivery receipt?

A)   AR
B)   RRR
C)   ADH
D)   U

29.   If city carrier Matt Kerns has ten accountable articles to deliver to Corporation XYZ, which of the following selections is true?

A)   All ten article numbers would be listed under item 5
B)   XYZ Corporation would be entered on line item 1
C)   Two separate business delivery receipts would be required
D)   None of the above

30.   Assume a COD package (article 17 180 16T) had been damaged in handling. All of the following represent accurate entries on the delivery receipt except:

A)   Article # 17 180 16T would be entered under item 5
B)   Itemized designation # for the COD would be F
C)   Assignment code ADH would be entered under item 6
D)   All of the above represent correct entries

ANSWER SHEET EXAMINATION 2 FORMS COMPLETION

1. Ⓐ Ⓑ Ⓒ Ⓓ   11. Ⓐ Ⓑ Ⓒ Ⓓ   21. Ⓐ Ⓑ Ⓒ Ⓓ

2. Ⓐ Ⓑ Ⓒ Ⓓ   12. Ⓐ Ⓑ Ⓒ Ⓓ   22. Ⓐ Ⓑ Ⓒ Ⓓ

3. Ⓐ Ⓑ Ⓒ Ⓓ   13. Ⓐ Ⓑ Ⓒ Ⓓ   23. Ⓐ Ⓑ Ⓒ Ⓓ

4. Ⓐ Ⓑ Ⓒ Ⓓ   14. Ⓐ Ⓑ Ⓒ Ⓓ   24. Ⓐ Ⓑ Ⓒ Ⓓ

5. Ⓐ Ⓑ Ⓒ Ⓓ   15. Ⓐ Ⓑ Ⓒ Ⓓ   25. Ⓐ Ⓑ Ⓒ Ⓓ

6. Ⓐ Ⓑ Ⓒ Ⓓ   16. Ⓐ Ⓑ Ⓒ Ⓓ   26. Ⓐ Ⓑ Ⓒ Ⓓ

7. Ⓐ Ⓑ Ⓒ Ⓓ   17. Ⓐ Ⓑ Ⓒ Ⓓ   27. Ⓐ Ⓑ Ⓒ Ⓓ

8. Ⓐ Ⓑ Ⓒ Ⓓ   18. Ⓐ Ⓑ Ⓒ Ⓓ   28. Ⓐ Ⓑ Ⓒ Ⓓ

9. Ⓐ Ⓑ Ⓒ Ⓓ   19. Ⓐ Ⓑ Ⓒ Ⓓ   29. Ⓐ Ⓑ Ⓒ Ⓓ

10. Ⓐ Ⓑ Ⓒ Ⓓ   20. Ⓐ Ⓑ Ⓒ Ⓓ   30. Ⓐ Ⓑ Ⓒ Ⓓ

CODING

TIME: 6 MINUTES

SERVICE RANGE	ROUTE ID
870-1390 CARLSON AVE. 1400-7570 S 16TH ST. 1299-4499 COLONIAL DR.	ROUTE A
7571-9250 S 16TH ST. 125-869 CARLSON AVE. 1550-2999 TAHOE BLVD.	ROUTE B
500-1399 S 16TH ST. 199-1549 TAHOE BLVD.	ROUTE C
ALL OTHER ADDRESSES THAT ARE NOT INCLUDED IN THE ABOVE RANGES	ROUTE D

STREET ADDRESSES	ROUTE CODE ANSWERS
1. 501 S 16TH AVE.	Ⓐ Ⓑ Ⓒ Ⓓ
2. 127 CARLSON AVE.	Ⓐ Ⓑ Ⓒ Ⓓ
3. 1311 TAHOE BLVD.	Ⓐ Ⓑ Ⓒ Ⓓ
4. 4000 COLONIAL DR.	Ⓐ Ⓑ Ⓒ Ⓓ
5. 7322 S 16TH ST.	Ⓐ Ⓑ Ⓒ Ⓓ
6. 809 CARLSON AVE.	Ⓐ Ⓑ Ⓒ Ⓓ
7. 2335 ESSEX LN.	Ⓐ Ⓑ Ⓒ Ⓓ
8. 1212 TAHOE BLVD.	Ⓐ Ⓑ Ⓒ Ⓓ
9. 37 OLD MILITARY RD.	Ⓐ Ⓑ Ⓒ Ⓓ
10. 1300 COLONIAL DR.	Ⓐ Ⓑ Ⓒ Ⓓ
11. 9199 S 16TH ST.	Ⓐ Ⓑ Ⓒ Ⓓ
12. 677 S 16TH ST.	Ⓐ Ⓑ Ⓒ Ⓓ
13. 1699 TAHOE LN.	Ⓐ Ⓑ Ⓒ Ⓓ
14. 470 APPLETREE DR.	Ⓐ Ⓑ Ⓒ Ⓓ

15. 7581 S 16TH ST. Ⓐ Ⓑ Ⓒ Ⓓ

16. 900 CARLSON AVE. Ⓐ Ⓑ Ⓒ Ⓓ

17. 3355 COLONIAL DR. Ⓐ Ⓑ Ⓒ Ⓓ

18. 1540 TAHOE BLVD. Ⓐ Ⓑ Ⓒ Ⓓ

19. 699 S 15TH ST. Ⓐ Ⓑ Ⓒ Ⓓ

20. 129 CARLSON AVE. Ⓐ Ⓑ Ⓒ Ⓓ

21. 8250 S 16TH ST. Ⓐ Ⓑ Ⓒ Ⓓ

22. 455 TAHOE BLVD. Ⓐ Ⓑ Ⓒ Ⓓ

23. 9250 COLONIAL DR. Ⓐ Ⓑ Ⓒ Ⓓ

24. 1111 CARLSON AVE. Ⓐ Ⓑ Ⓒ Ⓓ

25. 873 CARLSON AVE. Ⓐ Ⓑ Ⓒ Ⓓ

26. 2399 TAHOE BLVD. Ⓐ Ⓑ Ⓒ Ⓓ

27. 4250 EVEREST ST. Ⓐ Ⓑ Ⓒ Ⓓ

28. 1279 S. 16TH ST. Ⓐ Ⓑ Ⓒ Ⓓ

29. 1390 COLONIAL BLVD. Ⓐ Ⓑ Ⓒ Ⓓ

30. 919 CARLSON AVE. Ⓐ Ⓑ Ⓒ Ⓓ

31. 2105 TAHOE BLVD. Ⓐ Ⓑ Ⓒ Ⓓ

32. 131 CARLSON AVE. Ⓐ Ⓑ Ⓒ Ⓓ

33. 707 S 16TH ST. Ⓐ Ⓑ Ⓒ Ⓓ

34. 4040 BOSTON PL. Ⓐ Ⓑ Ⓒ Ⓓ

35. 4307 COLONIAL DR. Ⓐ Ⓑ Ⓒ Ⓓ

36. 1551 TAHOE BLVD. Ⓐ Ⓑ Ⓒ Ⓓ

MEMORIZATION   TIME: 3 MINUTES

SERVICE RANGE	ROUTE ID
870-1390 CARLSON AVE. 1400-7570 S 16TH ST. 1299-4499 COLONIAL DR.	ROUTE A
7571-9250 S 16TH ST. 125-869 CARLSON AVE. 1550-2999 TAHOE BLVD.	ROUTE B
500-1399 S 16TH ST. 199-1549 TAHOE BLVD.	ROUTE C
ALL OTHER ADDRESSES THAT ARE NOT INCLUDED IN THE ABOVE RANGES	ROUTE D

OPTIONAL WORKSHEET PROVIDED BELOW

STREET ADDRESS	ROUTE CODE
1. 860 CARLSON AVE.	Ⓐ Ⓑ Ⓒ Ⓓ
2. 205 TAHOE BLVD.	Ⓐ Ⓑ Ⓒ Ⓓ
3. 7501 S 16TH ST..	Ⓐ Ⓑ Ⓒ Ⓓ
4. 5075 COLONIAL DR.	Ⓐ Ⓑ Ⓒ Ⓓ
5. 407 PIEDMONT ST.	Ⓐ Ⓑ Ⓒ Ⓓ
6. 1304 S. 16TH ST.	Ⓐ Ⓑ Ⓒ Ⓓ
7. 888 CARLSON AVE.	Ⓐ Ⓑ Ⓒ Ⓓ
8. 9115 S 16TH AVE.	Ⓐ Ⓑ Ⓒ Ⓓ
9. 127 CARLSON AVE.	Ⓐ Ⓑ Ⓒ Ⓓ
10. 1105 CARLSON AVE.	Ⓐ Ⓑ Ⓒ Ⓓ
11. 1503 TAHOE BLVD.	Ⓐ Ⓑ Ⓒ Ⓓ
12. 1400 S 16TH ST.	Ⓐ Ⓑ Ⓒ Ⓓ
13. 2391 TAHOE BLVD.	Ⓐ Ⓑ Ⓒ Ⓓ
14. 536 CARLSON ST.	Ⓐ Ⓑ Ⓒ Ⓓ
15. 2000 COLONIAL DR.	Ⓐ Ⓑ Ⓒ Ⓓ

SERVICE RANGE	ROUTE ID
870-1390 CARLSON AVE. 1400-7570 S. 16TH ST. 1299-4499 COLONIAL DR.	ROUTE A
7571-9250 S 16TH ST. 125-869 CARLSON AVE. 1550-2999 TAHOE BLVD.	ROUTE B
500-1399 S. 16TH ST. 199-1549 TAHOE BLVD.	ROUTE C
ALL OTHER ADDRESSES THAT ARE NOT INCLUDED IN THE ABOVE RANGES	ROUTE D

MEMORIZATION

TIME: 7 MINUTES

1. 7370 S 16TH ST.
2. 1551 TAHOE BLVD.
3. 30575 HWY 16
4. 515 S 16TH ST.
5. 4113 COLONIAL DR.
6. 300 CARLSON AVE.
7. 2555 TAHOE ST.
8. 861 CARLSON ST.
9. 1666 S 16TH ST.
10. 9100 S 16TH AVE.
11. 2715 TAHOE BLVD.
12. 208 TAHOE BLVD.
13. 1607 S 160TH ST.
14. 3001 COLONIAL AVE.
15. 899 CARLSON AVE.
16. 859 CARLSON ST.
17. 605 CARLSON AVE.
18. 7892 S 15TH ST.
19. 910 CARLSON BLVD.
20. 3217 COLONIAL BLVD.
21. 1509 TAHOE BLVD.
22. 8050 S 16TH ST.
23. 676 CARLSON AVE.
24. 1518 S 16TH ST.
25. 4040 CLEARVIEW LN.
26. 1301 S 16TH ST.
27. 2650 TAHOE BLVD.
28. 800 CARLSON AVE.
29. 35007 COLONIAL DR.
30. 14-W COLONY CT.
31. 1244 S. 16TH ST.
32. 931-A CARLSON AVE.
33. 8703 S 16TH AVE.
34. 2100 TAHOE BLVD.
35. 1299 COLONIAL PKWY
36. 515-D S 16TH ST.

EXAM 2

ANSWER SHEET TO EXAMINATION 2 MEMORIZATION

#					#					#				
1.	A	B	C	D	13.	A	B	C	D	25.	A	B	C	D
2.	A	B	C	D	14.	A	B	C	D	26.	A	B	C	D
3.	A	B	C	D	15.	A	B	C	D	27.	A	B	C	D
4.	A	B	C	D	16.	A	B	C	D	28.	A	B	C	D
5.	A	B	C	D	17.	A	B	C	D	29.	A	B	C	D
6.	A	B	C	D	18.	A	B	C	D	30.	A	B	C	D
7.	A	B	C	D	19.	A	B	C	D	31.	A	B	C	D
8.	A	B	C	D	20.	A	B	C	D	32.	A	B	C	D
9.	A	B	C	D	21.	A	B	C	D	33.	A	B	C	D
10.	A	B	C	D	22.	A	B	C	D	34.	A	B	C	D
11.	A	B	C	D	23.	A	B	C	D	35.	A	B	C	D
12.	A	B	C	D	24.	A	B	C	D	36.	A	B	C	D

277

ANSWERS TO EXAMINATION 2 ADDRESS CROSS COMPARISON

1.	A	21.	A	41.	B
2.	B	22.	D	42.	A
3.	B	23.	D	43.	C
4.	D	24.	A	44.	A
5.	C	25.	B	45.	D
6.	C	26.	B	46.	B
7.	B	27.	C	47.	B
8.	D	28.	A	48.	A
9.	B	29.	C	49.	D
10.	B	30.	D	50.	B
11.	A	31.	B	51.	C
12.	C	32.	A	52.	A
13.	B	33.	C	53.	D
14.	B	34.	D	54.	A
15.	A	35.	B	55.	B
16.	D	36.	D	56.	D
17.	C	37.	A	57.	A
18.	C	38.	B	58.	B
19.	B	39.	C	59.	A
20.	B	40.	C	60.	D

ANSWERS TO EXAMINATION 2 FORMS COMPLETION

1.	B	16.	C
2.	C	17.	B
3.	A	18.	D
4.	B	19.	D
5.	D	20.	A
6.	D	21.	B
7.	C	22.	C
8.	B	23.	D
9.	A	24.	A
10.	D	25.	D
11.	B	26.	C
12.	C	27.	D
13.	D	28.	B
14.	A	29.	C
15.	B	30.	D

ANSWERS TO EXAMINATION 2 CODING

1.	D	13.	D	25.	A
2.	B	14.	D	26.	B
3.	C	15.	B	27.	D
4.	A	16.	A	28.	C
5.	A	17.	A	29.	D
6.	B	18.	C	30.	A
7.	D	19.	D	31.	B
8.	C	20.	B	32.	B
9.	D	21.	B	33.	C
10.	A	22.	C	34.	D
11.	B	23.	D	35.	A
12.	C	24.	A	36.	B

ANSWERS TO EXAMINATION 2 MEMORIZATION

1.	A	13.	D	25.	D
2.	B	14.	D	26.	C
3.	D	15.	A	27.	B
4.	C	16.	D	28.	B
5.	A	17.	B	29.	D
6.	B	18.	D	30.	D
7.	D	19.	D	31.	C
8.	D	20.	D	32.	A
9.	A	21.	C	33.	D
10.	D	22.	B	34.	B
11.	B	23.	B	35.	D
12.	C	24.	A	36.	C

Add together your correct answer count for each of the four test sections given.
   If they total:
151–162 correct, you have an excellent score.
138–150 correct, you have a good score.
137 or less correct, you need additional practice.

Personality and Experience Profiling

The last part of this test is intended to provide the Postal Service comprehensive insights into your personal character and background experience. People who take the Postal exams come from virtually every lifestyle, possess varied character traits, and have diverse work histories. With that said, applicants prefer to think of themselves as potentially perfect model employees. The truth, however, is that all individuals have their strengths and weaknesses. The questions on this part of the test are intended to quantify those characteristics and assess your potential work performance as a U.S.P.S. employee. It is very important to answer each of these questions truthfully because all of it can be crosschecked with a background investigation prior to hiring. You will find that a majority of the test questions offered are redundant in many respects. The questions may be worded somewhat differently; however, they address the same underlying themes. Your success will depend upon the continuity of your responses. If there is a marked variance in how you address safety issues, for example, that can be indicative of dishonesty. If you are an individual who prioritizes work safety, consistently mark your answers accordingly. Do not waffle on past exceptions or minor oversights. Be careful to avoid overstating your abilities as well. Examiners will most likely see that for what it is. This study guide cannot offer a one-way-fits-all approach in how these questions should be answered. Since the answers are based on your work background and character, there are truly no right or wrong answers. It may help you to understand, however, what the Postal Service is specifically searching for in a potential hire. In short, it can be summarized as follows:

- Integrity/honesty
- Flexibility/adaptability
- Safety on the job and at home
- Excellent learning proficiency
- Service minded ambitions
- Team focus

Candidates who demonstrate strengths in these given areas are the ones most likely to succeed in being hired. The sample questions that follow will be very similar to what will be on the actual exam, albeit an abbreviated version. The actual test has 236 questions and you will have 90 minutes to complete the exercise.

Below are 100 questions that serve as a representative cross-section. Again, answer each of the questions truthfully. In the event that more than one answer is possible, pick the one that best represents your character or situation. Take no more than 25 minutes to complete this exercise.

1.   Even under a great deal of stress, I am still able to perform efficiently on the job.

A)   STRONGLY AGREE
B)   AGREE
C)   DISAGREE
D)   STRONGLY DISAGREE

2. On the job safety is very important to the success of any operation.

A) STRONGLY AGREE
B) AGREE
C) DISAGREE
D) STRONGLY DISAGREE

3. Theft of any kind should immediately be reported to a supervisor.

A) STRONGLY AGREE
B) AGREE
C) DISAGREE
D) STRONGLY DISAGREE

4. Even when I know I am right, I will always listen to other people's opinions.

A) STRONGLY AGREE
B) AGREE
C) DISAGREE
D) STRONGLY DISAGREE

5. Speaking to a large group of people is very uncomfortable.

A) STRONGLY AGREE
B) AGREE
C) DISAGREE
D) STRONGLY DISAGREE

6. I work well within established deadlines.

A) STRONGLY AGREE
B) AGREE
C) DISAGREE
D) STRONGLY DISAGREE

7. I enjoy working at a faster pace than others do.

A) STRONGLY AGREE
B) AGREE
C) DISAGREE
D) STRONGLY DISAGREE

8. Boring or monotonous jobs can have a detrimental affect on my moral.

A) STRONGLY AGREE
B) AGREE
C) DISAGREE
D) STRONGLY DISAGREE

9.   While trying to focus on a particular task, I prefer not to have constant interruptions.

A)   STRONGLY AGREE
B)   AGREE
C)   DISAGREE
D)   STRONGLY DISAGREE

10.   If a co-worker suggests a better way to do something, it is very easy for me to change an established work habit.

A)   STRONGLY AGREE
B)   AGREE
C)   DISAGREE
D)   STRONGLY DISAGREE

11.   People who are close to me would say I am an optimist.

A)   STRONGLY AGREE
B)   AGREE
C)   DISAGREE
D)   STRONGLY DISAGREE

12.   If I do not agree with the handling of a work issue, I allow my frustrations to affect my attitude at work.

A)   STRONGLY AGREE
B)   AGREE
C)   DISAGREE
D)   STRONGLY DISAGREE

13.   I am not beyond taking a calculated risk to accomplish a given task.

A)   STRONGLY AGREE
B)   AGREE
C)   DISAGREE
D)   STRONGLY DISAGREE

14.   It is extremely irritating to hear criticism from a co-worker.

A)   STRONGLY AGREE
B)   AGREE
C)   DISAGREE
D)   STRONGLY DISAGREE

15.   I prefer not to wear seatbelts because they are too constrictive and uncomfortable.

A)   STRONGLY AGREE
B)   AGREE
C)   DISAGREE
D)   STRONGLY DISAGREE

16.   People who have worked with me would testify that my work ethics are superior.

A)   STRONGLY AGREE
B)   AGREE
C)   DISAGREE
D)   STRONGLY DISAGREE

17.   I get along with most everybody.

A)   STRONGLY AGREE
B)   AGREE
C)   DISAGREE
D)   STRONGLY DISAGREE

18.   Standing or walking for a long period would not be a problem for me.

A)   STRONGLY AGREE
B)   AGREE
C)   DISAGREE
D)   STRONGLY DISAGREE

19.   I never have to be reminded to attend meetings.

A)   STRONGLY AGREE
B)   AGREE
C)   DISAGREE
D)   STRONGLY DISAGREE

20.   It is important to me that my work performance is recognized.

A)   STRONGLY AGREE
B)   AGREE
C)   DISAGREE
D)   STRONGLY DISAGREE

21.   The quality of my work actually improves under tight deadlines.

A)   STRONGLY AGREE
B)   AGREE
C)   DISAGREE
D)   STRONGLY DISAGREE

22.   Once a project starts, it is important to see it through to its end.

A)   STRONGLY AGREE
B)   AGREE
C)   DISAGREE
D)   STRONGLY DISAGREE

23. If I had a choice, I prefer not to travel long distances for on-the-job training.

A) STRONGLY AGREE
B) AGREE
C) DISAGREE
D) STRONGLY DISAGREE

24. I prefer to work nights and weekends.

A) STRONGLY AGREE
B) AGREE
C) DISAGREE
D) STRONGLY DISAGREE

25. I consistently outperformed my classmates in school.

A) STRONGLY AGREE
B) AGREE
C) DISAGREE
D) STRONGLY DISAGREE

26. I do better when I work on one project at a time and not be required to multitask.

A) STRONGLY AGREE
B) AGREE
C) DISAGREE
D) STRONGLY DISAGREE

27. It is easy to be courteous when dealing with an angry customer.

A) STRONGLY AGREE
B) AGREE
C) DISAGREE
D) STRONGLY DISAGREE

28. I am always willing to go the extra distance to get the job completed.

A) STRONGLY AGREE
B) AGREE
C) DISAGREE
D) STRONGLY DISAGREE

29. I consider myself to be detail oriented.

A) STRONGLY AGREE
B) AGREE
C) DISAGREE
D) STRONGLY DISAGREE

30. If I witnessed a safety violation, I would bring it to my supervisor's attention immediately, regardless of how busy they were.

A) STRONGLY AGREE
B) AGREE
C) DISAGREE
D) STRONGLY DISAGREE

31. It is very easy for me to deal with an unpleasant co-worker.

A) STRONGLY AGREE
B) AGREE
C) DISAGREE
D) STRONGLY DISAGREE

32. Co-workers would agree that I work well under pressure.

A) STRONGLY AGREE
B) AGREE
C) DISAGREE
D) STRONGLY DISAGREE

33. While I was in school, I regularly dressed better than my classmates did.

A) STRONGLY AGREE
B) AGREE
C) DISAGREE
D) STRONGLY DISAGREE

34. I look forward to working with people who have a common goal.

A) STRONGLY AGREE
B) AGREE
C) DISAGREE
D) STRONGLY DISAGREE

35. I struggle to remain courteous toward co-workers who have a tendency to interrupt my conversations with others.

A) STRONGLY AGREE
B) AGREE
C) DISAGREE
D) STRONGLY DISAGREE

36. When others do not respect my opinion, I find it very aggravating.

A) STRONGLY AGREE
B) AGREE
C) DISAGREE
D) STRONGLY DISAGREE

37.   I have a genuine respect for authority.

A)   STRONGLY AGREE
B)   AGREE
C)   DISAGREE
D)   STRONGLY DISAGREE

38.   I find it very discouraging when something does not go my way.

A)   STRONGLY AGREE
B)   AGREE
C)   DISAGREE
D)   STRONGLY DISAGREE

39.   I enjoy change when it enhances my work performance.

A)   STRONGLY AGREE
B)   AGREE
C)   DISAGREE
D)   STRONGLY DISAGREE

40.   I carefully weigh all the risks prior to making a decision that affects others.

A)   STRONGLY AGREE
B)   AGREE
C)   DISAGREE
D)   STRONGLY DISAGREE

41.   I do not let the poor attitude of a co-worker have an affect on my performance.

A)   STRONGLY AGREE
B)   AGREE
C)   DISAGREE
D)   STRONGLY DISAGREE

42.   If a co-worker was struggling with a personal problem I would offer them encouragement and support.

A)   STRONGLY AGREE
B)   AGREE
C)   DISAGREE
D)   STRONGLY DISAGREE

43.   I am not reserved about making my co-workers aware of their mistakes.

A)   STRONGLY AGREE
B)   AGREE
C)   DISAGREE
D)   STRONGLY DISAGREE

44.   When necessary, I always wear hearing protection and safety goggles.

A)   STRONGLY AGREE
B)   AGREE
C)   DISAGREE
D)   STRONGLY DISAGREE

45.   I am more interested in doing my job the way that works best for me regardless of supervisory directives.

A)   STRONGLY AGREE
B)   AGREE
C)   DISAGREE
D)   STRONGLY DISAGREE

46.   I prefer work that has direct contact with the customers.

A)   STRONGLY AGREE
B)   AGREE
C)   DISAGREE
D)   STRONGLY DISAGREE

47.   I would not let a stressful week affect the quality of my work performance.

A)   STRONGLY AGREE
B)   AGREE
C)   DISAGREE
D)   STRONGLY DISAGREE

48.   When a supervisor does not listen to the opinions of others, I become frustrated.

A)   STRONGLY AGREE
B)   AGREE
C)   DISAGREE
D)   STRONGLY DISAGREE

49.   I would not hesitate to purchase an item that was priced lower than it should have been. After all, the pricing of merchandise is the store's responsibility, not mine.

A)   STRONGLY AGREE
B)   AGREE
C)   DISAGREE
D)   STRONGLY DISAGREE

50.   I consistently strive to improve my job performance.

A)   STRONGLY AGREE
B)   AGREE
C)   DISAGREE
D)   STRONGLY DISAGREE

51.   If I did not like the personal habits of a co-worker, I would let it be known to both the co-worker and my supervisor.

A)   STRONGLY AGREE
B)   AGREE
C)   DISAGREE
D)   STRONGLY DISAGREE

52.   I am open to suggestions from co-workers.

A)   STRONGLY AGREE
B)   AGREE
C)   DISAGREE
D)   STRONGLY DISAGREE

53.   I always wear my seatbelt when in a motor vehicle.

A)   STRONGLY AGREE
B)   AGREE
C)   DISAGREE
D)   STRONGLY DISAGREE

54.   I enjoy working on projects that take a lot of time and effort on my part.

A)   STRONGLY AGREE
B)   AGREE
C)   DISAGREE
D)   STRONGLY DISAGREE

55.   I would not enjoy finishing a job that someone else failed to complete.

A)   STRONGLY AGREE
B)   AGREE
C)   DISAGREE
D)   STRONGLY DISAGREE

56.   I only need to be told to do a specific task once.

A)   STRONGLY AGREE
B)   AGREE
C)   DISAGREE
D)   STRONGLY DISAGREE

57.   I am not bothered by doing the same kind of task every day.

A)   STRONGLY AGREE
B)   AGREE
C)   DISAGREE
D)   STRONGLY DISAGREE

58.   It is important to me to have some say about office policy.

A)   STRONGLY AGREE
B)   AGREE
C)   DISAGREE
D)   STRONGLY DISAGREE

59.   It is okay to keep the collection of government pens that I have inadvertently brought home.

A)   STRONGLY AGREE
B)   AGREE
C)   DISAGREE
D)   STRONGLY DISAGREE

60.   I do not like it when someone misconstrues something I have said.

A)   STRONGLY AGREE
B)   AGREE
C)   DISAGREE
D)   STRONGLY DISAGREE

61.   If I finish a particular job ahead of schedule, I will look for something else that needs to be done without being asked.

A)   STRONGLY AGREE
B)   AGREE
C)   DISAGREE
D)   STRONGLY DISAGREE

62.   A supervisor should be kept well informed of mistakes made by fellow workers.

A)   STRONGLY AGREE
B)   AGREE
C)   DISAGREE
D)   STRONGLY DISAGREE

63.   Supervisory directions should be followed without exception.

A)   STRONGLY AGREE
B)   AGREE
C)   DISAGREE
D)   STRONGLY DISAGREE

64.   I rarely have disagreements with people.

A)   STRONGLY AGREE
B)   AGREE
C)   DISAGREE
D)   STRONGLY DISAGREE

65. No matter how busy I may be, I will take the time needed to report a safety violation to an immediate supervisor.

A) STRONGLY AGREE
B) AGREE
C) DISAGREE
D) STRONGLY DISAGREE

66. I treat co-workers and customers the same way they treat me.

A) STRONGLY AGREE
B) AGREE
C) DISAGREE
D) STRONGLY DISAGREE

67. I work better alone than in a group setting.

A) STRONGLY AGREE
B) AGREE
C) DISAGREE
D) STRONGLY DISAGREE

68. If management grants a special favor to one person then everyone else should get the same benefit.

A) STRONGLY AGREE
B) AGREE
C) DISAGREE
D) STRONGLY DISAGREE

69. No matter how tired I might be, customer service is treated as a priority.

A) STRONGLY AGREE
B) AGREE
C) DISAGREE
D) STRONGLY DISAGREE

70. If a co-worker received undeserved praise, it would be important to set the record straight.

A) STRONGLY AGREE
B) AGREE
C) DISAGREE
D) STRONGLY DISAGREE

71. I look for new and improved ways to enhance my job performance.

A) VERY OFTEN
B) OFTEN
C) SOMETIMES
D) NEVER

72.   I render assistance to co-workers in need, even if they do not ask for help.

A)   VERY OFTEN
B)   OFTEN
C)   SOMETIMES
D)   NEVER

73.   I have used sick leave benefits for reason of preferential time off.

A)   VERY OFTEN
B)   OFTEN
C)   SOMETIMES
D)   NEVER

74.   I am quick to respond in kind to co-workers criticisms.

A)   VERY OFTEN
B)   OFTEN
C)   SOMETIMES
D)   NEVER

75.   I have received citations for speeding.

A)   VERY OFTEN
B)   OFTEN
C)   SOMETIMES
D)   NEVER

76.   I have been involved in fights with fellow classmates.

A)   VERY OFTEN
B)   OFTEN
C)   SOMETIMES
D)   NEVER

77.   I take issue with co-workers who do not show up for work on time.

A)   VERY OFTEN
B)   OFTEN
C)   SOMETIMES
D)   NEVER

78.   I get discouraged when a job has to be finished within an unrealistic time line.

A)   VERY OFTEN
B)   OFTEN
C)   SOMETIMES
D)   NEVER

79.   I like to plan things in advance and have contingencies in place, just in case.

A)   VERY OFTEN
B)   OFTEN
C)   SOMETIMES
D)   NEVER

80.   I apologize for other people's mistakes.

A)   VERY OFTEN
B)   OFTEN
C)   SOMETIMES
D)   NEVER

81.   Co-workers look to me for leadership.

A)   VERY OFTEN
B)   OFTEN
C)   SOMETIMES
D)   NEVER

82.   I will do tedious work that others neglect.

A)   VERY OFTEN
B)   OFTEN
C)   SOMETIMES
D)   NEVER

83.   I get irritated when I do not receive credit for my production or cost saving ideas.

A)   VERY OFTEN
B)   OFTEN
C)   SOMETIMES
D)   NEVER

84.   I use abusive language during times of frustration.

A)   VERY OFTEN
B)   OFTEN
C)   SOMETIMES
D)   NEVER

85.   I regularly maintain my personal vehicle with the intentions of avoiding safety hazards and costly repairs.

A)   VERY OFTEN
B)   OFTEN
C)   SOMETIMES
D)   NEVER

86.   I willfully avoid conversations that can be construed as gossip.

A)   VERY OFTEN
B)   OFTEN
C)   SOMETIMES
D)   NEVER

87.   I express concerns or problems as well as share successes with co-workers.

A)   VERY OFTEN
B)   OFTEN
C)   SOMETIMES
D)   NEVER

88.   I would resent not being personally informed of managerial decisions that directly affect the workplace.

A)   VERY OFTEN
B)   OFTEN
C)   SOMETIMES
D)   NEVER

89.   Regardless of what I am in the middle of, I am inclined to take a lunch break at a specific time.

A)   VERY OFTEN
B)   OFTEN
C)   SOMETIMES
D)   NEVER

90.   I will challenge managerial policies that do not seem to make sense.

A)   VERY OFTEN
B)   OFTEN
C)   SOMETIMES
D)   NEVER

91.   I make compromises to facilitate getting projects completed.

A)   VERY OFTEN
B)   OFTEN
C)   SOMETIMES
D)   NEVER

92.   I invite constructive feedback from others when work related issues are discussed.

A)   VERY OFTEN
B)   OFTEN
C)   SOMETIMES
D)   NEVER

93. I use sarcasm to deflect other people's criticisms.

A) VERY OFTEN
B) OFTEN
C) SOMETIMES
D) NEVER

94. Without reservation, I will perform duties outside of my job description.

A) VERY OFTEN
B) OFTEN
C) SOMETIMES
D) NEVER

95. I am flexible and accepting of frequent changes at work

A) VERY OFTEN
B) OFTEN
C) SOMETIMES
D) NEVER

96. I work long hours without complaint.

A) VERY OFTEN
B) OFTEN
C) SOMETIMES
D) NEVER

97. I held my last job for a period of

A) LESS THAN 1 MONTH
B) 1 TO 3 MONTHS
C) 3 MONTHS TO 1 YEAR
D) 1 TO 3 YEARS
E) 3 TO 10 YEARS
F) LONGER THAN 10 YEARS

98. I am currently searching for work because

A) I AM UNEMPLOYED NOW
B) I AM LOOKING FOR BETTER PAY AND BENEFITS
C) I WANT MORE CHALLENGING WORK THAN WHAT I HAVE NOW
D) I WANT TO RELOCATE DUE TO PERSONAL REASONS
E) I NEED SOMETHING FOR THE INTERIM WHILE I CONTINUE TO SEARCH FOR SOMETHING BETTER
F) OF OTHER REASONS

99.   Upon leaving a former job, how much notice did you give your employer?

A)   LESS THAN 24 HOURS
B)   1 TO 3 DAYS
C)   MORE THAN 3 DAYS BUT LESS THAN 1 WEEK
D)   1 TO 2 WEEKS
E)   MORE THAN 2 WEEKS
F)   I AM STILL WORKING FOR MY ORIGINAL EMPLOYER

100.   The highest level of education I have is

A)   NEVER COMPLETED HIGH SCHOOL OR RECEIVED A GED
B)   A GED
C)   A HIGH SCHOOL DIPLOMA
D)   AN ASSOCIATE DEGREE FROM COMMUNITY COLLEGE
E)   A BACHELOR DEGREE
F)   A MASTER'S DEGREE OR HIGHER

PERSONALITY AND EXPERIENCE PROFILING ANSWER SHEET

1. (A) (B) (C) (D)
2. (A) (B) (C) (D)
3. (A) (B) (C) (D)
4. (A) (B) (C) (D)
5. (A) (B) (C) (D)
6. (A) (B) (C) (D)
7. (A) (B) (C) (D)
8. (A) (B) (C) (D)
9. (A) (B) (C) (D)
10. (A) (B) (C) (D)
11. (A) (B) (C) (D)
12. (A) (B) (C) (D)
13. (A) (B) (C) (D)
14. (A) (B) (C) (D)
15. (A) (B) (C) (D)
16. (A) (B) (C) (D)
17. (A) (B) (C) (D)
18. (A) (B) (C) (D)
19. (A) (B) (C) (D)
20. (A) (B) (C) (D)
21. (A) (B) (C) (D)
22. (A) (B) (C) (D)
23. (A) (B) (C) (D)
24. (A) (B) (C) (D)
25. (A) (B) (C) (D)
26. (A) (B) (C) (D)
27. (A) (B) (C) (D)
28. (A) (B) (C) (D)
29. (A) (B) (C) (D)

30. (A) (B) (C) (D)
31. (A) (B) (C) (D)
32. (A) (B) (C) (D)
33. (A) (B) (C) (D)
34. (A) (B) (C) (D)
35. (A) (B) (C) (D)
36. (A) (B) (C) (D)
37. (A) (B) (C) (D)
38. (A) (B) (C) (D)
39. (A) (B) (C) (D)
40. (A) (B) (C) (D)
41. (A) (B) (C) (D)
42. (A) (B) (C) (D)
43. (A) (B) (C) (D)
44. (A) (B) (C) (D)
45. (A) (B) (C) (D)
46. (A) (B) (C) (D)
47. (A) (B) (C) (D)
48. (A) (B) (C) (D)
49. (A) (B) (C) (D)
50. (A) (B) (C) (D)
51. (A) (B) (C) (D)
52. (A) (B) (C) (D)
53. (A) (B) (C) (D)
54. (A) (B) (C) (D)
55. (A) (B) (C) (D)
56. (A) (B) (C) (D)
57. (A) (B) (C) (D)
58. (A) (B) (C) (D)

59. (A) (B) (C) (D)
60. (A) (B) (C) (D)
61. (A) (B) (C) (D)
62. (A) (B) (C) (D)
63. (A) (B) (C) (D)
64. (A) (B) (C) (D)
65. (A) (B) (C) (D)
66. (A) (B) (C) (D)
67. (A) (B) (C) (D)
68. (A) (B) (C) (D)
69. (A) (B) (C) (D)
70. (A) (B) (C) (D)
71. (A) (B) (C) (D)
72. (A) (B) (C) (D)
73. (A) (B) (C) (D)
74. (A) (B) (C) (D)
75. (A) (B) (C) (D)
76. (A) (B) (C) (D)
77. (A) (B) (C) (D)
78. (A) (B) (C) (D)
79. (A) (B) (C) (D)
80. (A) (B) (C) (D)
81. (A) (B) (C) (D)
82. (A) (B) (C) (D)
83. (A) (B) (C) (D)
84. (A) (B) (C) (D)
85. (A) (B) (C) (D)
86. (A) (B) (C) (D)
87. (A) (B) (C) (D)

[This page may be removed to mark answers.]

88. Ⓐ Ⓑ Ⓒ Ⓓ

89. Ⓐ Ⓑ Ⓒ Ⓓ

90. Ⓐ Ⓑ Ⓒ Ⓓ

91. Ⓐ Ⓑ Ⓒ Ⓓ

92. Ⓐ Ⓑ Ⓒ Ⓓ

93. Ⓐ Ⓑ Ⓒ Ⓓ

94. Ⓐ Ⓑ Ⓒ Ⓓ

95. Ⓐ Ⓑ Ⓒ Ⓓ

96. Ⓐ Ⓑ Ⓒ Ⓓ

97. Ⓐ Ⓑ Ⓒ Ⓓ Ⓔ Ⓕ

98. Ⓐ Ⓑ Ⓒ Ⓓ Ⓔ Ⓕ

99. Ⓐ Ⓑ Ⓒ Ⓓ Ⓔ Ⓕ

100. Ⓐ Ⓑ Ⓒ Ⓓ Ⓔ Ⓕ

What Follows After the Examination?

Once you have taken the exam, it will take two to eight weeks before your test results are mailed to you. If your score was 70 percent or better, your name will be placed on the Federal Register of the Post Office that offered the test. Your test score is not transferable to other post offices. Therefore, it is to your advantage to take as many of these exams as possible. The more registers you are on, the better your chances for an interview.

It should be noted here that veteran preference is granted for employment in the United States Postal Service. Five-point preference is usually given to honorably discharged veterans who served in active duty in the U.S. Armed Forces under any of the following conditions:

- During a period extending from April 28, 1952 to July 1, 1955
- During February 1, 1955, through October 14, 1976, for which any part of more than 180 consecutive days were served
- In any campaign or expedition for which a campaign badge was authorized, including Bosnia, El Salvador, Grenada, Haiti, Lebanon, Panama, Somalia, and Southeast Asia
- During the Gulf War from August 2, 1990 through January 2, 1992
- During the period beginning September 11, 2001 and ending on the final day of "Operation Iraqi Freedom" of which more than 180 consecutive days were served

Ten-point preference is given to honorably discharged veterans who served in active duty in the U.S. Armed Forces at any time and have a service-connected disability, for which they may or may not receive compensation. This preference may also be claimed by:

- Veterans who have been awarded the Purple Heart
- Spouses of certain veterans with a service-connected disability
- Mothers of certain disabled or deceased veterans
- Widows or widowers of an honorably discharged veteran, provided the deceased served in active duty during a war or died while in the Armed Forces

(Any veteran claiming ten-point preference eligibility must complete form S-F 15. The application is also available online at *www.opm.gov/forms/pdf_fill/sf15pdf.*)
NOTE: Gulf War veterans and medal recipients who enlisted after September 7, 1980 or entered active military duty on or after October 14, 1982 must have served 24 consecutive months or the full duration called or ordered to active duty. This requirement is not applicable to veterans separated for disability in the line of duty or veterans with compensable military-connected disabilities.

- Active duty for training under the six-month reserve or national guard program does not qualify
- Service retirees comprising the rank of major, lieutenant commander, or higher do not qualify for preference unless a service-related responsibility is claimed

For those who are eligible, five-point veteran preference grants an applicant five additional points to his or her total test score, provided the score was a 70 percent or above. Those who qualify for ten-point veteran preference are given ten additional points to their test score (provided the score was a minimum of 70 percent), and are also placed at the top of the hiring list (i.e., Federal Register), in descending order of their test scores. All other eligible candidates are listed below this group. For further information pertaining to veteran preference, contact the Department of Personnel at the post office where you intend to apply.

When you are among those to be considered for a postal position, you will be notified by mail about the time and place of your interview. Pay particular attention to the date and become familiar, in advance, with the location of the interview. One sure way to disqualify yourself is to arrive late for the interview. You don't want to begin your interview with excuses.

Appearance is important, as well. Interviewers gain a distinct impression from the manner in which a candidate dresses. If you are not well-groomed (e.g., soiled clothes, uncombed hair), interviewers perceive you as being uncaring and somewhat sloppy, before asking you even one question. Even though you may be the most hardworking and concerned candidate available, you may undo all your hard work in the application process if you neglect your appearance. Proper dress for men includes a nice shirt (tie is optional), slacks, and a pair of dress shoes. For women, an attractive blouse, dress pants (or suit or skirt), and shoes are appropriate.

Also, avoid smoking or chewing gum prior to or during the interview. Habits like these can create a poor appearance. The whole idea is to put your best foot forward to indicate that you are the most enthusiastic and best-qualified candidate for the job. Interview time is limited, so you'll want to make the most of it.

The beginning of the interview usually will focus on your application form. Your educational background, past employment history, and references will be examined. Before your interview, review everything you listed on your application form and have supportive reasoning for any career changes. If you can demonstrate that the direction you took has helped prepare you for work in the Postal Service, so much the better. However, do not deceive the interviewer regarding past choices. You may contradict yourself later in the interview. The best policy here is to answer all questions honestly, even if some past decisions were not necessarily the best ones. If you feel that you have made a questionable career move or have had a falling out with one or more past employers, explain why. If you can also show that something was learned or gained from a past mistake, point that out as well. Interviewers will appreciate your honesty and sincerity.

You will additionally be asked to sign an Authorization and Release Form (2181-A) for pre-employment screening. As permitted by law, this authorization is used to obtain information pertaining to your character and current or prior employment. This information is used to determine your suitability for employment in the Postal Service. If you deny the Postal Service consent to obtain this information, it may have an adverse effect on your employment eligibility.

Once the interview is over, thank the interviewer for his or her time and don't loiter to see how well you did. It takes a week or two to make a hiring decision. The United States Postal Service is an Equal Opportunity Employer. All qualified applicants receive consideration for employment without regard to race, religion, color, national origin, sex, political affiliation, age, marital status, physical handicap, or memberships in an employee organization.

Having worked as a letter carrier for the Postal Service for many years, I can attest to the fact that it is a fine employer. The job satisfactions are many and the service you provide to the public at large is considered invaluable.

—Norman S. Hall

Refund Policy

If you receive a score lower than 90 percent on the postal exam after having used this study guide, Adams Media will refund the purchase price.

The following conditions must be met before any refund will be made. All exercises in this guide must be completed to demonstrate that the applicant did make a real attempt to practice and prepare for the exam. Any refund must be claimed within ninety days of the date of purchase shown on your sales receipt. Anything submitted beyond this ninety-day period will be subject to the publisher's discretion. Refunds are only available for copies of the book purchased through retail bookstores. The refund amount is limited to the purchase price and may not exceed the cover price of the book.

If you mail this study guide back for a refund, please include your sales receipt, validated test results, and a self-addressed, stamped envelope. Requests for refunds should be addressed to Adams Media, Postal Exams Division, 57 Littlefield St., Avon, MA 02322. Please allow approximately four weeks for processing.